BOYCOTT
in
AMERICA

BOYCOTT

in

AMERICA

*HOW IMAGINATION AND IDEOLOGY
SHAPE THE LEGAL MIND*

Gary Minda

Southern Illinois University Press
Carbondale and Edwardsville

Library of Congress Cataloging-in-Publication Data
Minda, Gary.
Boycott in America : how imagination and ideology shape
the legal mind / Gary Minda.
p.   cm.
Includes bibliographical references and index.
1. Boycotts—Law and legislation—United States—Interpretation and construction.
2. Judicial process—United States. 3. Metaphor. I. Title.

KF3431.Z9M56 1999
340'.01'4—dc21   98-16474
ISBN 0-8093-2174-2 (cloth : alk. paper)   CIP

For Mom and Dad

The fact is, and every lawyer knows it, that *those judges who are most lawless, or most swayed by the "perverting influences of their emotional natures," or most dishonest, are often the very judges who use meticulously the language of compelling mechanistic logic, who elaborately wrap about themselves the pretense of merely discovering and carrying out existing rules, who sedulously avoid any indications that they individualize cases.*

—Jerome Frank, *Law and the Modern Mind*
(emphasis in original)

CONTENTS

CONTENTS

FIGURES

PREFACE

PREFACE

THIS BOOK EXAMINES how imagination and ideology shape the legal meaning of a word, *boycott*, in the law. As this book explains, *boycott*, the word, has taken on different substantive legal meanings as judges and lawyers have created different imaginative and normative understandings of boycott phenomena. These different imaginative understandings of boycott are the result of a reasoning process that relies upon prototypes, basic level categories, and conceptual metaphors to classify and categorize phenomena. The cognitive effects of legal imagination have remained concealed within law's official forms of reason, until now.

My basic thesis is that we can better understand how the ideology of law operates in boycott adjudications by considering the important cognitive role of legal imagination. What brought me to the study of the word *boycott* was an off-the-cuff remark by Justice Stevens in a famous civil rights boycott case, *NAACP v. Claiborne Hardware Co.*, 458 U.S. 886 (1982). In that case, Justice Stevens warned that "a court must be wary of a claim that the true color of a forest is better revealed by reptiles hidden in the weeds than by the foliage of countless freestanding trees" (458 U.S. at 934). Justice Stevens went on to remark that the word *boycott* was one of those words like *conspiracy* that, in the law, had a chameleon-like character (i.e., the word was capable of changing its meaning from context to context). These rather mystifying statements begged a nagging question: Why did Justice Stevens choose the metaphor of a chameleon to define what he meant by boycott, and what did he mean by his warning that a court should be wary of a reptile hidden in the weeds of the law?

In thinking about this, I soon realized that the clues for explaining the mystery of the word *boycott* were to be found not in the foreground of a legal text or opinion, but rather, in the background world of legal imagination and ideology. As Justice Stevens admonished, there is a reptile hidden in the weeds of the law. The reptile is the ideology of the law. The ideology of the reptile can be revealed by examining how the legal mind gives meaning to things. Understanding how this reptile conceals itself in the weeds of the law can provide us with important information about how judges deny their ideological role in adjudication. As it turns out, the word *boycott* is a rather good vehicle for examining how this reptile camouflages itself in the adjudication. Like a chameleon, the law is capable of changing the meaning it attributes to phenomena depending on the context and the ideological motivations of law's official interpreters.

Justice Stevens was quite perceptive in using the mental image of a chameleon to define the meaning of the word *boycott*. What Justice Stevens did not fully acknowledge, however, was that in using the metaphor of a reptile, he was providing us with a vivid metaphoric image of the hidden modality used for judicial law-making. To see why this is so, we need to consider the relevance of some of the recent insights that come from the developing field of cognitive science. The insights of cognitive science provide us with a highly useful framework for understanding the mechanism responsible for the denial of the ideological in adjudication, which has framed much of the critiques of adjudication advanced by the legal realist and critical legal studies movements in American legal studies this century.

The developments in cognitive science reveal three important insights: (1) cognitive reason is embodied and imaginative, (2) metaphor is a central modality of reason, and (3) human reason is grounded in human experience that is motivated by our interactions with the physical and social worlds. The insights of cognitive science challenge some of the basic notions about how language, concepts, and categories work to give meaning to things and in doing so establish a totally new critical framework for the study of law's reason. These insights have only recently been noticed in legal studies. My colleagues at Brooklyn Law School Steven L. Winter and Lawrence Solan, however, have engaged in some of the first serious efforts to bring the new learning of cognitive and linguistic theory into legal studies. Their work has been invaluable to me for gaining access to the ongoing revolution taking place in cognitive theory. I am also indebted to the work of my friends and colleagues in the critical legal studies movement; their work over the last two decades provides the paradigm for understanding how reason in the law operates as an ideological and political power in society.

Before beginning my study of boycott, I would like to raise some caveats. First, it should be noted that the book's focus will be on the meaning attributed to boycotts by private groups. Boycotts by nation-states, used as a tool of foreign policy, will not be specifically addressed, though the analysis herein offers a framework for analyzing the way nation-states may cognitively legitimate such activity. Second, it is important to alert the reader to the meaning of ideology that pertains to this study. For many readers, the word *ideology* is linked to the work of Karl Marx and his effort to develop a total theory to explain how social relations are economically structured by capitalism.

In this book, I will be using the word *ideology* in a much more narrow sense to describe the way ideas and representations of phenomena are distorted by mental images and imaginative models used in cognitive thought. For my purposes, the term *ideology* is used to refer to the way cognitive thought conceals information about phenomena, especially the interests and values that may be implicated. Here, I would refer the reader to the idea of ideology developed by Karl Manheim in his book *Ideology and Utopia* 55–60 (1936) or more recently by Duncan Kennedy in his book *A Critique of Adjudication {fin de siècle}* 290–91 (1997).

The ideas that led to this book germinated from a previously published legal essay on the subject of boycotts, Gary Minda, *The Law and Metaphor of Boycott*, 41 Buffalo Law Review 807–931 (1993). I benefited from comments of Lisa Eichhorn; Michael Frost; David Gregory; Leonard Gross; Larry Solan; Steven L. Winter; my editor, Carol Burns, at Southern Illinois University Press; and my copyeditor, Barbara Lund. I would like to thank a number of law students at Brooklyn Law School who provided superb research assistance on the manuscript: Deetza Benno, Valerie Ndekhedhe, Jamin Sewell, Joshua Zuckerberg. I would also like to thank my secretary, June Parris, whose devotion sustained my effort. Research for this book was supported by a summer research grant from Brooklyn Law School. I would like to thank the libraries of Trinity College, Dublin, Ireland, and of Galway University, Galway, Ireland, for allowing me access to their research facilities. Finally, I would like to thank the editors of the *Buffalo Law Review* for permitting me to draw from previously published material.

BOYCOTT

in

AMERICA

PROLOGUE
BOYCOTT AND THE REPTILE
HIDDEN IN THE WEEDS

A court must be wary of a claim that the true color of a
forest is better revealed by reptiles hidden in the weeds
than by the foliage of countless freestanding trees.
—Justice John Paul Stevens, *NAACP v. Claiborne Hardware Co.*

THE WORD *BOYCOTT* is steeped in mystery and clouded with ambiguity. Its origin is attributed to an infamous rent dispute between a small group of Irish tenants and an Englishman, Captain Charles Cunningham Boycott, a former soldier in the English Army who settled in northwest Ireland in 1853 and became a land agent for an important Irish landlord, the Earl of Erne. In chapter 1, I will trace the origins of the word to the events and cast of characters responsible for its coining. As we will see, a word created from an obscure set of events in northwestern Ireland at the end of the last century is now rather commonly used in English, French, Dutch, German, and Russian to define what we know as a boycott. Suffice it to say that the events involving Captain Boycott became the idealized cognitive model or central case for defining the meaning of the word *boycott* in law and culture. Even though the popular usage of the word has since broken free of its origins, the metaphoric markers of the central case continue to influence the way judges understood this word in the law.

In contemporary culture, the word has come to mean the collective withholding of relations of any kind, social or commercial, public or private, on account of political or other differences, so as to punish or influence someone or something. In the law, the word *boycott* has come to signify a host of different images, some negative, others positive, about the meaning of group activity associated with the boycotts of different boycotting groups.[1] As we will see, different legal understandings of boycott phenomena have been shaped by the colorful background images projected by imaginative metaphors judges use in the foreground of their opinions to characterize the meaning of boycott activity.[2] The chameleon-like nature of the word *boycott* in the law also offers a good illustration of how metaphoric reasoning serves ideological purposes in adjudication.

One would think that after more than a century of boycott activity, the legal meaning of the word *boycott* would no longer be a matter of serious controversy. And, yet, as we will see, judges continue to argue about the meaning of the word. The ongoing judicial disagreement over the meaning of the word has recently involved disputes about the meaning to be attributed to the historical origins of the word, as well as disputes about the way the word is now understood in our language. One point remains clear, however; the case law dealing with the right of groups to boycott has advanced conflicting judicial ideas about the nature of group boycotts, and these conflicting ideas of boycott phenomena have determined the way judges dispose of the stakes of ideological group conflict.

Consider, for instance, the doctrinal dissonance created by three modern Supreme Court decisions dealing with labor, antitrust, and civil rights boycotts. In *NAACP v. Claiborne Hardware Co.*,[3] the Supreme Court unanimously held that the organizers of a civil rights boycott could not be liable under state tort law because their boycott was protected by the First Amendment. In the same term, however, the Court again held unanimously, in *International Longshoremen's Ass'n v. Allied International, Inc.*,[4] that a political boycott organized by a labor union to protest the Soviet invasion of Afghanistan, was not protected by the First Amendment. More recently in *FTC v. Superior Court Trial Lawyers Ass'n*,[5] the Court held that a boycott staged by a group of criminal defense lawyers seeking an hourly fee raise constituted a *per se* (strictly illegal) offense under the federal antitrust laws. While the lawyers alleged that their acts constituted a protected political boycott, the Court found instead that the lawyers had engaged in a price-fixing conspiracy.

This confusing trio of cases has established a curious result: boycotts seeking political objectives are protected from governmental regulation unless a labor union is involved or unless the boycott is aimed at advancing the participants' own economic self-interest. Taken together, the Supreme Court's decisions in *Claiborne Hardware, Allied International,* and *Trial Lawyers* indicate that the Court distinguishes between political and economic boycotts, providing a higher degree of constitutional protection to boycotts perceived to be more political and less economic. Boycotts seeking political objectives are protected First Amendment expression unless a labor union is involved or unless the boycott involves lawyers who are seeking to advance their own economic self-interests in addition to the constitutional interests of their clients.

Scholarly explanations of boycott in the law have attributed inconsistency of the case law to either instrumental policy manipulation or a mistaken understanding about the nature and meaning of boycotts. While legal scholars have constructed legal theories of boycott, their theories have failed to explain the inconsistencies in the law. For some, the law of boycotts is but another black hole into which the problems of modern law have seemingly fallen, a place from which nothing can escape. One is left with the impression that Justice Stevens was right: the law applicable to boycotts is a chameleon that changes constantly, based on different conceptions and normative judgments about the acceptability of various forms of group behavior. The various legal meanings of the word are like the "reptiles hidden in the weeds" that Justice Stevens warned us about in the quote from *NAACP v. Claiborne Hardware Co.* quoted above.

One might conclude that the different forms of boycotts are explainable in terms of group identity. Labor, civil rights, and commercial boycotts would thus be explained by the identity of the group that is participating in essentially the same practice or activity—a boycott. But in the law, the legal meaning of phenomena known as *boycott* takes on a substantively different meaning when it is framed not by group identity, but a cognitive reference point oriented by an idealized understanding of the word.

Judges organize their knowledge and thoughts by reference to imaginative categories structured by idealized cognitive models (ICMs) of boycott. These models are used in adjudication to create legal categories that distinguish between boycotts of different groups. The legal categories operate as fixed points in legal reasoning, even though the imaginative boundary lines between the categories are quite transparent and hence highly revisable. The models give rise to distinct prototypical cognitive effects that enable judges to act as if the categories are capable of rendering legally correct answers in adjudication. The legal categories of boycott are defined in terms of group identity, but the meaning of each category is metaphorically constructed from an idealized understanding of boycott for that group.

I will be drawing from, directly and indirectly, the work of cognitive theorists and cognitive psychologists who have challenged some of the basic ideas about how we think, and what we think we know about the cognitive process. Eleanor Rosch's landmark work in cognitive psychology, for example, shows that people intuitively categorize things in terms of prototypes of categories, and that cognitive thought is influenced by choices made on the basis of a subjective judgment that some category types are better examples than others.[6] Rosch's study explains why many people categorize sparrows or robins as being in the bird category, but not ducks, owls, or penguins. Cognitive theorists, building on Rosch's work, have gone on to conclude that our idealized categories of phenomena have prototypical or gestalt-like effects in cognitive thought.[7] For example, the idealized cognitive model of a bird has certain predictable prototypical effects: Many people conclude that a chicken is a bird, but not an ostrich, and certainly not an airplane. The cognitive significance of prototypes can explain how we instinctively classify and categorize phenomena on the basis of idealized models of a common case or central example. As we stray farther away from the prototypical common case, ambiguity sets in, and new categories are needed to explain new situations.

The necessary and sufficient conditions of legal categories can not tell us why the courts treat labor, civil rights, or commercial boycotts differently. What can tell us why judges define the legal meaning of phenomena are the idealized cognitive models or conceptual frames that produce the cognitive reference points used by judges to classify and give meaning to phenomena. The legal categories of boycott are thus imaginative categories created by the legal mind for different idealized understandings of boycott. Boycott categories operate as framing concepts much like the words *mother* or *trial* function to frame the meaning of complex phenomena like *motherhood* and *litigation*. One objective of this book is to explain how the framing concept of classification works in the law of boycott to produce different legal meanings of the word *boycott*.

The law's classification of boycott can also be elucidated by considering how language and power are mediated by an imaginative form of reason structured by metaphor. The imaginative structure of this form of reason developed from *default* metaphors that initially associated the collective activity of labor boycotts with ideas about the destructive force of a bomb or an unruly, rioting mob. These metaphors have had *default consequences* because they influence legal opinion in deciding highly contestable legal interpretations of boycott phenomena.

I will show how the default consequences of the metaphors have served to imaginatively establish and define what cognitive theorists call a *radial category*.[8] The notion of radial category is derived from Wittgenstein's insight that categorization in cognitive thought is based on imaginative similarities and relationships based on "family resemblances."[9] To use Wittgenstein's famous example, games such as poker, monopoly, football, and so forth, share a family resemblance based on common characteristics that have little to do with the rules of a particular game. We categorize games based on their common similarities, relationships, to a family resemblance category, rather than according to rule.

Cognitive theorists have developed the idea of radial category to explain how the cognitive process of categorization can defy rationalist criteria of necessary and sufficient conditions, and they have shown how categories are framed by an imaginative normative background.[10] A radial category is therefore a central model or common case with various extensions. Although the extensions are related to the common case by similarities and relationships, they are neither defined by necessary and sufficient conditions nor explained by definitional rules. For example, understanding the rules of a particular game like poker fails to explain why football is a game, but similarities and relationships of football and poker as a common model of game (e.g., all games involve competitive performance, scoring is usually involved, players take turns, etc.) enables one to comprehend the gamelike nature of the sport. The extensions from the common case or family resemblance category create prototypical effects that enable us to cognitively classify phenomenon on the basis of the central case.[11]

Take, for example, the word *hand*.[12] The word *hand* is a common model that we use to make sense of expressions such as "lend me a hand" or "she has the upper hand." The linguistic meaning of these statements is related to a radial category, the meaning of which has certain prototypical effects (i.e., gestalt awareness) of understanding *hand* as an appendage to a human limb. The hand as human limb has unique prototypical effects that enable us to ground or give meaning to expressions and things that may have little or nothing in common with each other beyond their common relation to the common case. What enables us to see similarity and relation is the radial category of the common case.

In this book, I will explain how the common case involving Captain Boycott has established a series of radial categories or family resemblances for attributing different legal meanings to boycotts of different groups. These radial categories have unique normative consequences for the adjudication of boycott controversies. The prototypical effects of the radial categories of boycott, shaped by default metaphors, are what define the legal meaning of the word *boycott*. These different boycott metaphors exclude other meanings of boycott from legal decision making, and hence the metaphors have *default* consequences in adjudication. The legal meaning of the default metaphors can be shown to be normatively infused by ideological values and assumptions. The metaphors are not value-neutral.

One could think of the word *boycott* to be like the word *mother*. As with the category *mother*, there are a number of subcategories or radial categories for defining the meaning of *working* mothers, *unwed* mothers, *biological* mothers, *birth* mothers, *genetic* mothers, *surrogate* mothers, *single* mothers, *adoptive* mothers, *foster* mothers, and good old-fashioned *stepmothers*. As George Lakoff has noted, the subcases of the word *mother* cannot be explained in rationalist, deductive terms: "There is no general rule for generating kinds of mothers. They are culturally defined and have to be learned."[13] An unwed mother is simply not a mother who is not married, and we would not normally regard egg donors as *mothers*. To understand the relation between the category *mother* to the subcases, one must examine how the central concept of mother, like the central concept of boycott, is a *cluster model* of several different culturally defined normative models, including a labor model, a civil rights model, and a commercial model.

The central concept of boycott, like the central concept of mother, is capable of generating a cluster model of different imaginative ideas of boycott: boycott as destructive force, boycott as political expression, boycott as competitive process, and so forth. These different normative ideas of boycott have created different legal categories of boycott in the law, but the legal categories can be shown to be a radial extension of what cognitive theorists call an idealized cognitive model. Proof of the radial extension can be seen by examining the normative traces of the colorful conceptual metaphors that judges use in constructing different legal meanings of boycott as law-enforcing or law-threatening activity, and targets as predators or victims. In essence, then, judges have used a family resemblance category to mediate and justify the different legal treatment they have accorded boycotts by various groups in society.

As we will see, from the very first time the word *boycott* was used to describe the events involving the famous Captain Boycott in Ireland, metaphor shaped the meaning of the word in terms of a normative background. The word was normatively shaped by metaphors that had certain prototypical effects. For example, in Ireland, as soon as the word *boycott* was used for the first time, it was associated with colorful and highly normative metaphors drawn from the context of the contemporaneous Zulu uprising in Southern Africa. Irish tenant boycotters were thus characterized in the Irish press as a "host of Zulus thirsting for blood."[14] An otherwise peaceful and nonviolent tenant boycott, involving an obscure and hardly threatening group, was found to be conceptually like the bloody Zulu resistance to British rule in Africa. Shortly thereafter in America, a Connecticut judge made reference to the events involving Captain Boycott in Ireland in a labor boycott case and compared an otherwise peaceful labor boycott to a wild bloodthirsty tiger. In using the "tiger" metaphor, the Connecticut judge concluded that boycott was akin to murder.[15]

Why would anyone think that Zulus and wild tigers share something in common with a boycott, and why did those categories enable judges, or anyone else, to understand the meaning of the word *boycott* as murder? This is, in a nutshell, the puzzle I am purporting to solve in this book. I will explain how the metaphors of boycotters as "savage Zulus," "wild tigers," or "murder" have obvious normative prototypical cognitive effects for giving legal meaning to group boycott phenomena. The imaginative representations of boycotters as "savage Zulus," "bloodthirsty tigers," and boycott as "murder" seem strange, but they can be shown to make perfect sense in light of the prototypical effects of an imagined category of boycott that equates labor-boycott phenomena with uncivilized, animalistic behavior.

As this book will explain, judges have used the word *boycott* to call up inflammatory, as well as sublime, connotations. On one hand, judges have compared group boycotts to bloodthirsty tigers, and they have analyzed boycott activity as if it were a disease, infecting the internal biological system of the body. On the other hand, judges have compared group boycotts to soapbox oratory, and they have concluded that boycott activity is a special form of political speech. Boycotts have thus been associated with ideas of criminality as well as with sublime and majestic ideas of free expression and mass assembly. Conceptual metaphors of boycott used in the adjudication of boycott disputes reveal how imagination and ideology shape the legal mind.

Metaphor is the cognitive engine that permits the legal mind to classify group boycotts differently in the law. The landlord-tenant dispute involving Captain Boycott marks the metaphoric origins of the word, and, as I will argue, these early metaphoric origins of the word establish the central case from which the radial categories of boycott in American law can be traced. What shapes how these categories operate in particular cases, however, are default metaphors, imaginatively created from an understanding of some, but not all, of the prototypical properties of the central case involving Captain Boycott.

What's more, the boycott metaphors judges use to define and classify different boycott phenomena can be shown to be based on normatively loaded ideas about the meaning of group activity. In the boycott case law, metaphors of boycott have thus had an important role in shaping legal outcomes. Judges treat metaphor as if it were a tool, like language and grammar, to be deployed by a neutral judge/interpreter. However, because the metaphors are themselves normatively loaded, the tool is itself normative, and consequently, the judge/interpreter is acting in an ideological manner when he or she uses the tool in an impartial and nonideological manner. As Gary Peller in his "The Metaphysics of American Law" has insisted, "legal discourse can present itself as neutral and determinate only to the extent it denies its own metaphoric starting points."[16]

This study of boycott[17] reveals that judges are more prone to recognize a legal right to boycott when the boycotting group is seen to be furthering the authority of the law (of the state or the market). When the group boycotting is perceived to be a threat to the authority of the law (of the state or of the market), a number of colorful default metaphors are deployed to either condemn the boycott or to deny the boycotting group constitutional or other legal protection. This book will explain how these legal results are the prototypical effects of a metaphoric form of reason.

At this juncture, it may be helpful to define more specifically what I mean by metaphoric reason. In its most common understanding, metaphor is a figurative form of expression used to convey meaning by comparing one object with another, as Romeo does when he rhapsodizes, "Juliet is the sun." This metaphor is based on a riddle that can be solved by making a comparison between seemingly unrelated things: Juliet and the sun. Metaphor and simile (an explicit form of comparison) allow us to gain insight by drawing cognitive comparisons between what is known and what is unknown. In comparing Juliet to the sun, for example, Romeo expressed the depth of his love for Juliet. In the act of comparison, Romeo enables us to understand that Juliet was at the center of his universe in the same way that the sun is at the center of the planets in our universe. Hence, what Shakespeare may have meant by the metaphor "Juliet is the sun" is that Romeo's day begins and ends with Juliet.

The fact that similarity and comparison are of fundamental importance for solving the riddle of metaphor does not mean that metaphoric comprehension is simply a matter of the logic of a literal simile or comparison. As John R. Searle has argued: "How are we supposed to know, for example, that the utterance, 'Juliet is the sun,' does not mean 'Juliet is for the most part gaseous,' or 'Juliet is 90 million miles from the earth,' both of which properties are salient and well-known features of the sun?"[18]

Metaphoric reason, unlike a literal comparison, relies upon an implicit background understanding that the reader shares with the author to give meaning to the metaphoric utterance. Thus, in stating "Juliet is the sun," we know that Romeo means that his day begins and ends with Juliet because we share a cultural understanding of romantic love that enables us to select the proper properties of the sun (the sun as central to our universe) for comprehending the meaning of the metaphor. What may distinguish metaphor from simile is that cognitive insight generated by metaphoric utterance is dependent upon an unstated background of meaning that relies upon something that is absent in the metaphor statement. An analogy or simile is thus a metaphoric mapping that is so well established in our conceptual system that background assumptions necessary for cognition are taken for granted.

The ability of metaphor to generate meaning based on a shared background understanding of how things are in reality, is central to our cognitive process. We use metaphors in everyday conversations, sometimes without much conscious reflection; we know that *up* is more, and *down* is less, even though we may not know why we think this way about such things. We use poetic expressions like "Love is a flower" or "Love is a madness" to convey the meaning of love, even though the literal meaning of the metaphor can't be objectively proved or analyzed. In ancient times, classical rhetoricians understood metaphor as a means for "giving names to nameless things."[19] Indeed, metaphor may be the only way to comprehend the meaning of complex phenomena like love or boycott.

Human emotion known as love, of course, is neither a flower nor madness, but we instinctively understand the meaning of these metaphors. In speaking this way, we create meaning. Metaphor creates meaning by enabling us to better understand an unfamiliar domain by reference to a domain that is known. If Shakespeare wrote instead that, "Love is a journey," we might come to appreciate another idea about Romeo's love for Juliet. We instinctively understand the cognitive meaning of statements like: "This relationship is not going anywhere" or "The love she once had is dead" or "The relationship has moved to a new level of commitment." What gives meaning to these statements is a cognitive model that relates the phenomena of love and relationship to a more basic conceptual metaphor, "Life is a journey." For Romeo, love, like life itself, is a journey that ends in death.

The metaphor "Life is a journey" structures an idealized cognitive model that gives meaning to expressions such as: "He will *go far* in his career as a lawyer." "She will *get over* him in due time." "He has reached the *final stage* of his recovery." The metaphor "Life is a journey" enables us to understand the meaning of these statements in reference to an embodied experience of time and space. The metaphor also provides us with a model or theory for understanding the meaning of many seemingly unrelated phenomena, including love (e.g., the "Love is a journey" category extension).

By invoking the metaphor "Love is madness," however, we instinctively know the meaning of other statements like "He is *crazy* about her" and "She's gone *mad* about him." In thinking of "love" as "madness" rather than as a "journey," we focus on particular features of the subject of the metaphor and suppress others. The suppression of difference helps us to see an aspect of the subject domain that would otherwise be hidden from our mind's eye. When we think of "Love is madness," we begin to understand an aspect of love hidden by the metaphor "Love is a flower." Metaphor is thus more than just a simile or comparison between two unrelated things; it is an imaginative system for transferring background knowledge and normative vision from one conceptual domain to another. Metaphor is, in this important sense, a cognitive device that is essential for comprehending the meaning of our reality.

However, because metaphors are only partial representations of one of many possible conceptual domains, metaphor also restricts cognitive insight. The suppression of different conceptual domains facilitates the psychological experience of denial in the cognitive process. We may consciously choose which of these two metaphors to use in our discourse about love, and we may do so strategically. But we are rarely aware of what our metaphors exclude and how they may mislead us. Hence, we are only half conscious about our choice because the strategic use of metaphor in argument and discourse keep from us the full implications of what our metaphors leave out from our cognitive thoughts and actions.

"Love is a journey" and "Love is madness" are but two of many different ways of conceptualizing love. As we conjure up more and more different metaphors of love, the phenomena of love becomes more complicated and much more difficult to understand. By focusing on the limited domain of a metaphor, however, we forget the possibilities of other metaphors and thus ignore information and ideas that would ordinarily cause us to have doubts about the certainty of our thoughts and normative understandings of phenomena.

In the law, this form of metaphoric forgetting enables judges and lawyers to overcome the anxiety of their ideological role in adjudication. Metaphor thus facilitates a psychological form of denial in adjudication. By examining how metaphoric-induced denial operates in adjudication, we can come to appreciate how judges conceal the true ideological nature of their work. The study of metaphor in adjudication can thus affirm the analogy recently drawn by Duncan Kennedy between his "analysis of the ideological in adjudication and the Freudian tradition of hunting out sexual motives where people are most concerned to conceal them."[20]

Classical rhetoricians understood, long before there was a discipline known as a cognitive science, that metaphors work subtly to enable not only logical meaning (what they called *Logos*) but to also reveal knowledge about the emotional (*pathos*) and normative (*ethos*) character of the author.[21] Metaphor can provide a context for evaluating how the author's choice of metaphor reflects the author's emotional and normative perspective, revealing to us something about the author's psychological perspective and ideological character.

Three classical dimensions of metaphor—Logos, pathos, and ethos—enable us to access the lawmaker's reasoning process, stylistic strategies, and the decision maker's perspective hidden in adjudication. We can, in other words, gain insight about the law's ideology by evaluating the particular ethos and pathos as well as the logical integrity (Logos) of metaphoric reason used in adjudication. By exploring the imaginative metaphors judges have used in defending their legal conclusions, we can come to understand the modalities of the politics of law. In contemplating other possible metaphors in terms of ethos, pathos, and Logos, we can discover what is missing in judges' legal analyses of group boycotts.

In law, metaphors are everywhere. As Thomas Ross has put it, "We live in a magical world of law where liens float, corporations reside, minds hold meetings, and promises run with the land. The constitutional landscape is dotted with streams, walls, and poisonous trees. And these wonderful things are cradled in the seamless web of law."[22] I will show how the "seamless web" of the law of boycott includes in its fibers an intriguing set of decisions dealing with a relatively new word in our language. The mystery of the word *boycott* begins with the history of the word *boycott*. In examining that history, we will be able to unravel the different meanings of boycott in the law, and with the unraveling, we will discover what is missing in the law's regulation of boycott practices of various groups in society.

Part 1 surveys the origins of the chameleon-like nature of the word *boycott* in Ireland and in America, explores cognitive theory, and examines how ideology operates in adjudication. Chapter 1 will trace the word from its early Irish origins. Chapter 2 will examine how the word came to influence the way American judges understood the meaning of labor boycotts during the formative era of the labor union movement. Chapter 3 will offer a new analysis of the boycott case law, developed from cognitive theory and cognitive psychology. Chapter 4 will then explore how metaphoric reason operates to conceal ideology in the adjudication. Part 2 examines how metaphor has shaped the contemporary legal meaning of boycott in labor, civil rights, and business boycotts. These three categories of boycott are treated in chapters 5, 6, and 7 respectively. Part 3 is aimed at evaluating the social meaning of boycott phenomena in law and contemporary society. Chapter 8 will first review the various ways legal scholars have attempted to make sense of boycott phenomena. Chapter 9 will examine boycott practice in light of the norm literature used to evaluate legal regulation of societal practices. Chapter 10 will examine the ethos of the legal mind reflected within the norm regulation that judges have used to regulate boycott practices of different groups. This chapter will also seek to uncover an alternative ethos of boycott evident in the private norm regulation of boycott practices.

The current boycott practices examined in part 3 suggest that the metaphors judges use no longer capture what boycott represents to those who are boycotting. The law needs new boycott metaphors to clarify the legal meaning of new forms of *cyberboycott* on the Internet as well as the new practices of labor/consumer boycotts occurring on the streets of America. The epilogue develops the basis for the discovery of new legal meanings of boycott to be found in new forms of boycott practices.

The mystery of the word *boycott* therefore raises high ideological stakes for the law. At stake is whether the meaning of an important cultural practice, boycott, should be left hidden in the weeds of the law, or whether it should be brought out into the light of day so that others might have a constructive role in its determination. In the following chapters, we will examine how the reptile, the ideology of the law hidden in the weeds of law's imagination, conceals itself and how it can be brought out into the light of day so that its true meaning can be ascertained.

Part One

ORIGINS OF BOYCOTT AS METAPHOR

CHAPTER 1
CAPTAIN BOYCOTT, THE IRISH
REVOLUTION, AND METAPHOR

THE WORD BOYCOTT can be traced to a particular place and time. It came into the English language at the end of the last century in Ireland during a time saturated with clashes between the powerful and the disenfranchised. The word was invented in the fall of 1880 to describe a rather minor rent dispute between poor Irish tenants and their landlord. The word that was born out of this dispute has since come to define a conflicting set of ideas about the meaning of a group's refusal to deal with another.

To this day, whenever the word boycott is used, it is usually encoded with metaphoric images derived from conflicting ideas about group refusals to deal. One image, derived from the events during the Irish Revolution at the end of the last century, associates collective action of boycotts with popular will against tyranny and injustice. An alternative image, which has come to dominate the legal meaning of labor boycotts in America, associates boycott activity with the dangers of unseemly and uncontrollable mobs and carries with it the threat and fear of violence and even murder in the background. These conflicting images of boycott have established prototypical properties of the central case or common model used to define the meaning of the word. The model of boycott derived from the central case of boycott establishes the metaphoric and normative ground for understanding the legal meaning of boycott in America.

To understand why this word is laden with different imaginative metaphoric themes, we must return to the place of its birth, County Mayo in northwest Ireland. This chapter thus returns to the origins of the word in order to retrace the historical events that gave rise to a new word that has come to influence law and culture. This chapter will explain how the cognitive power of metaphor has influenced the subsequent history of the word as well.

CAPTAIN BOYCOTT AND THE LAND WARS IN NINETEENTH-CENTURY IRELAND

The specific dispute that led to the coining of the word involved an infamous Irish land agent, Captain Charles Cunningham Boycott, who unwittingly became a central character in the struggle between the Irish landlord class and the Irish peasantry in the late 1880s.[1] Boycott seems to have been a brutal land agent, exacting fines on his hapless tenants if their livestock strayed onto his property, ruthlessly collecting rent, and ordering evictions of entire families during one of the worst harvest seasons in western Ireland. Boycott was not himself a landlord; he was instead a land agent who leased a 1,000 acre farm and a house, the Lough Mask House, from an Irish landlord, the Earl of Erne of Mayo.[2] Lord Erne was an absentee landlord,[3] who like other landlords of his time was land rich and money poor. He owned 40,000 acres in Counties Donegal, Fermanagh, Mayo, and Sligo, but the expenses of maintaining large houses, foxhunting, preserving game, and other extravagances imposed a heavy debt burden.[4] The most visible aspect of his wealth was the various mansions, such as the Lough Mask House, that represented the "centers of employment and social power."[5]

To afford such expenses, Lord Erne, like other landlords of his time, depended on rental incomes derived from small leaseholds held by tenant farmers. As Lord Erne's agent, Boycott had the primary responsibility of collecting rents from thirty-eight tenants who had small leaseholds on Lord Erne's Mayo estate. Most of the Irish farmland was owned at this time by a small group of Anglo-Irish landlords like Lord Erne who, with the aid of their agents, had absolute control over the land. The Irish tenants lived on the estates of their landlords and were in fact more like agricultural laborers than like independent farmers.

Captain Boycott had the misfortune to be in the wrong place at the wrong time during an extremely turbulent period in the history of landlord-tenant relations in Ireland.[6] Only forty years after the Potato Famine had caused the death of more than 1 million Irish citizens, a profound struggle for land, known as the Land War, was spreading throughout rural Ireland, precipitating a social, political, and economic conflict between the Irish landlord class and the Irish peasant tenants, who had been living under a feudal-like caste system for centuries.

The Land War followed a series of catastrophic potato crop failures in 1877 and 1879 that put many small tenant farmers into arrears with their rents. Landlords, squeezed by high costs of estate management and indebtedness, were economically dependent on the rents from their estates and had to recover arrears on back rents and seek eviction if necessary.[7] One of the worst-affected counties in 1879–1880 was County Mayo. Rent evictions and widespread poverty spread fear and deep-seated anger among tenants who clung to survival, especially as rents were increasingly harder to collect, evictions increased, and farms changed hands.[8] As the Irish priest Father John O'Malley of County Mayo (a key organizer of the boycott against Captain Boycott) explained to the traveling American journalist and crusader James Redpath, "When I was a young priest there were 1,800 families in the [County Mayo] Parish. There are only six hundred now. They were driven out by famine and the landlords."[9]

The fears and anger reported by Father O'Malley supported the impression that landlords were to blame for the plight of peasant farmers. The economic conditions in rural Ireland were bad, and in County Mayo, they were even worse. Tenants were severely pressed, but these same economic conditions weighed heavily on the landlord class, who were pressed for cash. Irish landlords were adversely affected by falling agricultural incomes as were the tenants. There was no factual basis, for example, to support the tenant view that landlords were "rackrenting," that is, charging monopoly rent.[10] In case of Lord Erne, there was no evidence to suggest that either he or his land agent, Captain Boycott, were rackrenting. Indeed, Lord Erne had granted, as other landlords had done, a series of rent reductions during the depressed agricultural season of 1879–1880 in recognition of the plight of tenant farmers.[11]

The traditional picture of landlordism was more likely shaped by the conflict between the Irish people along the lines of religion, class, and land. There were many reasons for this conflict and division. Absentee landlords made little effort to make improvements on the land,[12] and in leaving the administration of their estates to a professional class of land agents, they allowed estate management to exercise dictatorial power over tenants.[13] Deep conflict was created by the fact that some landlords and their agents were either British or were educated in Britain.[14] Captain Boycott was, for example, an expatriate British soldier, and the Earl of Erne, although Irish, identified himself with the feudal landlord class in England. Both were Protestants, as were most landlords and their agents. The peasant tenants, on the other hand, were primarily Catholics. Given these differences, it is still understandable that the Catholic Irish tenantry would picture landlords and their agents as foreign ambassadors of England and Protestant Ulster. Religious conflict was so central to the divisions in Ireland that it colored the way most people perceived the landlord-tenant system. James Redpath perhaps accurately captured what most Irish people believed when he wrote that "there was a fierce spirit brooding among [the tenants of Mayo] . . . that if some bloodless, but not pitiless, policy was not advocated—there would soon be killing of landlords and land agents all over the west of Ireland."[15]

Against this backdrop of conflict, a wave of tenant agitation broke out in County Mayo in the fall of 1880. The dispute, which led to the first use of the word *boycott*, involved a social, political, and economic struggle over control of land.[16] But the controversy was not just about land; it also symbolized a fundamental move toward the rise of Irish nationalism and the end of landlord feudalism in Ireland. Landlords sought to maintain their absolute power over land at the very time a united tenantry laid claims to it, and the only way that the question over land could be answered was by resolving the larger issue concerning the tenants' claims to a distinctive Irish nationality and a Catholic identity. The land question, framed by the relation between landlords and tenants, thus became a metaphor in the nineteenth century for Irish nationalism.[17]

Out of this agrarian discontent came a united mass movement, the Irish Land League,[18] organized on the basis of a nonviolent technique of resistance. The mass movement represented the tenantry class and was committed to the idea that "the land of Ireland [should be] for the people of Ireland."[19] The Land League, represented by two early Irish nationalists, Charles Parnell and Michael Davitt, mobilized the tenant class and organized boycotts throughout Ireland in the 1880s. In their view, boycott was "the law of the land," and it was thus a justified form of resistance against landlords.[20] The struggle that swept Ireland in the fall of 1880, however, came to be identified with the personality and character of one man, Captain Charles Cunningham Boycott of County Mayo.

Captain Boycott had earned the reputation as one of Ireland's worst land agents long before he came to County Mayo to work for Lord Erne. Living on Achill Island (a small but majestic piece of land off the western shores of Ireland) before coming to Lord Erne's estate,[21] Boycott was known to exact "fines on hapless tenants if their livestock strayed on to his lands; even fowl such as geese were in danger of being run down by his side-car, or horse, if they were caught grazing [on his property]."[22] He fined laborers on his land if they were late for work, and "the fines sometimes exceeded their wages."[23] On one occasion, Boycott tried to prevent local fisherman from fishing in the bay near his land, and on another occasion, he was brought to court for illegally stripping a wrecked ship in the Bay of Achill. Hence, by the time Captain Boycott became a land agent for Lord Erne, he was already known as a brutal and unsavory character.[24]

When he came to Lord Erne's Mayo estate, Captain Boycott further advanced his reputation by compelling tenants on the estate to work for him on his own farm at reduced rates, reduced even more drastically through the use of fines and penalties. "Boycott conceived efficiency in a military sense as disciplined orderliness and rigidity; and there was much petty friction with tenants and laborers over trivial fines for infringement of rules—late starting, mislaid tools, straying stock and trespassing children."[25] He soon became known in County Mayo as a rigid and authoritarian agent who cared more about the rules than about efficient farming. In fact, Boycott knew little about farming and agricultural matters. He was primarily a military man who cared more about racing horses than about the mundane tasks of farming.

As Lord Erne's agent, it was Boycott's duty to collect rents from tenants and to administer the affairs of the estate. His was not an easy position since he had all of a rent collector's responsibilities but little real power. "Avoiding disputes, rather than exacerbating them, was probably the aim of most agents."[26] Captain Boycott's military demeanor, however, placed him in a rigid position with his tenants. He was firm in enforcing his Lordship's orders, and this firmness made dispute resolution difficult. Further, because he was an Englishman living in Ireland, he symbolized the historical English landlord class and the Protestant faith. As a land agent, he also resided on the land and thus placed himself at the mercy of hostile neighbors, many of whom worked on Lord Erne's estate. He was in one sense an island of English power in a sea of Irish resistance. The tenants, living in small dark stone cottages, saw Boycott, living in Lord Erne's stately Lough Mask House, as a symbol of predatory landlordism.[27]

Significantly, the dispute that eventually gave the captain's name to the word *boycott* took place in the very county that was the birthplace of both the Land League and one of its most vocal founders, Michael Davitt.[28] Michael Davitt was born in a small village in County Mayo. His parents were evicted from their humble farm during the potato famine, and Davitt had vivid firsthand experiences of living under the arbitrary control of Irish landlords. These life experiences helped to bring Davitt into two Irish revolutions during his lifetime. First, there was the Fenian movement, which advocated armed resistance as a means for establishing a democratic Irish republic. At age twenty-five, Davitt was sentenced to fifteen years of hard labor for running guns as a member of the secret Irish Republican Brotherhood, the secret Fenian organization that eventually evolved into the Irish Republican Army. The other Irish revolution, which involved tenant boycotts, was represented by the Land League. The Land League advocated the use of nonviolent strategies for the immediate purpose of protecting tenants and for the ultimate goal of converting the tenant class into land owners.[29] The two movements were, of course, connected, affecting the way they were perceived by those who wanted to maintain the status quo.

In County Mayo, Davitt along with Charles Parnell organized the Land League as a mass resistance movement to counter the power of Irish landlords, to advance the cause for a new Irish State, and to argue the case for land reform. The Land League represented a new departure from the high Fenian orthodoxy and its commitment to armed rebellion.[30] It was Davitt's Land League that had decided to use a form of nonviolent "excommunication" as a means for bringing social pressure against predatory landlords. As Davitt explained the idea to a crowd in Mayo:

> If a landgrabber comes to town and wants to sell anything, don't do him any bodily harm. . . . If you see a landgrabber going to a shop to buy bread, or clothing, or even whiskey, go you to the shopkeeper at once, don't threaten him . . . Just say to him that

under British law he has the undoubted right to sell his goods to anyone, but that there is no British law to compel you to buy another penny's worth from him, and that you will never do it as long as you live.[31]

Initially, Davitt had neither a word nor a particular landlord in mind when he first described his technique of "excommunicating" or "shunning" land-grabbers. It was not until the rent dispute involving the tenants under Captain Boycott's authority erupted that Davitt found a word and a person to describe his idea. The spark that lit Davitt's imagination sprang not from a rent increase but rather from the effort of a landlord to *reduce* rent. Lord Erne had instructed Captain Boycott to allow a 10 percent rent abatement, but his tenants instead demanded a 25 percent reduction.[32] Why such a minor and in some ways petty dispute would attract the presses of Dublin, London, and eventually New York, result in the bringing of military troops to Boycott's Lough Mask House, and usher the word *boycott* into the international vocabulary requires explanation.

The dispute was at first an entirely local matter, directed by a parish priest, Father John O'Malley. Father O'Malley, however, turned out to be a rather gifted political organizer who evidently had a special talent for political strategy. At this time, Catholic priests were active in the Land League, and they served as important political figures for the tenant class. Janet Marlow noted that O'Malley was a "forceful character" who was "loved by his parishioners, probably as much for his weakness for the bottle as for his humor and conviviality."[33] Marlow also notes that it was O'Malley "who pointed the (first) finger in the direction of landlord ostracism and withdrawal of labor."[34] Addressing crowds at Boycott's Lough Mask House, O'Malley called for a united tenant action if Lord Erne did not accept the tenant demands for a rent reduction.

It was Lord Erne and his faithful land agent Captain Boycott, however, who raised the first hand leading to the inauguration of boycotting. Lord Erne stood firm in rejecting the idea of a further rent reduction, and Boycott was more than willing to act as his Lordship's faithful agent. He let it be known that he would evict any tenant who failed to pay rent in accordance with the offered 10 percent abatement. The two sides were thus locked into positions that created an atmosphere of conflict and agitation.

The harvest of 1879 had been one of the worst in the west of Ireland, and by May of 1880, when rents were to be collected on the Mayo estates, many tenants were unable to pay even reduced rents. Conditions were reported to be reminiscent of the Great Famine of thirty years before when Ireland lost a quarter of its population (about 1.5 million) through starvation and disease.[35] A series of dismal harvests had combined with a steady fall in agricultural prices to make farming uneconomical at the prevailing rent. Sympathy for the tenants, however, was strong given that many were still trying to recover from the potato famine. Perhaps it was the vivid images of more than a million starving Irish farmers who died during the Great Potato Famine that lent the greatest weight to the tenants' position. Tenant farmers were literally starving to death, while landlords were merely suffering the hardship of reduced income and rising debt. It would be hard, indeed, to show sympathy for landlords who were living the life of English royalty in their manor houses while Irish laborers working in their estates and living in cold stone houses were starving.

Struggling to survive a bad year, tenants found themselves forced to pay rent they could hardly afford. Some were completely unable to pay. Nevertheless, Captain Boycott threatened to evict anyone, and entire families, if they did not pay. After posting notice of the rent reduction, Captain Boycott found on his gate a crude drawing of a coffin with a demand for a greater reduction of rent. A tenant petition for a greater rent reduction was then sent to Lord Erne, but his Lordship refused to grant further abatements, and then, without further warning, Captain Boycott posted eviction notices against eleven tenants who had failed to pay their rent. Some of these tenants paid their rent in due course, but three families were subsequently evicted for nonpayment.[36]

The eviction of three tenants and their families became a rallying cause for Michael Davitt and his Land League. Outraged by the events in Mayo, the Land League called a mass meeting, and with the aid of Father O'Malley and local Land League organizers, a united tenantry rose to take action. The Land League called a general rent strike and induced everyone in the community to desert Captain Boycott and cease all relations with him.

Some called it "moral excommunication," "social ostracism," or "sending to Coventry" (that is, Coventry, England). The idea was to force Captain Boycott off the land by cutting off all social and economic relations and communications with him. The idea of shunning an offender of the community was an old idea, and it had been used before in Ireland, but never had it been used in an organized way and on a national scale. More significantly, this technique had never been named until the events leading up to the boycott of Captain Boycott.

Tenants, with the aid of organizers of the Land League, were able to bring national attention to a local rent dispute by focusing on Captain Boycott's "bad reputation" and using it as a symbol of predatory landlordism. Captain Boycott found himself isolated in his community. No one would buy from him; no one would sell to him. He and his wife were socially isolated by their neighbors. He was unable to harvest his own land or transact business of any kind in the community. Quite suddenly, the struggle of landlord and tenant had come to be focused on a single man, Captain Boycott.

Captain Boycott sought and was given relief in the form of government regiments of several hundred armed soldiers and fifty paid laborers from Ulster, the equivalent of modern day strike replacement workers, to harvest his crops at an expense, far in excess of their actual worth.[37] The entire episode proved to be a complete disaster, however. In the ensuing days, soldiers camped in tents on his land, chopped down trees for firewood, ate some of his livestock, and effectively took possession of the estate. Captain Boycott and his wife were prisoners in their own home. Eventually, they secretly fled from Lord Erne's estate in an army ambulance wagon escorted by twenty troopers in the early morning hours.[38] They headed back to Achill Island, where they lived out the remainder of their days under the shadow of an infamous word derived from their name.[39]

These events soon became an international news story as reporters from Dublin, London, and New York arrived in Mayo. One such journalist, a crusading American, James Redpath, had come to Ireland in 1880 as a special correspondent of the *New York Herald* and *Inter-Ocean*.[40] Marlow notes that "Redpath brought all the enthusiastic one-sidedness of the convert to the tenants' version of Irish ills."[41] Redpath already had a national reputation for covering the abolitionist John Brown story in America. Soon after arriving in County Mayo, Redpath wasted little time publicizing Father O'Malley's call for excommunicating land-grabbers like Boycott. Redpath put the first spin on the events by portraying Davitt and the Land League as champions of the Irish and Captain Boycott and Lord Erne as "lackeys" and "executioners" of the English Parliament.[42]

Interest in the dispute was further stimulated by a letter by Boycott to the London *Times* detailing how crowds of people from Mayo had descended on his property and were preventing him from using the land. As Captain Boycott explained in the *Times* letter: "I can get no workmen to do anything, and my ruin is openly avowed as the object of the Land League unless I throw up everything and leave the country."[43] Boycott's position was enthusiastically defended in the Ulster press, and Dublin's *Daily Press* published letters calling for a Boycott Relief Fund. Analogies between what had happened at County Mayo and tribal uprisings in Africa subsequently appeared in national papers covering the Boycott story.[44] The tenants boycotting at County Mayo were characterized in the press as a "host of Zulus thirsting for blood."[45]

Within days of these events, people began using the word *boycott* to describe Captain Boycott's social and economic ostracism, and the Zulu metaphor stuck. For those who identified with Captain Boycott, the word signified the dangers of what can happen when "uncivilized" people assert their collective power against a defenseless individual. For some, the boycotting mobs in County Mayo were like Zulus in Africa, who were then resisting British rule by killing British soldiers. For the vast majority of Irish tenants, however, Captain Boycott represented the evil and tyranny of arbitrary power of estate ownership, and it was the Land League and its boycotting that symbolized law and order. The popular image of boycott stemmed from the perspective of the Irish peasants who were either boycotting other landowners and their agents, or sympathized with the boycott effort.

Capitalizing on these events, Charles Parnell, Michael Davitt, and the Irish Land League were eventually able to organize tenants throughout Ireland and promote land reform. Boycotting of other landlords took place in other counties as news of the Land League's successful boycott against Captain Boycott spread throughout Ireland. Criminal mischief increased, but no serious criminal activity attributed to boycotting as such was reported.[46] The primary tactic used by the Land League was social and economic boycotting of landlords and their agents. In fact, Davitt, as a leader of League, urged tenants to remain nonviolent and to refrain from using boycotting to settle old disputes between individuals.[47]

A criminal prosecution was eventually brought against the leaders of the boycotts for inciting citizens to withhold rents. Evidence produced by the prosecution consisted of speeches by boycotters and the slogans displayed on banners and placards carried during meetings and during actual boycotting.[48] After many hours of deliberation, an Irish jury failed to find a verdict; "they were unanimous," as the jury foreman put it, "in being unable to agree."[49] This legal victory for the Land League became the first judicial test in Ireland of the legality of the Land League's boycotting.[50] Meanwhile, Captain Boycott sought political relief for the expenses he incurred during the boycott. He made appeals to the prime minister of Ireland, and he petitioned the Bessborough Commission, a landlord-tenant agency. But, in the end, Captain Boycott was never officially compensated, though he did recover some money by selling the lease he had with Lord Erne and by accepting a small amount of money raised on his behalf by public subscription.[51]

It is difficult to say for sure who was responsible for coining the word *boycott*. The frequently stated account in the secondary literature is that the word was invented by Father O'Malley, who organized the boycott against Captain Boycott on behalf of the Land League.[52] In discussing events involving the boycott, James Redpath recounted that it was Father O'Malley who coined the term. Redpath documented a conversation he had with Father O'Malley as follows:

> "When people ostracize a landgrabber we call it social excommunication, but we ought to have an entirely different word to signify ostracism applied to a landlord or a land agent like Boycott. Ostracism won't do, . . . and I can't think of anything," (complained Redpath). "No" said Father John, "ostracism wouldn't do." He looked down, tapped his big forehead, and said, "How would it be to call it 'to boycott him'?"[53]

And, as Redpath put it, from the "big forehead" of Father John O'Malley came a label for this powerful form of "excommunication" by workers of their landlord and employer. This colorful tag traveled the seas and remains with us today.

Whether Redpath's account is true or not, it is significant that a new word had to be created to define what we know today as a boycott. Social ostracism and what we now know as boycott had been utilized by the Land League as early as 1851, but the word was not coined and made popular until the incidents involving Captain Boycott.[54] Apparently, there was no other word in the English language to describe this dispute. The uniqueness of the word is illustrated by the fact that foreign languages also lacked comparable words for it. The word *boycott* thus passed into Dutch, French, German, and Russian without linguistic alteration.

CAPTAIN BOYCOTT AS METAPHOR

The Land League's boycott against Captain Boycott is now legendary in Irish history and culture. The story of the boycott is retold in the schools of modern Ireland and is as well known to the Irish as any story about Washington or Jefferson has become known in America. Captain Boycott has become a dark cult figure in Irish culture, popularized by a novel and even a movie.[55] In today's Ireland, Captain Boycott remains a symbol of predatory landlordism, tyranny, and injustice. The technique of boycotting that carries his name is linked to the struggle for justice and economic freedom.

The boycott of Captain Boycott illustrates how this word became associated with the high ideological stakes of group conflict involving popular protest and civil unrest.[56] From Captain Boycott's perspective and that of the landlord class in Ireland, the Irish tenants' refusal to deal represented a serious breach of duty owed to the authority of the property class in England. To the landlord class, the poor Irish tenants' boycott may have resembled the Great Mutiny, when English sailors refused to obey the orders of the superiors.[57] The boycotting in County Mayo was probably viewed by the ruling class as a dangerous threat to civil society, capable of inciting otherwise peaceful people to commit crimes as serious as murder. Landlords were greatly outnumbered by tenants, and occasional incidents of violence against landlords and their agents, though isolated and sporadic,[58] helped to create the impression that the tenantry class was more dangerous and formidable than reality would dictate. Captain Boycott as "victim" became a metaphor for the way the landlord class understood the meaning of the boycott.

For the Irish tenants, however, boycotting was a defensive measure aimed at protecting and defending their economic position as well as establishing their right to determine their own fate. For the boycotting tenants, the metaphor "Captain Boycott is predator" was the appropriate metaphor. Boycotting against Captain Boycott gave the Irish tenants a way to advance legal claims of *right*. Boycotting was to them the law of the land, and Captain Boycott was the law-violator. And, because the tenants' boycott was effective, it quickly became known as a way to enforce the popular will of the community against tyranny and injustice. "Captain Boycott is predator" thus became the dominant metaphor of the tenant class for understanding the meaning of the boycott.

Captain Boycott thus served to establish a basic-level or central cognitive model for categorizing different linguistic meanings of the word *boycott*. The central case of Boycott is capable of generating two contrary imaginative narratives. One narrative creates a conceptual metaphoric structure or stock story that imagines Captain Boycott (the target of the boycott) as "predator" and imagines the boycotting group as being engaged in law-enforcing activity. The alternative narrative creates a conceptual metaphoric structure or stock story that imagines Captain Boycott as "victim" and imagines the boycotting group as being engaged in law-threatening activity. The central *idealized cognitive model* of Captain Boycott, a cluster model of different imaginative narratives, is mapped in figure 1.1.

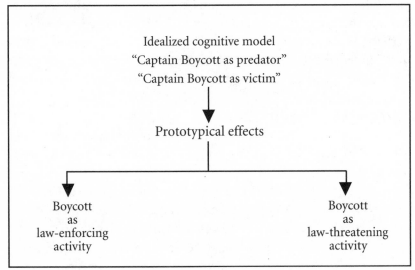

Figure 1.1
Captain Boycott as Central Case

The image of Captain Boycott as predator and boycott as law-enforcing activity nurtured the orthodox view of this era held by Irish historians for decades.[59] Orthodox Irish historians assumed that predatory land-lords were responsible for agrarian agitation during the Land War era and that this predatory behavior necessitated the use of boycotts.[60] The "evil" character of Captain Boycott, whether it was evil or not in fact, became a metaphor for associating boycotts by tenants with the law-enforcing and libertarian impulses of the Irish masses for decades.

Interestingly, however, a new history has been written by historians who question the historical accuracy of the Captain Boycott "landlord as predator" metaphor. Irish historians now argue that the landlords of nineteenth-century Ireland were not predatory but were rather rational economic actors who were responding to the market forces of their day. These revisionist historians have examined the estate records of the period, and they report that landlords in the nineteenth century were not powerful but rather were themselves distressed by the agricultural depression of the time. W. E. Vaughan's analysis of estate records, for example, shows that landlords during the nineteenth century were not "rackrenters," that evictions were not common, and that landlords were neither as "bad" nor as predatory as they have been made out to be.[61] Barbara Solow, in turn, has shown that most Irish tenants during the nine-teenth century paid below market rent and that the failure of landlords to charge reasonable rents placed the landlords in a weak economic posi-tion, rendering them unable to make necessary improvements on the land.[62] The historical work of these historians attempts to establish empirical support for the metaphors of Captain Boycott as victim and boycott as law breaking.

The new Irish histories provoke a number of puzzling questions. Why did the orthodox view of predatory landlords hold firm through-out the 1960s and 1970s? If rents were not unreasonably high and evic-tions infrequent, what caused the Land Wars, and what precipitated the tenant boycotting? "Why," as Professor Vaughan has asked, "should so many nineteenth-century witnesses condemn the landlords?"[63] One answer is that the predatory landlord thesis was based on inaccurate data. Vaughan's research attempts to show, for example, that the orthodox his-torians had ignored important data in the collections of estate papers that had accumulated over time. Further, Vaughan argues that if they had also acquainted themselves with double-entry bookkeeping, the ortho-dox historians would have discovered the actual size of rent increases at each estate failed to support the predatory landlord thesis.[64] In Professor Vaughan's judgment, the orthodox historians "had got it wrong," and if they had only checked the estate records and used the proper accounting methods, they would have "come to radically different conclusions."[65]

And yet, as Professor Vaughan admits, the orthodox view of nineteenth-century landlordism "was what most people believed."[66] Strongly held beliefs may have validated the predatory landlord thesis even in the face of empirical research. Others have tried to explain the tenant agitation that broke out in County Mayo by offering up ideas about "rising expectations" and anger among the tenants or by emphasizing the indebtedness of both landlords and tenants ("landlords trying to recover arrears and shopkeepers trying to have their bills paid").[67] Professor Vaughan ultimately concludes that Parnell and Davitt were crucial in mobilizing the tenant class to rise up against their landlords.[68] In mobilization, according to Vaughan, "clear, simple personal leadership was required, something easily identified with—*faces* rather than principles."[69]

There is no doubt that Parnell and Davitt had a lot to do with popularizing the conception of landlords as predators. But it was not their faces that mattered, but rather the face of a landlord agent, the infamous Captain Boycott. The publicity of the boycott against the Captain embedded the predatory landlord thesis in the imagination of the Irish. As explained above, it was the metaphor of predatory landlordism, shaped by the events involving the notorious Captain Boycott, that probably influenced the way many people thought of this era in Irish history. Captain Boycott became an ideological metaphor used by activist nationalists to mobilize the tenantry class to challenge the system of hierarchy based on ownership of land.

As metaphor, Captain Boycott shaped the orthodox view of historians for much of this century. The explanation for the long-standing influence of the predatory landlord thesis lies in the ideological power of metaphor in shaping the way large numbers of people, including professional historians, understood the meaning of the Irish tenants' boycott. The very belated appearance of a new critical scholarship of the Land Wars suggests that the boycott metaphor, symbolized by the deeds of Captain Boycott, has had an immense power to shape attitudes and beliefs by focusing attention on some phenomena while hiding others.

As we will see, boycott metaphors carried equal power when the word *boycott* reached the shores of America, but these metaphors emphasized very different aspects of the legal meaning of group boycotting in the American legal system. American judges, confronted for the first time with boycotts by workers and unions, drew on their own imaginations to characterize the legal meaning of a labor boycott. New imaginative ideas of boycott developed in the context of peculiarly American events, and these new ideas of boycott were also shaped by metaphors that could be traced to perceptions or misperceptions of the 1880 tenant uprisings in County Mayo.

CHAPTER 2

ORIGINS OF BOYCOTT IN AMERICA

> To most Americans "boycott" is a word of ill-omen.
> The pictures it calls up are of acts like those
> charged against striking coal miners.
> —Harry W. Laidler, *Boycotts and the Labor Struggle:*
> *Economic and Legal Aspects*

> If this is a correct picture, the thing we call a boycott
> originally signified violence, if not murder.
> —*State of Connecticut v. Glidden*

BY THE END of the last century, labor disturbances and violence in the United States had reached epidemic proportions. American society was on the edge of anarchy.[1] The relation between labor and capital at this time was not unlike the relation between tenants and landlords in nineteenth-century Ireland. In both countries, judges had reasons to think that boycotting represented a threat to society. The imaginative stereotypes of an unruly working class enabled judges to rely upon prototypical properties for understanding the meaning of collective-worker activities, and these properties were consistent with at least one set of imaginative ideas attributed to boycotts in Ireland.[2] This chapter will examine how the central case of boycott came to define the meaning of labor boycotts in America.

In Ireland, boycott was a technique of protest used to advance Irish nationalism, and in America, boycott became a strategy used by labor unions to advance worker solidarity, worker rights, and a trade union movement. Boycott activity, without the name boycott, had, of course, been used in the United States before the Declaration of Independence. The Sons of Liberty, for example, had used nonimportation agreements blocking British goods as a cornerstone to their independence movement.[3] Any person who was found to have violated the nonimportation policy of the colonies was vilified in posted handbills and local papers; some violators were tarred, feathered, and driven out of town. Such action was viewed by many American colonists as an appropriate, non-violent, form of lawful group action.[4] What we now know as a boycott was thus used in the years immediately preceding our revolution as a legitimate form of political action.[5]

More than a century later, however, *boycott* became one of the most vilified words in the vocabulary when it came to be used to describe actions by labor unions to organize large masses of workers in industrial America. In the late nineteenth century, American judges adopted notions of property rights to side with the interests of capital against labor, and metaphor became the ideological legitimator of their opinions.[6] Judges invoked Captain Boycott's name to justify the implementation of rigid legal limitations on peaceful labor boycott publicity and activity in order to stifle labor union organization and growth.[7] Judges in effect became the legal representatives of capital as they devised a series of default metaphors that operated ideologically to pit labor boycotts against the property rights of capital and hence the authority of the Rule of Law itself.

In America, unions were viewed by most judges as an outsider to the employment relation,[8] and the common law rules of contract, property, and tort were invoked as a justification for protecting the employer's property and managerial interests. The fear of class solidarity and conflict motivated judges to think this way.[9] Injunctions against picketing, and the traditional opposition to labor boycotting, were justified by an imaginative legal discourse that associated even peaceful concerted labor activity with acts of violence and trespass. The rules were skewed, but legal discourse justified the rules as the "naturalized" consequences of the "American system."[10]

American judges reacted negatively to labor boycotts, viewing such activity as criminal conspiracy, but American juries, consisting mainly of working people who experienced labor dispute first hand, were more sympathetic to the plight of the boycotters. American juries thus identified with the plight of the boycotters, saw the target of the boycott as predator, and refused to return convictions or to impose harsh penalties.[11]

Hence, there was in America different imaginative understandings of the meaning of boycott: one created by the legal imagination of judges, the other the product of citizen experience. The restraining effect of the jury system, however, became less significant in America as the American legal system began to rely on labor injunctions to regulate boycotts.[12] Labor injunctions enabled judges to control the meaning of boycott because injunctions and restraining orders were issued exclusively in judicial proceedings without juries.

Many historical justifications have been given for the development and application of the labor boycott rules,[13] but invariably metaphor can be shown to have played a role in justifying the substantive legal outcome. The cognitive role of metaphor enabled judges to rationalize and justify what they thought they knew about the labor boycotts, at the same time allowing them to be in denial about what they failed to know about the labor boycotts. To understand how the cognitive engine of metaphor worked in the early labor cases at common law, we must first examine how boycott metaphors developed at early common law. The story of Captain Boycott established a central case for analyzing labor boycott problems, but the judicial interpretation of the story was a normatively loaded reading.

LABOR BOYCOTTS AT EARLY COMMON LAW

When the word *boycott* was first used in a legal opinion in America, the events in Ireland involving Captain Boycott's confrontation with the Irish tenants were well known. Captain Boycott's name quickly became in America a word to describe the destructive nature of strikes, work stoppages, and labor violence. The Irish boycott had obvious connections to labor boycotts in America. Leaders of the Land League had, for example, studied trade union strikes in industrial England and used what they learned to plan a strategy to counter the actions of landlords. Disputes over wages and working conditions in England were manifestations of a deeper conflict over the power and authority of an employer, just as they are today. Collective work stoppages by employees have always been one of the chief means for resolving such conflict. The strike, for example, enabled workers to assert economic pressure against their employer by cutting off the employer's labor supply unless certain terms were agreed to by the employer (normally higher wages and/or reduced working hours).

A strike can be general in the sense that workers refuse to work for all employers who have failed to recognize their union or refuse to deal with an employer that has a dispute with another union. In such cases, a general strike is not unlike a boycott. In either case, the workers withhold their services and request others to cease having relations with the target so as to punish the target for the position it has taken, or coerce the target into abandoning it. As a general refusal to work, a strike is like the general refusal to deal involved in every boycott, a point that has caused great confusion in the subsequent development of modern labor law.

CAPTAIN BOYCOTT, WILD TIGERS, AND DANGEROUS THINGS

The word *boycott* first appeared in America in a published judicial opinion decided by the Connecticut Supreme Court in the 1887 decision in *State v. Glidden*.[14] The case involved a boycott called by a union seeking to unionize a publishing company in Connecticut. The union solicited the support of the public in an effort to force the publisher to recognize the union. In their effort to unionize the firm, union sympathizers distributed leaflets to induce the public not to patronize the firm. The leaflets carried slogans such as, "A word to the wise is sufficient, boycott the *Journal* and *Courier!*"[15] The leaflets were dropped on the streets by two persons who walked together on public sidewalks.

The Connecticut Supreme Court, in an opinion written by Justice Carpenter, upheld an injunction and criminal conspiracy charges against the union sympathizers. In considering whether the defendants had a legal right to act as they did, Justice Carpenter observed that "[t]he bare assertion of such a right is startling."[16] As he explained:

> If the defendants have the right which they claim, then all business enterprises are alike subject to their dictation. No one is safe in engaging in business, for no one knows whether his business affairs are to be directed by intelligence or ignorance,—whether law and justice will protect the business, or brute force, regardless of law, will control it. . . . If a large body of irresponsible men demand and receive power outside of law, over and above law, it is not to be expected that they will be satisfied with a moderate and reasonable use of it. All history proves that abuses and

excesses are inevitable. The exercise of irresponsible power by men, like the taste of human blood by tigers, creates an unappeasable appetite for more.[17]

In Justice Carpenter's mind, the defendants had acted irresponsibly because they had allowed their collective desire "for more," that is, higher wages, to become an animal-like passion of brute force. The boycott activity was thus analogized to that of a wild tiger, thirsting for human blood, much in the same way that the Irish peasants boycotting in Ireland were analogized to a hoard of Zulus thirsting for blood. In *Glidden*, the mental image of a wild tiger structured the legal meaning the court attributed to the collective action of the defendants. In Ireland, the mental image of Zulus structured the meaning of the Irish boycott, at least in the minds of those who sympathized with the position of the target, Captain Boycott. Animalistic images of the behavior of animals and savages thus shaped one meaning of boycott in the law.

Clues for uncovering the metaphoric sway of the court's *Glidden* opinion lie in the descriptive phrases Justice Carpenter used in telling the story of the boycott against Captain Boycott. According to Justice Carpenter:

Captain Boycott was an Englishman, an agent of Lord Erne, and a farmer of Lough Mark, in the *wild* and beautiful district of Connemara. In his capacity as agent he had served notices upon Lord Erne's tenants, and *the tenantry suddenly retaliated in a most unexpected way* by, in the language of schools and society, sending Captain Boycott to Coventry in a very thorough manner. The population of the region for miles round resolved not to have anything to do with him, and as far as they could prevent it, not to allow any one else to have anything to do with him. His life appeared to be in danger—he had to claim police protection. His servants fled from him as servants flee from their master in some plague-stricken Italian city. He and his wife had to work in their own fields themselves, in most unpleasant imitation of theocritan [*sic*] shepherds and shepherdesses, and play out their grim eclogue in their deserted fields with the shadows of the armed constabulary ever at their heels. The Orangemen of the north heard of Captain Boycott and his sufferings, and the way in which he was holding his ground, and they organized assistance and sent him down armed laborers from Ulster. *To prevent civil war the authorities had to send a force of soldiers and police to Lough Mark,* and Captain Boycott's harvest were brought in and his potatoes dug by the armed Ulster laborers, guarded always by the little army.[18]

This passage provides clues for understanding the meaning and source of the "boycott is tiger" metaphor. Justice Carpenter's rendition of the story of Captain Boycott begins with the observation that the District of Connemara (County Mayo) was "wild and beautiful."[19] He then notes that the poor Irish tenants who were evicted by Captain Boycott from his estate "suddenly retaliated in a most unexpected way."[20] The tenants retaliated, boycotting Captain Boycott in a "very thorough manner."[21] Captain Boycott and his family were depicted as helpless victims; their "[lives] appeared to be in danger" and, according to Justice Carpenter, soldiers and police had to be sent in order to "prevent civil war." In the wild district of Connemara (where Lord Erne's Mayo Estate was located), workers suddenly retaliate like wild tigers, forcing helpless property owners off their land.[22] This image of the Irish boycott was thus stigmatized with negative images of boycott as uncivilized and animal-like behavior, characterizing the boycott as wild and dangerous.

The hidden conceptual meaning of the court's tiger metaphor can be explained in light of the metaphoric reason of the *Great Chain of Being* proverb.[23] As George Lakoff and Mark Turner have explained, the *Great Chain of Being* is a cultural model that concerns kinds of beings and their properties, and places them on a vertical scale with "higher" beings and properties above "lower" beings and properties.[24] The *Great Chain of Being* has been used in storytelling since ancient times, and it provides a commonplace theory for understanding our place in the universe. Our common-sense understanding of the nature of things allows us to think of humans as "higher-order beings" than animals.[25]

What makes the *Great Chain of Being* metaphoric is that we tend to rely upon our knowledge of the generic attributes of lower-order beings to comprehend specific behaviors of people.[26] The English proverb "All bark and no bite," for example, uses our commonplace understanding about dogs to convey a specific understanding about certain people. Conversely, the *Great Chain of Being* also allows us to comprehend the nature of animals and objects in terms of better-understood human characteristics.[27] In comparing the worker boycott in *Glidden* to a bloodthirsty tiger, the court associated the boycott with a lower-order being, thus placing it on a level with animals known to have bestial instincts and drives. The lower-level attributes of a wild tiger were identified with the workers' boycott and consequently helped legitimate the need for the court's injunction.[28]

The *Great Chain of Being* proverb permitted the court in *Glidden* to endow boycott activity with the vivid image of a wild tiger, thereby shaping the meaning of the activity by placing the boycott in the order of things. The tiger metaphor would have worked even without the *Great Chain of Being* proverb so long as one had a model of tigers as wild and bloodthirsty. However, because some models of tigers are more appealing and less threatening (consider, for example, the less threatening, almost human image of tiger in William Blake's poem "The Tyger,")[29] more was needed to link the workers' boycott to the dangerous tiger model.

The metaphoric reason of the *Great Chain of Being* proverb permitted the court to connect the force of the workers' boycott with the "brute force" of a bloodthirsty tiger.[30] The workers had utilized a "dangerous instrumentality"[31] because they had acted, in concert, on their bestial instincts and animal drives. The workers' boycott in *Glidden* was thus perceived as dangerous since some people were felt threatened much in the same way that one would be threatened by the incomprehensible instincts of a wild beast who thirsts for human blood.

The *Great Chain of Being* also explains the cognitive meaning of the "Zulu" analogy made in the Irish Press to describe the meaning of the tenant boycott against Captain Boycott. In analogizing the tenants to "savage Zulus," the Irish Press[32] encouraged its readers to comprehend the meaning of that boycott as a serious threat to civilized society. Uncivilized savages may be higher up on the chain than wild tigers, but they are still imagined to be lower when compared to the predominantly white civilized society of Great Britain. Boycotting workers were imaginatively placed in a dangerous category created for explaining the behavior of uncivilized and unpredictable "lower-level" beings.

Hence, when the *Glidden* court attributed the characteristics of lower-level beings to people, the court used the tiger image to deny human rights. A lower-level being was associated with the activity of a higher-level being to downplay the significance of a human activity. Persuasive as rhetoric, the *Great Chain of Being* proverb and the image of a bloodthirsty tiger provided the emotional or pathetic appeal of the *Glidden* decision.

In addition, the *Glidden* court, through its tiger metaphor, highlighted the idea of violence as the distinguishing characteristic of boycott. The court described the nature of the boycott in terms of the unruly behavior of an animal to justify its legal conclusion that an otherwise peaceful boycott had a propensity for violence. Focusing on the instinctual propensity that tigers have for violence, Justice Carpenter was able to equate boycott with ideas of bloodshed. As Justice Carpenter put it, "[t]he exercise of irresponsible power by men, like the taste of human blood by tigers, creates an unappeasable appetite for more."[33] Ideas of wildness and mental images of uncontrollable animals thus colored the court's legal analysis of the labor boycott, much in the same way that the Ulster press attempted to color the meaning of the tenant boycott in Ireland by comparing it to the bloody Zulu uprising in South Africa.

It is true that wild animals are unpredictable and uncontrollable. They may seem cute and docile one minute, but they can suddenly turn and bite the hand that feeds them, for no reason that humans can understand. Even wild animals domesticated by humans will eventually grow up and fail to conform to human codes, unlike a dog or a cat. It's in their nature, and there is nothing we can do about it. What seemed like violence to the *Glidden* court, however, was just ordinary business to the tiger. In the tiger's world, it is not murder to kill for food; it is just part of the day-to-day business of survival. Similarly, the proud warriors in the tribe of Zulu had lived for centuries as the rulers of their land; their behavior in attacking British troops at the end of the last century was quite understandable given the invading intentions of the British.

The tiger's world was thus governed by a code of behavior that was incomprehensible to the judge in *Glidden*. And the same could be said of the Zulus in Africa who were fighting the British for control of their land and their culture. What might seem like wildness or lack of civilization to judges in America or Ireland may simply be the result of a different code of conduct. This gap in understanding may explain why the court failed to appreciate the value of the workers' boycott. The gap between the powerful (judges) and the powerless (workers) was so broad that the court was unable to grasp the meaning of boycott from the perspective of those who were boycotting. This gap in the judicial understanding enabled the court to think in terms of ideas of wildness and images of bloodthirsty tigers or Zulus in comprehending the meaning of a workers' boycott. The social gap between judges and workers was as wide as the gap between different species or different cultures. What was missed was the fundamentally different understanding of boycott gleaned from the perspective of boycotting workers.

In Justice Carpenter's mind, the instinctual nature of wild tigers was linked conceptually to boycott, and this association drove his narrative of Captain Boycott. The tiger metaphor caused Justice Carpenter to also perceive the Irish boycott as supremely dangerous: "[I]f this is a correct picture the thing we call a boycott originally signified violence, if not murder."[34] If boycotts are like a wild tiger thirsting for human blood, then boycotts are like the violence of murder.

Since Captain Boycott's time, there have been at least two basic ways to metaphorically describe the legal meaning of boycott. One, illustrated by Justice Carpenter's *Glidden* opinion, utilizes a picture of animalistic behavior to explain the meaning of boycott. Here the court's tiger metaphor is consistent with the way Irish Protestants, who were sympathetic to Captain Boycott, probably understood the meaning of the Irish tenants' boycott. The other way to understand the meaning of boycott can be found in the images of boycott projected from the boycotters' perspective (the tiger's perspective in the tiger metaphor).

Labor boycotts might have been seen as courageous and noble rather than wild and violent. The courts might have then understood the Irish boycott as it was initially understood by tenants in County Mayo or as it was understood by American colonists immediately before our revolution, as an example of citizen solidarity and political struggle, a story about the courageous effort of a group engaged in peaceful political and economic struggle for mutual aid and self-protection. The boycott could have been seen as an alternative to violence and murder.

The Irish Land League, unlike the I.R.A., or the "Mollies," advocated acts of peaceful civil disobedience and rejected the ways of the gun and bomb. Their boycott effort was a transformative act aimed at changing the economic system that favored a particular class, an event in an ongoing political struggle that was transforming fundamental social and economic institutions in Ireland and in America. However, because the court's common folk understanding of the nature of tigers was negative (wild tigers are normally thought to be dangerous and unpredictable) the *Great Chain* led Justice Carpenter to view labor boycotts as dangerous.

Justice Carpenter's opinion was subsequently followed by the Supreme Court of Virginia in its 1888 decision in *Grump v. Commonwealth*.[35] In *Grump*, Judge Fauntleroy consulted the *Glidden* decision, adopted Justice Glidden's narrative of Captain Boycott, and concluded: "The essential idea of boycotting, whether in Ireland or the United States, is a confederation, generally secret, of many persons, whose intent is to injure another, by preventing any and all persons from doing business with him, through fear of incurring displeasure, persecution and vengeance of the conspirators."[36]

Glidden and *Grump* thus illustrate one way judges at early common law imaginatively created a radial category for giving legal meaning to labor boycotts. This radial category was extended from a subset of prototypical characteristics from the central case of Captain Boycott. Imaginative metaphors of "wild tigers," "murderous behavior," and "illegal conspiracy" were chained to this radial category to define the legal meaning of labor boycott to an imaginative view of Captain Boycott as victim, and an imaginative view of the boycotters as "murdering Zulus."

FORCE, MOTION, AND UNCONTROLLABLE APPEAL OF GROUP EXPRESSION

The Supreme Court's 1911 decision in *Gompers v. Bucks Stove & Range Co.*[37] highlights a *force* image that has also been highly influential in shaping legal notions about labor boycotts in the formative era of the labor union movement. In *Gompers*, the Supreme Court concluded that the mere promotion of a threatened boycott by workers could be legally enjoined. The Court reached this curious result by adopting a metaphor that compared the verbal acts of boycott publicity to the physical acts of hypothetical boycott violence. As the Court explained, the "verbal acts of a boycott" are like the "use of any other *force* whereby property is unlawfully damaged."[38] This legal conclusion can be shown to be the cognitive entailment of the imaginative conceptual metaphor "Boycott is violent force" and the related conceptual metaphor "Actions are motions."

The case arose out of a bitter labor campaign to prevent the Bucks Stove & Range Company from ordering members of the stove polishers' union to work a ten-hour day instead of the accustomed nine hours. The controversy was highly publicized because James Van Cleve, president of the Bucks Stove & Range Company, was also president of the National Association of Manufacturers, an organization characterized within the labor movement as "a kind of antilabor chamber of commerce and Lions Club combined."[39]

The stove polishers went on strike, ignored a court injunction against the strike, and declared a boycott of Bucks Stove & Range's products. The leadership of the American Federation of Labor (AFL) was subsequently asked by the strikers to put the company on its "We Don't Patronize" list, published regularly in the AFL's trade union newspaper, *American Federationist*.[40] The union's president, Samuel Gompers, and the AFL agreed that a national boycott should be called against the company.

The Bucks Stove & Range Co. responded by obtaining an injunction against the AFL and its officers proscribing any interference with the sale of Bucks Stove & Range Co. products "in any manner," including "declaring or threatening any boycott . . . or assisting such boycott."[41] Gompers and several high-ranking officials of the AFL were subsequently convicted of civil contempt for violating a court injunction that had prohibited them from publicizing the boycott "in any manner." The Supreme Court reversed the contempt convictions of Gompers and two other union officials on procedural grounds,[42] but the Court's approval of the use of injunction to stop the promotion of a boycott constituted a stinging precedent for organized labor.[43]

Writing for a unanimous Supreme Court, Justice Lamar reasoned that the publication of the boycott publicity carried a "force not inhering in the words themselves," and served as an implied "agreement to act in concert when the signal [to boycott] was published." In rejecting the union's claim that the publicizing of a boycott was entitled to First Amendment protection to preserve "liberty of speech," the Court reasoned that the union's publicity involved "verbal acts" causing a "force" subject to legal injunction like any other act of "force" whereby property is damaged.[44]

Two reasons were found to justify associating the union's verbal acts with physical acts of force. First, because the boycott publicity intended to incite group action, the publicity was seen to create the potential for a "force not inhering in the words themselves, and therefore exceed[ing] any possible right of speech which a single individual might have."[45] Second, the Court concluded that the boycott publicity was coercive because the only way that the employer could comply was by "purchasing peace at the cost of submitting to terms which involve the sacrifice of rights protected by the constitution; or by standing on such rights and appealing to the preventive powers of a court of equity."[46] According to Justice Lamar, "When such appeal is made it is the duty of government to protect the one against the many as well as the many against the one."[47]

There were obvious problems with the logical integrity of Justice Lamar's idea of force. One problem was that mere publicity was enjoined; no evidence of actual physical coercion appeared in the record of the litigation. Another was that the Court upheld the injunction despite there being no lower court finding that the union had even directed its membership to coerce or threaten anyone. The case involved only the legality of the AFL's publication of the boycott notice. While the Court recognized that the judges may "differ as to what constitutes a boycott that may be enjoined," Justice Lamar failed to explain the basis for concluding that the mere publication of a boycott was "a means whereby a boycott is unlawfully continued, and . . . amount[s] to a violation of the order of injunction."[48]

Further, while Justice Lamar attempted to justify his conclusion that the AFL, a powerful union with "multitudes of members," was threatening to boycott someone, he also expressly recognized the "right of workingmen to unite and to invite others to join their ranks."[49] However, if boycott publicity is coercive merely because a group disseminates a message that causes others to act, as the Court suggested, then the ostensibly Court-affirmed legal right of workers to join for a common cause would seem hollow indeed.[50] Boycott slogans such as "Unfair" and "We Don't Patronize" would be a force every time the workers' message persuaded audiences. The reason why the promotion of a labor boycott should be interpreted as a forceful act, even in the absence of actual or potential coercion or physical force, was not explained.[51]

In *Glidden*, the court seemed to be concerned that the vast power of the multitudes of members of a labor organization could render an individual helpless in the face of a boycott threat. Labor boycott slogans such as "Unfair" and "We Don't Patronize" were thus interpreted as signals for concerted action to be taken against a defenseless target. These boycott signals must have seemed to Justice Lamar like a bomb waiting to explode. All that was needed was a call to action, such as a notice of a boycott, to light the fuse. These normative orientations in the background can explain why Justice Lamar saw the boycott publicity as a dangerous force, and it created an appealing pathos to justify his decisions.

A metaphor, however, was needed to explain why Justice Lamar understood the force of the boycott to be dangerous. A conceptual model of "boycott is violent force" and a conceptual metaphor "Actions are motions" provided the logic for Justice Lamar's legal conclusion that peaceful boycott publicity is a dangerous force. The spatial image of a path of motion from boycotters to a single target is the image schema that gives their unique meaning. The experience of physical motion is "mapped" onto labor boycott activities. The mapping is systematic, which "means that each of the entailments from the domain of physical mobility—the experience of blockage, containment, and movement through space toward desired objects—is also carried over to the target domain of abstract social action."[52]

The source of the *Gompers* boycott, the starting point, was the boycott organizers. The goal or ending point was Bucks Stove & Range Co. The communication of and response to boycott publicity aimed at the company was the path connecting the source with the goal. Because the boycott participants were numerous, and the target, the Bucks Stove and Range Company, was a single entity, the Court perceived the movement of the boycott to carry the force of a stampede. The force of the stampede of workers, which fuels itself, is reminiscent of the tiger in *Glidden*, whose "taste of human blood creates an unappeasable appetite for more."[53] In addition, a "corporation is person" metaphor humanized the target in this stampede, Bucks Stove & Range Co., and enabled the Court to see the target as a single entity. Thus, human actors protesting corporate action became nonhuman actors stampeding a solitary human victim.

It never occurred to Justice Lamar to consider other boycott images. The request of boycotters to cease doing business with the Bucks Stove & Range Company might have been imagined as peaceful protest. Some listeners might have grasped the boycott publicity as a command for action, but others might have interpreted the boycott as communicative expression about a dispute. The publicity might have caused some to laugh at the boycotters. The Court might have also considered the fact that a business entity is itself an organization made up of many individuals, with considerable power to counter a worker boycott. The Court emphasized other facts, however, because judges were predisposed to see the force of the boycott moving in a particular direction, toward an individual, helpless target.

In *Gompers*, as in *Glidden*, a metaphor shaped the legal meaning of the boycott in light of the judge's knowledge about physical force moving along a trajectory. Boycott publicity was viewed as force, the entity acted upon was an individual target, and the trajectory was the compulsion of the appeal of the boycotters. In this way, the mental schematic of a boycott as a compulsory force led the courts to the outcome that boycott activity had to be legally restrained. The court's opinion reasoned metaphorically, treating boycott as something that sweeps people along to compel them to do things they might not otherwise do.

In *Gompers*, the Supreme Court was thus able to conclude that publicity of a boycott involved a moral force, and in *Glidden*, the court understood the boycott as a physical force. The idea of force can thus be seen to be structured by the experience of physical as well as moral compulsion. Individuals can be forced to take action through physical compulsion, the meaning of which is linked to knowledge about how our bodies interact with external and internal physical forces. The meaning of force can also be understood, as it was in *Glidden*, as social or ethical force, such that action is brought about through moral persuasion or group peer pressure. It is, however, the basic conceptual metaphor "Actions are motions" that enabled the *Glidden* court to recognize this meaning of force.

Gompers has never been overruled, and the legal meaning of boycott upon which the decision rests is now deeply entrenched in labor law discourse despite heavy criticism. It is now well accepted, for example, that state or federal governments may regulate peaceful labor boycotts in order to protect society from economic disruption. While the Supreme Court recognized in its 1940 *Thornhill v. Alabama*[54] decision that picketing is a form of speech that cannot be absolutely prohibited by government, the Court has also held that picketing and boycotting involve nonspeech elements that can be regulated because they may affect a compelling governmental interest.[55] The courts have also accepted the notion that the signaling effects of boycott publicity can be regulated as "verbal acts."[56] Courts have found these signals to be coercive, and therefore subject to regulation, by adhering to the pathos of the "force" metaphor of boycott, and ignoring the obvious weakness of its Logos or logic. What would motivate judges to use these curious metaphors of boycott in cases like *Glidden* and *Gompers*?

THE CULTURAL BACKGROUND FOR LABOR BOYCOTT METAPHORS

In this section, I will identify what I believe to be the defining social moment in American labor history that grounds the meaning of these curious metaphors. When the courts first grappled with the conflicts of labor boycotts in *Glidden* and *Gompers*, there was a cultural history that sedimented the background assumptions and normative orientations of the judges. The background culture provides insight for understanding the normative orientation of the metaphors judges used in their opinions. There was, in other words, a "sedimented background" that had distinctive normative orientations for shaping the "foreground" of legal decision making.[57]

The origins of labor union strikes, picketing, and boycotting date to the early 1800s.[58] The earliest reported American labor case was tried in 1806, when the Philadelphia Cordewainers (shoemakers) were indicted for engaging in a criminal conspiracy for calling a strike for higher wages.[59] The first organized labor boycott in America was organized by the Baltimore hatters in 1833.[60] According to newspaper stories of the day, journeymen hatters protesting a 25 percent reduction in wages issued an appeal to all other workers and consumers in Baltimore to cease doing business with the employers who were reducing their wages. These events preceded the coining of the word *boycott*, but they were the first signs of labor unrest precipitating boycott activity at an ever greater level of intensity.

As Christopher Tomlins has observed: "For labor and management the last years of the nineteenth century and the first years of the twentieth were an 'era of sharp conflict.'"[61] It was a time of acute conflict in America between the owners of capital, the state apparatus that supported them, and the vast majority of working people. Conflict between owners of capital and labor engendered a sense of urgency on behalf of business leaders, the government, and the judiciary. State court judges tended to view the collective action of workers as a bomb waiting to explode or a riot threatening to erupt. The bomb and riot metaphors had their source in numerous violent strikes and disputes involving the history of organized labor, but one highly publicized and politically intense event in the history of the labor movement stands out from all others—the bloody incident known as the *Haymarket Riot*.

THE HAYMARKET RIOT AND THE FEAR OF CLASS CONFLICT

In 1877, during a period of economic depression, railroad workers throughout the country struck and boycotted for higher wages. This general strike began in Baltimore, where at Camden Junction the strikers stopped a freight train and convinced the fire and brake men to leave their posts. The mayor responded by arresting the union leadership, who were quickly set free by the militia, many of whom were friends and relatives of the strikers. This forced the mayor to bring in federal troops who would be more willing to fire upon strangers. On July 20, 1877, a running battle ensued between the police and federal troops and striking workers. The police and federal troops killed ten people and wounded at least fifty.[62] In Pittsburgh, where the strike had spread, one thousand troops sent from Philadelphia engaged stone-throwing youths to help them implement martial order. At one point, a division of the militia, surrounded by enraged citizens in a roundhouse, blasted their way out, killing twenty people. These blood-drenched clashes were a perennial occurrence in the early labor history of the United States.

The use of labor boycotts in disputes with employers coincided with the rise of the American labor union movement. The Noble Order of the Knights of Labor, founded in 1869 by Uriah S. Stephens, for example, claimed a membership of some six hundred thousand by 1886 and had a number of successes in conducting strikes and boycotts against employers. The Knights of Labor looked primarily to boycott and strikes in maintaining its collective actions. The ultimate goal of the Knights was the abolishment of the wage system.[63] However, the initial success of the Knights of Labor soon turned sour as judges came to understand labor boycott activities as either a bomb waiting to explode or a riot threatening to erupt. What enabled judges to invoke these images was an underlying fear of class conflict.

The judicial image of a labor dispute as a bomb was shaped by the famous Haymarket Riot. The so-called riot took place in Chicago on May 4, 1886, six years after Father O'Malley coined the word *boycott* in Ireland and one year before the word was used in the Connecticut decision in *Glidden*. This riot epitomized the violent reaction against labor boycotts that had been developing in the United States since the railroad strikes. The incident was a *cause célèbre* for American labor. The Haymarket Riot developed out of a workers' rally in support of the eight-hour day.[64]

The government and press had widely denounced the strike as a ridiculous socialist daydream. From the union's perspective, the idea of striking for an eight-hour day was as sensible as striking for pay without hours. From the perspective of the business community, however, there was the fear that a strike to enforce the demand for eight-hours work a day would paralyze industry, depress business, and check the reviving prosperity of the country. As Samuel Yellen, a labor historian, documents, much industry was stalled by the strike: "The building interests, then enjoying a boom, were suddenly paralyzed. The great metal foundries and vast freight yards were tied up."[65] During the years leading up to the Haymarket Riot, passions and prejudices were heated to the boiling point.

The Haymarket incident occurred after a peaceful rally at which the leading anarchist labor leaders of Chicago had spoken in Haymarket Square under the watchful eyes of hundreds of police officers. As the night wound to a close, the governor went home, pleased that all had gone smoothly. Unfortunately, an overly zealous Inspector Bonfield decided prematurely that the rally was over. Despite the fact that one of the leaders remained at the speakers wagon addressing the workers, the inspector ordered 180 troops to approach the workers. The captain of the contingency of police ordered the speaker to step down and the workers to go home. The speaker refused, and moments later, orders were shouted to the police, and a bomb was thrown, from the area of the speakers wagon, in the police ranks. The bomb exploded and sent the police into a frenzy of return fire that left several dead and two hundred injured. The police themselves lost seven officers and had sixty-six wounded.[66]

There was wide speculation as to the identity of the bomber. In the end, the most likely suspects were released in favor of holding the union leadership responsible for organizing the rally. Four anarchist leaders were hanged despite the fact that there had been little evidence of guilt and many judicial irregularities. A fifth defendant committed suicide. The rally and explosion subsequently came to be known as the Haymarket Riot, and for the next generation, organized associations of workers were associated in the minds of many with the violence of mob action, riots, and exploding bombs. Dynamite and mob action thus came to characterize the meaning of otherwise peaceful labor activity.

The Haymarket Riot sedimented a number of cultural assumptions that permitted judges to imagine the collective activities of labor as a threat to status quo. An underlying fear of class conflict, graphically illustrated by the bombing at the Haymarket Riot, established the normative orientation for treating the collective activity of workers as a dangerous force to be curtailed by law. It didn't take much of a stretch for American judges to fear class conflict and to think of labor groups as a destructive force in society. The labor problem in America was, after all, coming to the forefront of public attention at the same time that land wars in Ireland were projecting images of an unruly tenantry class as savage Zulus, murdering the civilized agents of British society. Perhaps images of class, combined with an unarticulated subtext of race and foreignness, nurtured the idiom of boycott in the eyes of the establishment in both Ireland and in America.

The organizational impulse of the labor movement was the same impulse that motivated a united tenantry class at the end of the nineteenth century in Ireland, and created the background for the boycott against Captain Boycott. What emerged as class conflict in America, however, was co-opted by a legal culture that accommodated labor to the interests of large-scale corporate capitalism.[67] As we will see, class conflict was mediated in adjudications that gave corporations the rights of individuals, and unions the stigma of criminal conspiracy.

As labor boycotting swept over the country in 1885, modern labor unions came to use the word *boycott* in organizing workers on a regular and national basis.[68] In that year, the newspaper *Bradstreet's* documented the use of 196 boycotts by labor unions.[69] The use of the phrase "boycott as weapon" colored the way the press and courts came to characterize the labor boycott problem. The idea that collective action was being used to pressure employers to recognize labor union demands was seen by judges and the media as a weapon used by unruly mobs to bring down the capitalist system. To some, the very existence of an organized working class, largely immigrant, was viewed as a subversive threat made up of individuals who were using the weapon of a boycott to undermine the sanctity of private property in a free market.

The tiger model of boycott in the *Glidden* case, used to characterize an otherwise peaceful and nonthreatening boycott as an act of murder, thus makes perfect sense when one considers the prevailing popular views of labor boycott in late-nineteenth-century America.[70] Moreover, by the time *Glidden* was decided, stories about Irish-American mine workers known as the Molly Maguires, or "Mollies," had imprinted in the mind of many Americans a picture that associated labor groups with acts of violence and murder. The Mollies were a violent and highly secret society of Irish workers, some of whom emigrated from the region of Ireland near County Mayo, where the boycott against Captain Boycott had taken place.[71] The Land League nationalists involved in the actual boycott against Captain Boycott eschewed the use of violence that had been practiced by the "Molly Maguires nearly forty years earlier."[72] Nonetheless, in the popular conception of many Americans, County Mayo, Ireland, must have seemed like a wild and dangerous region, where uncivilized Irish peasants, operating in secret societies, were prone to use violence against their employers and agents. It was not all that surprising then that Justice Carpenter, writing in *Glidden* shortly after the word *boycott* was first used in Ireland, would choose to use the words *tiger* and *murder* to describe the meaning of a peaceful and nonthreatening boycott action. What the tiger model misrepresented was the reality that boycott in Ireland and America was a nonviolent act of civil disobedience necessary to bring reform to the social relations between labor and capital. The Haymarket Riot, itself a misrepresentation of an actual event,[73] served to solidify the accuracy of the labor boycott images and metaphors used by judges to restrict labor union activity during the formative period of the labor movement.

When the word *boycott* first appeared in America, judges made reference to the Irish tenants' boycott, but they associated the word with what they viewed as the revolutionary and dangerous tendencies of working people prone to violence. Exceptional and marginal labor organizations such as the Industrial Workers of the World (IWW) and the Molly Maguires helped to justify these stereotypes. Hence, when judges first confronted boycotts by labor, they used every rhetorical arrow in their judicial quiver to invalidate the use of the boycotts by identifying with the targets of the boycott instead of the boycotting actors. The horrifying images of riotous mobs and of bombs exploding, made famous by the Haymarket Riot, became the linguistic source for the legal vilification of labor boycotts and the workers who were associated with them. Labor boycotts were quickly identified as criminal activities, and the word became associated with the dangers of an unruly mob threatening to hurl bombs at peaceful citizens.[74]

An Ohio court in 1897 concluded, for example, that even peaceful labor boycotting represented a coercive combination that extended beyond "the limits of law and order."[75] While it was recognized that workers had the right individually to engage in peaceful assemblies to persuade others not to enter into a relation with the employer, it was also recognized that "persuasion, with the hooting of a mob and deeds of violence as auxiliaries, is not peaceable."[76]

Labor boycotts were associated in the courts with images of illegality, disorder, insurgency, and hooting mobs. Hence, "[s]ome judges denounced boycotters' motives as 'wicked,' 'insolent and truculent.' Others described their behavior as 'cruel, heartless and unrelenting,' or showing 'wantonness and malice' with the 'grossest tyranny.'"[77] As one court boldly proclaimed: "Intimidation and coercion are essential elements of a [labor] boycott."[78] Another court declared that the "word 'boycott' [was] itself a threat,"[79] and yet another concluded that the term carries with it a "menace, as acquired in popular vocabulary."[80] These images of labor boycott reflected an underlying fear of unions as outsiders and collective labor activity as violent class conflict.

When *Glidden* and *Gompers* are read within their cultural context, it is understandable that judges might find otherwise peaceful labor boycotts to represent a dangerous force not unlike the threat of a bloodthirsty tiger or a herd of stampeding beasts. The images of violence evoked by the exploding bomb in Chicago during the Haymarket Riot were vividly inscribed in the judicial imagination, and those images misrepresented the nature of most labor boycotts.

TRANSCENDING CULTURAL CONTEXT

The negative images of boycott found in the early reported legal opinions in America were consistent with the way the Irish legal system and the Irish landlord class understood the meaning of Captain Boycott. Subsequent tenant boycotts were the subject of criminal prosecutions in Ireland, and the Irish legal system, like the American legal system, viewed boycotts as a danger that had to be restrained by orderly legal process. However, prosecutions of boycotts in Ireland and in America, tried before juries, failed to produce convictions or serious penalties. In Ireland, the dominant image of boycott in popular culture was associated with law and justice, whereas in America, the legal image of boycott was associated in legal culture with law-breaking and violence.

A new idealized cognitive model of labor boycott was eventually created by American judges from the central case involving Captain Boycott. Imaginative ideas about the central case created a radial category of boycott for understanding the legal meaning of labor boycotts. This model of boycott was a radial category because it was related to the central case involving Captain Boycott. Figure 2.1 maps the radial category of labor boycotts in America.

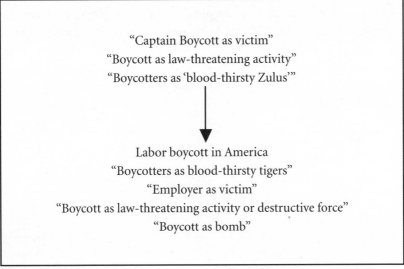

Figure 2.1
Radial Category of Labor Boycott

Captain Boycott consequently became a model or cognitive template used by American judges to assimilate the legal meaning of labor boycott to the prototype effect of violence. In *Glidden*, the Connecticut Supreme Court revisited the story of Captain Boycott and discovered the imaginative metaphors of "Captain Boycott is victim" and "boycotting is law-threatening activity." The cultural metaphors in the establishment press describing the boycotting tenants as "bloodthirsty savage Zulus" was in keeping with the Connecticut court's description of boycotting workers "as bloodthirsty wild tigers." In *Gompers*, the United States Supreme Court used the same imaginative model for relating the prototypical effects of boycott publicity to the destructive force of a bomb. Metaphoric reason used to give meaning to boycott thus transcended language and culture by essentializing and motivating the legal meaning of labor boycott as violence.

Because the central case of boycott was capable of portraying boycott as either law-enforcing or law-threatening activity, it generated diverse legal meanings of boycott. A number of default metaphors have defined how the central case operates in a particular legal field. The way in which these default metaphors operate requires further analysis of the way metaphoric reason functions in the law to give rise to different prototypical cognitive effects of labor, civil rights, and commercial boycotts. At this point, it is sufficient to emphasize that there is no single, correct metaphor for characterizing the legal meaning of boycotts in the law.

CHAPTER 3
BOYCOTTS AND
COGNITIVE THEORY

O NE MIGHT THINK today, more than a hundred years after the Glidden decision, that labor boycotts would be cleansed of their early negative images in the law. For example, a pair of linguistic scholars, Eve V. Clark and Herbert H. Clark, writing in 1979, concluded that the "noun origins" of the word *boycott* had become "completely lost" in popular expressions, such that when the word is used today as a verb ("boycott the store"), the word has become an "opaque idiom" of speech lacking any connection to Captain Boycott, or any particular historical or cultural context.[1]

As I have shown in chapter 2, however, judges at early common law did consider the meaning of the word in light of Captain Boycott, and Captain Boycott as the central case continues to influence the way the word is understood in the law today. Indeed, in chapter 7, we will have occasion to review a recent Supreme Court decision where Justice Scalia once again consults the story of Captain Boycott to ascertain the meaning of the word.[2]

In going back to the origins of the word, American judges have rediscovered metaphoric images for giving meaning to the word *boycott*— images that are far from opaque. The metaphors used by judges for describing the origins of the word help to explain the ideology of adjudication. In the law, the word has become an *ideological* idiom with distinct normative roots that have ideological consequences for adjudication. If the word is opaque, it is because the chameleon-like metaphors used by judges to give legal meaning to boycott phenomena conceal their metaphysical groundings. Because the legal meaning of the word *boycott* changes from context to context, it has the appearance of being an opaque idiom of speech.

In this chapter, I will offer an explanation for boycott case law that links the structure and ideology of legal doctrine to the forms of metaphoric reasoning used by judges. My objective will be to explain how the word *boycott* can be interpreted *metaphorically*—that is, as a structure of symbolic representations or socially constructed mental images shaped by conceptual metaphors, image schemas, and idealized cognitive models. When viewed metaphorically, boycott opinions can be interpreted as imaginative narratives that are both constrained and facilitated by imaginative ideas about force, balance, containment, parts and wholes, and the like. These imaginative ideas are central to the cognitive process in the law, and they have a particular grounded source derived from bodily experience and cultural context. Moreover, the metaphoric transference of this cognitive process creates opportunities for judges to engage in lawmaking activity in adjudication without ever having to reveal their true ideological role.

What Justice Stevens saw as the chameleon-like nature of boycott doctrine turns out to be the intelligible product of an imaginary and ideological process structured by an embodied legal imagination.[3] Boycott metaphors appearing in written legal opinions are thus more than interesting metaphors or similes; metaphor has shaped judicial opinion by performing a silent, but important, legitimating role in the law, through which judicial reasoning is made conceptually possible. Metaphor is what gives boycott its chameleon-like character.

METAPHOR AS A COGNITIVE ENGINE

In analyzing boycott problems in the law, judges, lawyers, and legislators, like everyone else, use words of a language system to define and give meaning to observable phenomena. The unstated assumption is that words can mirror, or objectively represent, fields of reality out there in the world. Language is commonly understood to be a relatively reliable framework or tool for analyzing and evaluating real-world events. Legal decision makers use words to solve problems, but they never bother to consider whether the words they use can bias the preferred framework for conceptualizing problem solutions. The problem of bias is never presented to us because we share the judge's framework for conceptualizing language as a mirror for reflecting the reality of phenomena.

Recently, however, cognitive theorists working with new ideas about metaphor have questioned the objectivist assumptions embedded within the traditional literal theories that structure our conceptions of language.[4] George Lakoff, Mark Johnson, Mark Turner, Michael J. Reddy, and others have shown that language is not a mirror of an objective, autonomous reality, and that our commonly held ideas about human communication are, in fact, the imaginative construct of human imagination. Language cannot operate as a mirror because, as cognitive theorists insist, many, if not all words we use are "fundamentally and ineradicably metaphoric."[5]

Cognitive theorists thus insist that the reasoning process is conceptually "metaphoric" rather than analogical, logical, or objectively rational.[6] They argue that metaphors function conceptually by evoking images that become the logical determinants of comprehension and communication. For them, metaphor is the engine that gives meaning to experience. They claim that we think, act, and even dream by using metaphors. A favorite example is the conventional meaning of the word *argument*, as it is used in everyday language. What lawyers and most people mean when they argue is not based on a literal, objective definition, but rather on a basic conceptual metaphor "argument is war."[7] This metaphor explains statements such as "Your claims are *indefensible*. He *attacked every weak point* in my argument. I *demolished* his argument." Such sentences have meaning because argument is conceptualized in law as a form of combat. The metaphor "argument is war" structures, at least in part, what lawyers do and how lawyers understand what they are doing when they argue.

The metaphor "argument is war" is a basic-level metaphor that explains, only in part, how lawyers, and nearly everyone else, comprehend an important quality of legal argument. Some metaphors, however, are so powerful that they create an "entire metaphoric system" for understanding many different aspects of some phenomenon. The cognitive theorist Michael J. Reddy, for example, has shown how the conduit metaphor has structured our understanding of human communication itself.[8] The conduit metaphor transfers information about the physical domain of a conduit or container to give meaning to the intellectual domain used to understand human communication. We thus understand the domain of language by reference to the physical domain of the embodied experience of *containment*. Ideas are metaphorically understood as "objects," words are "containers," and language is a "conduit." As Reddy explains: "Each of us is a container, with a bounded surface and an in-out orientation."[9] We experience our bodies as object containers like a box. Basic bodily experiences like *up* and *down* thus provide us with an experiential frame for understanding that "up is more" and "down is less." The metaphor "body is container" is also a powerful semantic structure that enables us to imagine language as a receptacle used to carry ideas from speaker to listener. The container metaphor influences the way lawyers and judges give meaning about language and legal arguments: The metaphor structures the meaning of statements such as "this argument lacks *content*," or "lacks *substance*," or that this argument "won't *hold* water."

The conduit metaphor performs a *constitutive* role in establishing the preferred frame for conceptualizing what we know about language and communication.[10] Unlike analogical reasoning, which proceeds from "case to case," metaphoric reasoning is capable of producing "fully realized ideas."[11] The conduit metaphor, for example, provides a fully realized model for understanding the nature of human communication itself—how it works, the problems it sets for practical solution, and the type of issues likely to be presented for debate and analysis. Hence, in the law, freedom of speech becomes a "fully realized idea" as a result of the conduit metaphor—speech is a conduit for carrying ideas and information to a receiving public; ideas exist within the words, and hence, free speech is about words not action.

When judges use a metaphor to conceptualize phenomena, they invoke a "complete image and apply it to a situation as a means of conceptualizing that situation in its entirety."[12] As legal theorists Edward Rubin and Malcolm Feeley have explained: "There is a visual quality to metaphor; it is like a picture, where one sees the totality at a glance and then fills in the details upon closer examination."[13] Unlike linear forms of reasoning that proceed from point-to-point, metaphoric reasoning evokes a complete picture without the need for filling in the details and points in the image. "The metaphor of a chilling effect in First Amendment law, for example, brings to mind in an instant a complete mental image of a cold wind emanating from the offending governmental agency and of potential speakers, like pedestrians in Chicago, withdrawing in discomfort to protect themselves from its effect."[14]

The real power of metaphor, however, is its ability to ingrain in the imagination a picture that is used over and over again to categorize different phenomena. We use metaphors to categorize objects, not in linear theoretical terms, but in terms of *prototypical effects* of *idealized cognitive models* of a common case or base-line example, stock story, or conceptual frame for making comparisons, seeing resemblances, and reasoning across different domains. George Lakoff and Mark Johnson, borrowing from the landmark research of the cognitive psychologist Eleanor Rosch, cite a popular example to illustrate how the theory of prototypes and basic-level categories entail important cognitive qualities or what they call "prototypical effects" of idealized cognitive models. As they explain: "For example, small flying singing birds, like sparrows, robins, etc., are *prototypical birds*. Chickens, ostriches, and penguins are birds but are not central members of the category—they are nonprototypical birds. But they are birds nonetheless, because they bear sufficient family resemblances to the prototype; that is, they share enough of the relevant properties of the prototype to be classified by people as birds."[15]

The prototypical effect of the idealized cognitive model *bird* is what enables us to instantly classify different types of birds we observe in nature. Our category for bird is constructed from a cognitive model structured by a basic-level metaphor, "generic is specific." Hence, the generic-level structure of the metaphor "bird is a flying object" enables us to intuit that a robin is a bird, but maybe not a penguin, and certainly not an ostrich. Lakoff and Johnson conclude that the prototypical effects of idealized cognitive models are experienced as a gestalt-like response of a conceptual metaphor used to classify phenomena.[16] When judges use the word *boycott*, they have in mind a generic-level image of what they understand to be a prototypical boycott, and they then use the prototype category or model to classify the legal meaning of different boycott phenomena.

Prototype analysis allows the observer/judge to form a partial theory of meaning based on prototypes and central cases. Boycott as murdering Zulus becomes a theory of boycott that enables judges to understand a peaceful labor boycott as a variant of the Zulu prototype—boycotting workers are conceptualized as bloodthirsty tigers, and boycott itself is classified as a form of murder. Because we are never completely conscious of the way prototype analysis operates to influence our cognitive analysis, judges—like everyone else—assume a neutral stance with respect to the prototypical analysis they use to justify their legal decisions. When judges use the word *tiger* to explain the legal meaning of a labor boycott, they are never completely clear about the cognitive link between boycott and wild tigers, and it is thus understandable that the normative consequences of the metaphor would remain unstated in their opinions and in their cognitive thoughts.

Prototype theory also explains how judges conceptually classify and categorize on the basis of what cognitive theorists call a *radial category*.[17] Subcategories imaginatively derived from the central case, learned not from logical deductions from rules but rather from conventions of a particular culture and human experience, is what is meant by the idea of a radial category. As Steven L. Winter has explained: "A radial category consists of a central model or case with various extensions that, though related to the central case in some fashion, nevertheless cannot be generated by rule."[18] Hence, we can think of the central case involving Captain Boycott as having prototypical properties like rays that move along different narrative paths to give different meaning to the word *boycott*. One ray of meaning maps an understanding of boycott that views boycott as a response to predatory conduct of the target. Another ray of meaning moves along a different narrative path that views the boycott as a destructive force, threatening to innocent victims.

The relation between the legal meaning of the word *boycott* and the man Captain Boycott involved more than just the linguistic use of a name to label what we know as a boycott. A family resemblance category for characterizing legal meaning of a labor boycott was generated from the central case involving Captain Boycott to establish a radial category extension or *ray* for defining the legal meaning of the boycott. Different linguistic meanings of the radial categories have since been created by different default metaphors used to define the fault lines between the radial categories of boycotts of different groups in the law. The default metaphors applicable to the labor boycott create prototypical mental images that enable judges to distinguish a labor boycott from boycotts of civil rights or business groups.

In *Glidden*, the court's legal meaning of the workers' boycott was the product of a default metaphor created by the domain of dangerous wild animals (the tiger analogy) and a metaphor of force derived from embodied physical experience. The legal understanding of labor boycott thus became a radial category extension of the central case with its own unique prototypical effects structured by the default metaphors of "Boycott is tiger" and "Boycott is force." These default metaphors combined in *Glidden* to create a new radial category extension for associating the legal meaning of otherwise peaceful labor boycott activity with inherently violent if not murderous activity. The radial extension from one narrative ray of the central case (Captain Boycott as victim, boycotters as bloodthirsty Zulus, boycott as law-threatening activity) enabled the *Glidden* court to make what many would see today as a strange category association—peaceful boycott as murder. In *Glidden*, we thus have an example of what cognitive theorists call "*chaining* with a category: some extensions are incorporated on the basis of their relation to an existing category-member rather than to the central case."[19] The central case defined by the prototypical effects of knowledge about wild tigers and the physical experience of force is chained to the radial category, giving it a meaning marked by the normative orientation of another radial category (wild animals, destructive force, mobs, bombs, etc.). The important ramification is that boycott categories do not operate on the basis of rules as such since the categories are constructed from prototype effects of imagined default metaphors.

The legal analysis of labor boycotts did not proceed rationally at all. Instead, the analysis developed on the basis of a metaphoric image that permitted judges to see a limited subset of prototypical properties of the central case or model of boycott. In the early history of the labor movement, the image of violent, unruly mobs, exploding bombs, and riots created a common model or central case for understanding the legal meaning of collective labor activity. The meaning of the common model was used to extend the radial category of the word *boycott* to imaginative metaphors of "animalistic behavior," "murder," "exploding bombs," and the like. The prototypical effects of the radial category served to establish legal meaning for an idealized cognitive model of labor boycotts. Labor boycott metaphors thus permitted judges to cognitively experience different prototypical effects, to extend radial categories, and to *chain* new default metaphors to create new radial categories.

Judges instinctively use the radial category to classify labor activities as either lawful or unlawful. They extend the central case to define the legal meaning of new boycott phenomena, and they chain their imaginative models of boycott to other radial categories. What animates this imaginative process are metaphors used to give meaning to things. Metaphoric reasoning thus creates a number of colorful imaginative images of boycott that recur in case after case as judges classify and analyze collective activities of different boycott groups. This is why boycotts of labor, civil rights, and business groups are analyzed differently in the law; each legal category of boycott is an extension of a common case based on different prototypical effects of default metaphors of boycott.

While the prototypical effects of boycotts change over time (judges no longer classify boycotters as "wild tigers"), the basic idealized cognitive models (the central imagined case) remain relatively constant as judges develop new imaginative metaphors to give meaning to central case (e.g., boycott is "weapon," "mob," "force," etc.). Consequently, with the use of a new default metaphor, judges can restructure the frame of the central case so that it appears as a different kind of case. What was a "tiger" is now "soapbox oratory;" what was "irresistible force" is now "natural competition." The thrust of the default metaphor shapes the way judges manipulate and classify objects and phenomena.

Hence, in labor law, the basic default metaphor of "boycott as violence" controlled the way judges manipulated prototypical properties of labor boycotts. Civil rights and business boycotts, as we will see, were analyzed under different default metaphors that have given rise to different perceived prototypical properties of these boycotts. The legal doctrine of *stare decisis* operates on the basis of manipulations of prototypical effects, but the substantive treatment of labor boycotts remained controlled by deeply ingrained default metaphors that created the distinguishing features of observed boycott phenomena.

Recognizing metaphor as a cognitive engine can lead to a better understanding of how law changes over time. Metaphoric shifts in the imaginative models used to comprehend the reality of phenomena loosen the imaginative moorings of a rule or doctrine such that it becomes possible to see the same phenomena from a totally new perspective. The change *in* perspective enables law to move to new substantive positions. Metaphor is thus a type of reason that needs to be studied in order to comprehend legal reason in its entirety. The conceptual role of metaphor can then be described, understood, and evaluated.

THE DYNAMIC NATURE OF METAPHORIC REASON

The dynamic nature of metaphoric reason is thus two-fold: metaphor simultaneously constrains and facilitates legal reasoning. First, metaphor constrains legal thought by relating judicial understanding of one subject in terms of another. Thus, metaphors are, by their very nature, only partial representations of reality. The partiality of metaphoric reasoning can lead to distortion and category mistakes. Judges make category classification based on metaphors. On the one hand, in focusing on the central case of the metaphor, judges may create an overinclusive or underinclusive category that fails to adequately fit the disputed events and phenomena at issue in litigation. On the other hand, if the metaphor fits the category or phenomena reasonably well, the metaphor created will do a good job in capturing the important prototypical properties of the disputed event or phenomena. Metaphors that become embedded in legal precedent, however, may no longer depict modern phenomena accurately, and they may fail to capture the full complexities of new events and phenomena. Hence, a relentless intellectual assault is possible whenever the foundations of old beliefs based on old metaphors are challenged by new metaphors.

Second, by constituting relevant prototypical categories and properties, metaphors facilitate efficient decision making by enabling judges to reach results without explicitly working through the complexity of disputed events and phenomena. To understand how this works, we must consider how metaphor can shape the frame of legal analysis on the basis of *image schemata*. Legal categories and doctrinal distinctions used in the boycott cases can be shown to have developed from recurring mental pictures or what cognitive theorists call image schemata.[20] These pictures or *image schema* are simply codes of common sense that we use subconsciously in cognitive thought. Elemental image schemata operate in the law to create different metaphoric domains or idealized cognitive models[21] of boycotts in the law, and these models have remained relatively constant.

An image schema is a "means of structuring particular experiences schematically, so as to give order and connectedness to our perceptions and conceptions."[22] Image schemata is a mental picture that provides us with general information for organizing our understanding of the world. Hence, our understanding of ideas such as container, path, cycle, link, balance, and so forth, allows us to make sense of relations among diverse experiences. Steven L. Winter provides a helpful example of the *source-path-goal* image schema structured by the conceptual metaphor "Life is a journey":

> Early in life, we discover that we can obtain objects by moving toward them through space. We imagine a *source-path-goal* structure to this experience. We then use this experience and its projected structure to elaborate all kinds of more abstract purposive activities. Thus, when we complete fifty percent of an intellectual task, like writing an article, for example, we say that we are *at the midpoint in our efforts* or that we are *halfway there*. As we near the end of our writing project, we see *the light at the end of the tunnel*. And, when we finish that article, we say that we have achieved our *goal*, or that we have completed what we *set out* to do.[23]

The source-path-goal schemata serves to motivate us to think in terms of a "systematic set of *journey* metaphors that are elaborated to conceptualize life" (emphasis added). As Winter has explained,

> Thus, we give our children an education to give them a good *start in life*. If they act out, we hope that it is *just* a stage (or something they are *going through*) and that they *will get over it*. As adults, we hope they won't be *burdened* or *saddled* with financial worries or ill health. We hope that they will *go far* in life. And we know that, as mortals, they will eventually *pass away*.[24]

An image schema creates the recurrent patterns that structure our actions, perceptions, and conceptions of life as a journey. "Image schematas [*sic*] are those recurring structures of, or in, our perceptual interactions, bodily experiences, and cognitive operations."[25] The structure of schemata can be traced to fundamental embodied experiences that we all share. The power of schemata is that it "colors and controls our subsequent thinking about its subject."[26]

Early in life, we rely upon information about how our bodies interact in the physical world in processing our worldly experiences. The image of verticality, based on the bodily experience of standing up, for example, allows us to employ an up-down orientation for understanding quantity in vertical terms: more is up, and less is down. The schema of "in-out" and "parts-whole," based as they are on the experience of body as containment, allows us to comprehend events and activities in terms of a container. The image schema of balance, derived from knowledge of body movement, creates prototypical effects that influence our basic notion of justice. Justice, symbolized by a scale, is understood as the maintenance of "proper balance."[27] The balance schema also structures the way we understand rational legal argument: "[L]awyers want the jury to *lean* in their favor, so they employ a confusing *mass* of facts, encourage *weighty* testimony, *pile* one argument upon another, add the *force* of acknowledged authorities, and summon the *weight* of the legal tradition."[28]

Judicial images about labor boycotts can be interpreted in light of the most common image schemata of force and force relationships.[29] We experience physical force as our bodies interact with gravity, light, heat, wind, bodily pressure, and other external physical objects and phenomena.[30] We associate these experiences in the process of making sense of the idea of force. They become the prototypical properties of the idea of force. The idea of boycott as force originates from basic bodily experiences such as the experience of being moved by a crowd of people.

As the cognitive theorist Mark Johnson has explained, "When a crowd starts pushing, you are moved along a path you may not have chosen, by a force you seem unable to resist."[31] We learn from what happens in a crowd that the idea of force relates to basic bodily experiences such as compulsion,[32] attraction,[33] or blockage.[34] The force of ideas can thus be understood in terms of physical force (e.g., the bodily experience of being swept away by a crowd moving in a particular direction). The idea of force can also involve moral and ethical persuasion or peer group pressure.[35] Responsible people can be swept along by the passion of a mob. Justice Holmes in *Moore v. Dempsey*,[36] for example, once argued that a mob-dominated atmosphere at a capital murder trial was such that "counsel, jury and judges *were swept to the fatal end by an irresistible wave of public passion*."[37] Boycott force may thus be the result of *social* force—compelling conformity with the group's objectives.[38]

Cognitive meaning of metaphoric reason does not, however, take place in a vacuum. Innumerable background conceptions and normative orientations of culture, contextual relation, and institutional setting influence the cognitive meaning of image schema and idealized cognitive models. Just as surely as facts are the product of selective observation, the mental process used to reason about facts is also the product of a highly selective imagination. In the early labor boycott cases, for example, the background conceptions and normative orientations of events like the Haymarket Riot, and deeply ingrained fears of class conflict, created a highly selective imaginative understanding of boycott. Labor boycotts, the most effective collective activity of labor unions were rendered illegal by a metaphoric form of reason that was normatively shaped by background assumptions that tended to treat organized labor activities as criminal conspiracies. Desired results were thus justified on the basis of a highly selective imaginative process.

The default metaphors used in adjudicating boycott cases were normatively loaded by background assumptions that explain why certain facts of boycott activity were heavily weighed and others not. Judges adjudicated boycott litigation under an analysis that seems nonideological even when the analysis was itself skewed by the imaginative tool that judges used in their analysis. Judges were quite effective in using their tools of analysis to deradicalize class conflict by using legal metaphors and cognitive models developed from a market-driven culture to accommodate the rights of workers to the rights of large-scale corporate capitalism. James B. Atleson's study *Values and Assumptions in American Labor Law*[39] has revealed, for example, how assumptions and values about the economic system, and the prerogatives of capital, underlie many contemporary labor decisions. These background assumptions and values have had the effect of accommodating interests and rights of workers to those of large-scale corporate capitalism. These assumptions and values can be explained in terms of the judicial concern for protecting the managerial control of the owner's interest in the business, and the corresponding "fear of anarchy" if workers were allowed to exercise their statutory rights fully.[40]

The ideological sway of metaphoric reason provides insight for understanding a central claim of the legal realist and critical legal studies movements;[41] namely, that legal decision making and adjudication is an intensely political activity.[42] A central assertion of the critical legal studies critique of adjudication is that adjudication is a "forum of ideology."[43]

Judicial opinions and the arguments of lawyers are what critical legal studies scholars regard as "the ideological documents, or texts" of the forum. As Duncan Kennedy has insisted, ideological conflict is a continuous "discursive process" that is managed and rationalized by deductive and policy modes of analysis that are presented as part of an abstract authoritative system that purportedly constrains ideology.[44] The normative character of the forum is masked by a discursive process created to give the appearance that law and its process is separate from politics.[45] The notion that labor disputes should be resolved in light of the stated purposes and policies of federal labor legislation, the "received wisdom" in labor law, has in fact been "deradicalized" by background assumptions of a market-driven economy that trump statutory rights of workers.[46]

Cogent policy analysis in adjudication is thought to turn on instrumental goals, but in labor law, as in many other areas of the law, policy is merely a way to rationalize ideology in legal decision making.[47] Critical legal scholars have defended the use of policy argument against the charge that it is necessarily a Trojan horse for ideology, even though no one can offer a compelling argument for why and how policy differs from ideology.[48] Most judges, however, believe that policy analysis is nonideological. Judge Richard A. Posner, for example, believes in the possibility of cogent policy analysis; he imagines that the pragmatic judge "rolls up his sleeves and does policy, hoping that the bar or the academy will provide him with the resources for making sensible policy analysis."[49] But, policy analysis requires agreement on instrumental goals and agreement often requires confronting the highly contingent images and metaphoric models that shape the way judges find consensus or goals. The selective choice of goals is itself a product of the imaginative process that motivates judges to see the world in a particular way such that certain goals are weighed more heavily than others. The Trojan horse is thus one of the theoretical unmentionables that is swept under the rug of serious pragmatic analysis about what judges do in fact.

What enables judges to conceal the ideology of their policy analysis is the normative sway of metaphoric reason. An example of how metaphoric reason can do this is illustrated by the way judges at common law imaginatively conceptualized the nature of boycotting groups and their targets. In chapter 4, I will explain how judges cognitively use policy to conceal their ideology in adjudication.

In *Glidden*, as we have seen, the court's characterization of the boycott as a wild tiger made sense in light of the concealed logic of the *Great Chain of Being* proverb. The proverb enabled the court to attribute the characteristics of a wild beast to the workers' boycott, and thus identify the radial category of labor boycotts with prototypical characteristics of the central case involving Captain Boycott (boycotters as wild Zulus, and Captain Boycott as victim of an uncivilized and unruly mob). The use of metaphor in *Glidden* provided more than just a linguistic aid for describing a cultural practice; metaphor created a fully realized metaphoric system for concealing an obviously biased normative understanding about the nature of peaceful labor boycotts. The ideological nature of the decision was concealed in information about the boycott derived from embodied experience.

As cognitive theorists have demonstrated, a key to uncovering the meaning of metaphor is the human body, and information that emerges from our embodied experience. Metaphors in the law are no different; embodied experience thus shapes legal doctrine. For example, by the late nineteenth century, judges advanced the idea that industrial organizations were like people, entitled to liberties that the law would protect under a free-trade policy. Metaphors such as "Corporation is a person" permit us to understand an abstract entity such as a corporation as a person. The metaphor "allows us to refer to it, quantify it, identify a particular aspect of it, see it as a cause. . . . Metaphors like this are necessary for even attempting to deal rationally with our experiences."[50]

The metaphor "Corporation is a person" became a rich and thickly textured imaginative device that enabled judges to socially construct a law of corporations based on the powerfully simple idea that the corporation is an entity, having rights like a person.[51] In talking about business entities as people, judges have linked corporations to humans, thus endowing them with human qualities. If a corporation were like a person, then it would be possible to understand how it might have a presence in a particular location or a will capable of reason and of being coerced by force.[52] As a fictional person, the corporation was accorded the legal recognition accorded to individuals but not groups. Also important was the fact that the act of incorporation was originally a matter of royal prerogative. Since the authority of the King ultimately derived from God, only the sovereign could create a legal person. Other groups and private associations could not claim to be created by the sovereign, and thus, they lacked legal recognition as a legal person. Since the law did not recognize groups but only individuals, private associations, such as labor unions, lacked legal rights as entities.

In the labor boycott cases, the "Corporation is a person" metaphor worked silently to enable judges to see worker boycotts as constituting a physical interaction between a group and a fictional person. This metaphor allowed Justice Lamar in the *Gompers* case to conclude that a labor boycott constituted a power that had been "used against one." Thus, in viewing a business entity as a person, the Supreme Court has been able to reason that a large business entity is a helpless individual needing protection from the superior force of many. Boycott was thus understood as a force directed against the body of a single person. This image has enabled courts to ignore contrary facts (e.g., the fact that a business entity was itself an organization made up of many individuals, with considerable power to counter a workers' boycott). What was ignored was the image of a mob of capitalists, subtly organized and united in their common interest of maintaining their authority over their investment. Judges did not visualize capitalists as a mob because they were not demonstrating on the streets as were labor groups. The activity of the owners of capital were viewed as the activity of individuals who acted alone in their offices even though the collective decisions reached had violent results for those workers who had no offices and who had to rely on direct action to advance their interests.

The reality is that the targets of the labor boycotts had their own collective organization, the National Association of Manufacturers, which historically was devoted to the cause of defeating organized labor.[53] Business entities had access to powerful allies that might have been more than sufficient to countervail whatever power a labor combination might assert with its boycott. It was also the case that the targets of a number of labor boycotts were able to persuade their employees and customers to ignore the boycott. Boycott calls, then as now, often fall short of their objectives. In treating a corporation or business entity as if it were a single person, however, judges were able to characterize labor boycotts as a one-sided struggle of the many against one. In conceptualizing a large corporate organization as a person, judges were able to make their policy arguments about the coercive nature of group action seem logically cogent and persuasive. The rhetorical sway of the metaphor, "corporation as person," was quite effective in concealing the ideological sway of the judge's policy perspective of the labor-capital dispute. Like the tiger metaphor in *Glidden*, the person metaphor humanized the corporate target while dehumanizing the combination of human workers. From this reversal, the court derived a powerful and persuasive negative *pathos* of labor boycotts for advancing what looks on the surface of the opinion to be a balanced and fair policy conclusion.

Judges did *not* apply the same metaphors to boycotts organized by business groups. Business combinations, organized as a single entity, were generally not perceived by judges as inherently coercive groups because they created relatively silent, less visible pressures of inducement and promise. Business boycotts were usually covert, involving only a handful of key individuals. Business organizations, structured as they were by charter and state law, exhibited to the world an orderly, legal appearance that could hide the actors, whereas labor unions had the appearance of potentially moblike collectives. These outward appearances explain the different attitudes of common-law judges in dealing with labor and capital in the late nineteenth century. The image of the labor union as a rowdy and passionate mob of workers, and the image of the corporation as a rational and reasonable person, explains why judges initially applied a double standard to labor and business boycotts.

The metaphoric representation of the modern corporation as a person is quite consistent with the way metaphor functions in law and culture generally. In *Metaphor and Reason in Judicial Opinions*, Haig Bosmajian observed that "the tropes, especially the metaphor, are not simply rhetorical flourishes and ornaments used to embellish discourse."[54] And as George Lakoff and Mark Johnson have warned, "Political and economic ideologies are framed in metaphoric terms. Like all other metaphors, political and economic metaphors can hide aspects of reality. But in the areas of politics and economics, metaphors matter more, because they constrain our lives. A metaphor in a political or economic system by virtue of what it hides can lead to human degradation."[55]

As Haig Bosmajian has also observed, "[T]he Nazis relied heavily on the disease and illness metaphors in their attacks on the Jews, Communists and other 'enemies.'" The Nazis spoke of the "Jewish bacillus," "the Bolshevist poison," "the Jewish plague," "the Jewish parasites," and the "Jewish cancer."[56] And as to the cancer metaphor, Susan Sontag has noted that it has been widely used in political discourse:

> Trotsky called Stalinism the cancer of Marxism; in China . . . the Gang of Four have become, among other things, "the cancer of China." John Dean explained Watergate to Nixon: "we have a cancer within—close to the Presidency—that's growing." The standard metaphor of Arab polemics—heard by Israelis on the radio every day for the last twenty years—is that Israel is "a cancer in the heart of the Arab world" or "the cancer of the Middle East."[57]

Interestingly, in the labor boycott case law, judges have used a cancer metaphor in explaining their prohibitions of boycott phenomena. As we will see, the cancer metaphor has driven the suppression of labor boycotts by judges. Secondary boycotts by labor unions have thus been analyzed by courts as if they were cancerous metastases spreading throughout the body. The visual quality of the metaphor provides a fully realized idea that urges the proscribing of secondary labor boycotts. It purports to conceptualize the entirety of all secondary boycotts.[58]

Metaphor has thus performed an important ideological role in framing negative or positive images judges attribute to boycott activity. Boycotts were tagged with negative images (diseases, wild animals, etc.) as judges decided that collective activity of groups should be suppressed. Boycotts were similarly tagged with positive images (soapbox oratory, free competition, etc.) as judges decided that collective activity of groups should be legally protected. There was a strong visual quality to the meaning of boycott, a meaning created at a glance through the picture of the metaphor used in boycott opinions.

METAPHORS ARE EVERYWHERE

If metaphors smuggle ideology into the policy deliberations of the law, as I have argued, then why haven't judges ruled metaphors out of the law's discourse? The simple answer is that they can't! Metaphors are embedded in our language and our thoughts; metaphors are everywhere. We need metaphors to gain insight about the meaning of boycott phenomena, and yet, the fact that metaphors can distort and sway opinion means that metaphors are neither neutral nor benign. Moreover, because metaphors are everywhere, they can not be avoided, even if we wished to do without them. We talk about communication as a process of transmitting substantive information across "conduits" from a sender to a receiver.[59] We thus say we wish *to get our thoughts across* so we *use as few words* as possible so that our listener can *extract the meaning out of our words*. The conduit metaphor frames these ideas and hence influences our understanding of language itself. We implicitly presume that language objectively mirrors reality and that the meaning of things can be transported objectively from a sender to a receiver. Metaphor is thus embedded within our concept of speech itself.

Because the conduit metaphor is embedded within our very concept of language, we cannot easily escape the influence of metaphor even though it may mislead and confuse our understanding about the nature of human communication. We ignore other alternative ways of conceiving of human communication because we mistakenly assume that communication is about sending and capturing ideas with words.[60] We can, however, critically examine the ways that metaphors frame problems and present them to us. The stories that we tell with metaphors may be the wrong stories we need to be telling in the law. Deeply held beliefs can be shaken by revealing how metaphoric reason leads to category mistakes and misrepresents important facts.

We can use metaphor to analyze how metaphoric reason works and to reveal the preferred frames of analysis that it generates. For example, in writing this book, I use metaphors to get my ideas across. I invoke the metaphor of an "engine" to emphasize the central importance of metaphor in the legal analysis of boycott decisions. I use the image of "default" to denote the courts' tendency to rely on particular metaphors without considering other options. The visual image of default, represented by the failure to pay a debt, and to forfeit by such failure, offers an alternative story for explaining how a basic conceptual metaphor can result in a "forfeit" of other possible legal interpretations of boycott phenomena.

Judges use metaphors because they are central to our cognitive process. But when judges use metaphors to justify their policy conclusions in the law, metaphors become part of the authority judges purport to enforce in the name of the Rule of Law. The radical implications of this is that judges use metaphors in their policy analysis to exercise a type of "private sovereignty"[61] in the law, and those metaphors can be called into question by raising the appropriateness of other metaphors. Metaphors can become a way to exercise authority and power in the law, but they can also become an effective tool for exposing the preferred frame of analysis of law's authority, and this can shed light on aspects of reality ignored by law's preferred metaphors. Judges choose metaphors they use in their legal work, but they are not always fully conscious of their choices because the metaphors they use ignore what is left unstated and unexpressed.

Judges use conceptual metaphors to focus their audience's attention on domains of social reality they find supportive of their policy choices, but in the process of mapping from one conceptual domain to another, metaphor hides from the audience, and sometimes even the judge, aspects of social reality that would be revealed by other metaphors drawn from other domains of social reality. In using the same metaphors from prior cases, judges are able to commit the doctrinal field to a particular ideological position, whether or not they are aware of the ideological position taken. As the next chapter explains, the cognitive role of metaphor in legal thought helps to explain Duncan Kennedy's claim that "neutral" judges are ideological performers: "The Neutral judge is an ideological performer in this sense: he or she develops the solution to a legal problem and then justifies it in a legal language that is also ideological language."[62] As we will see, the cognitive role of metaphoric thought in adjudication helps to explain why even an intelligent, pragmatic judge like Judge Richard A. Posner might persist in maintaining his faith in cogent policy analysis, and in doing so utterly fail to appreciate why policy analysis is ideology by another name.

CHAPTER 4
METAPHOR AND ADJUDICATION

NE MIGHT THINK that lawyers and judges, who spend a great deal of their professional lives writing, arguing, and thinking conceptually with words, would have developed by now an appreciation of the cognitive powers of metaphor. After all, legal writing is, as Judge Richard A. Posner has correctly observed, full of "legal fictions," and these fictions are a "form of metaphor."[1] Judge Posner, insisting that law and literature are separate disciplines, nevertheless argues that metaphor has no essential cognitive content.[2] Following the view of Donald Davidson, Judge Posner concludes that metaphor has a limited rhetorical role in law. According to his view, metaphor is part of the surface glitter that provides rhetorical support to the judge's legal prose.[3] Judge Posner's view of metaphor is, in fact, representative of the prevailing misunderstanding about metaphor in adjudication; metaphor is thought to be an interesting rhetorical device used to spice up the nononsense rational prose used by judges to do things in the law.

In this chapter, my objective will be to explain why and how metaphor performs not just an important cognitive role in adjudication, but also an ideological function as well. An examination of the cognitive role of metaphor in adjudication leads to some rather radical insights that challenge the conventional wisdom about adjudication, specifically about what judges think they do when they are doing law. The prevailing view of adjudication accepts the notion that judges make and change law, but that logic, reason, and the paramount duty to decide cases in accordance with the authority of the law limit the degree of discretion a particular judge can exercise. The pragmatic task of deciding cases is thought to provide great leeway for judicial creativity, but the paramount duty to decide cases in accordance with the law is thought to constrain judges. Surprisingly, many judges are not ready to abandon the ancient dream that the way out of intellectual perplexity is hard thinking. Hence, when they are in their professional role, at the podium, before the bar, behind the bench, judges project, with great convenience, their ability to exclude their subjective motivations from their pragmatic analyses of law.

Judge Posner, a former law professor from the University of Chicago Law School, a renowned legal scholar and prolific writer, and an active appellate judge of the federal courts, personifies the contemporary view of what judges say they do when they are doing law.[4] Eschewing formalistic logic and abstract theory, Judge Posner adopts a pragmatic stance and argues that judges should use theory and legal philosophy as a tool to get a job done.[5]

In Judge Posner's view, the merit of every legal analytic must be tested by asking whether it works instrumentally in maximizing human goals and aspirations. Judge Posner thus argues that judges should use empirical methods in their policy analysis and take a more practical approach in deciding hard cases.[6] In adopting a no-nonsense pragmatic stance, Judge Posner accepts the idea that metaphor is a way of thinking, but in the law, metaphor is often "undisciplined and misleading."[7] Posner thus understands metaphor to be, at times, an effective rhetorical device that can jolt a person "out of his existing frame of reference by getting him to look at something in a fresh, and perhaps illuminating, way."[8]

THE LINK BETWEEN METAPHOR AND ADJUDICATION

When a judge uses an interesting metaphor in a legal opinion, the metaphor operates to do more than just provide rhetorical support for the judge's prose, as Judge Posner believes. Judge Cardozo's legal prose, for example, is full of metaphoric meaning that goes beyond the function of rhetoric. Professor Richard Weisberg has shown, for example, how Judge Cardozo's prose in one famous case, *Hynes v. New York Central R.R. Co.*,[9] uses geological and spatial metaphors (quicksand, planes, concentric spheres, etc.) for poetic purposes that had an important cognitive sway in persuading the reader to accept the judge's position. Unsurprisingly, Judge Posner finds Cardozo's use of metaphor to be an annoying source of doctrinal distortion and inaccuracy in Cardozo's legal compositions.[10] Of course, sometimes a good metaphor can be extremely powerful in shifting the relevant frame of analysis to enable judges to create new legal doctrine. As Judge Posner realizes, the mental picture of a good metaphor can loosen the doctrinal moorings of a rule sufficiently to enable judges to see how a new doctrine might establish a more solid foundation for a new rule.[11] Judge Cardozo's use of geographic and spatial metaphors in the *Hynes* case, for example, enabled Cardozo to shift the frame of legal analysis, for determining the liability of a railroad for children playing on the railroad property, from the old trespass rules (which favored the defendant railroad's legal position) to the modern framework of reasonable care under the circumstances (which favored the plaintiff's legal position).[12]

Doctrinal creation and rhetoric persuasion, however, are merely two minor roles that metaphor can perform in adjudication. As we have seen, cognitive science offers insight for understanding how metaphor enables judges to perform an ideological function in shaping the analysis of law and policy, as well as coordinating and generating new ideas for the creation of new doctrine. As a conceptual tool, metaphor performs a cognitive function that both facilitates and constrains doctrinal and policy analysis in the law. The cognitive role of metaphor in law offers us a glimpse into the background assumptions that judges use when they analyze real-world controversies. In the adjudication of boycott cases, for example, we saw how metaphor was a concealed form of authority that was as important to judicial lawmaking as are legal doctrine, policy, and logic. Metaphor performs a subtle legitimating empowerment and mediating function in adjudication in addition to providing the operative force for law's reasoning process.

The legitimating and empowerment effects of metaphor may not always be as central as I claim it to be in the boycott case law, but my examination of the cognitive role of metaphor in those cases leads me to believe that metaphor may be one of the most important unexplored determinants of adjudication in American law. Metaphor may turn out to be as influential as law or policy. Rather than saying that legal decisions are constrained by law and policy, it may be more apt to say that legal decisions are mediated by a form of legal imagination structured by *law's metaphors* (the internal cognitive and normative mechanisms that are hardwired into law's reason).

The link between metaphor and ideology in adjudication can be discovered only by considering how metaphoric reason operates within the institution of adjudication. For the judge, the duty to decide a case establishes, as Judge Posner has forcefully put it, the "paramount duty" of the judge.[13] That role is thought to require judges to bring the imaginative and rational powers of their minds to the case at hand. The imaginative nature of the legal mind, assuming we can talk of such a thing, is the product of a particular context, a particular culture, and a unique institutional setting. The way institutional, cultural, and subjective factors influence judicial imagination demonstrates that the so-called rational modes of legal analysis are in fact the product of a highly selective legal imagination. It is only recently that legal scholars have begun to inquire into the institutional setting in which adjudication takes place, and to study the objective motivation of judges seriously.

ADJUDICATION AND JUDGES

At one time, legal thinkers believed that judges were constrained by the law they applied in deciding cases. During the era of legal jurisprudence known as Langdellian formalism, it was assumed that judges were "living oracles" who performed an essentially passive role in deciding the cases before them.[14] Later, after the legal realist movement in legal studies,[15] legal thinkers came to realize that judges had considerable discretion in interpreting the law laid down, and that they made law by interpreting it in view of their life experiences. The rules of decisions found in authoritative legal texts required interpretation, and through the act of interpretation, judges translated law in light of their life experiences in giving meaning to legal and factual phenomena. *Hard cases* (cases where the doctrinal and legal materials failed to provide an easy answer, i.e., indeterminate law) enabled judges to use *policy analysis*, a mode of analysis normally used by legislators (lawmakers) that requires choices to be made about instrumental goals. Most modern legal thinkers continue to believe that judges cannot do whatever they like because law, legal policy, and the institutional setting constrain the degree of discretion judges can exercise.

From the judge's perspective, constraint is experienced as fidelity to the duty to decide a case fairly and within the accepted bounds of the orthodox legal materials and methods for decision making. Institutional legitimacy, reasoned argument, and the practical need to get a job done

---

are what judges think they do in adjudication. Again, as Judge Posner puts it, "For law is, among other things, the activity of judges in deciding cases."[16] The activity of deciding cases, however, does not take place in a vacuum. Judges are not just pragmatic technocratic programmers who tune in the right instrumental goal for their policy analysis or make the right deduction from orthodox materials. There is a legal culture, an institutional setting, and psychological motivation in the background that influences what judges really do when they are doing law.

THEORIES OF ADJUDICATION

One explanation for what judges do in adjudication was given with considerable confidence by the school of jurisprudence known as legal process during the 1950s and 1960s.[17] The process school of jurisprudence, which has had a recent revival of sorts,[18] attempts to define what judges do in adjudication in terms of processing values. A key idea of the legal process is that the institution of the judiciary possesses a unique methodology for legal decision making that encourages judges to imagine themselves as masterful process technocrats. A more normative breed of legal scholar, however, inspired by the work of the philosopher Ronald Dworkin rejects the emphasis on process and argues instead that judges should see themselves as "philosopher kings," purveying in adjudication the "practical wisdom" of the legal culture.[19] More recently, new interest in the ideas of American pragmatism has also influenced legal thinkers and judges such as Judge Posner who reject theoretical models and explanations of adjudication altogether and have instead turned to a pragmatic approach that sees the judge as a policy maker who does what all lawmakers do when they are confronted with difficult social problems; they "roll up their sleeves" and get a job done.[20]

None of these explanations of what judges do actually tells us much about what judges really do in adjudication. Process theory merely provides us with a set of phrases like "reasoned elaboration" or "neutral principles" that do little to explain decision making in the vast majority of cases. These legalisms are merely legal illusions that operate as conversation stoppers that put to rest a serious question about what judges actually do in deciding cases. In response to an inquiry about how cases are actually decided, the legal process theorist is prone to say "Why, of course, the judge would decide the case on the basis of reasoned elaboration and principal argument," as if the uttering of those words was enough to silence further inquiry about method. Ronald Dworkin's normative approach, though infinitely more sophisticated philosophically, is really not that different from the process approach. Dworkin sets out what he believes to be the best normative solution to a problem, writes off contrary arguments as lacking "good judgment," and proceeds to advocate what he believes to be "the best available political theory." Dworkin's view of adjudication reduces to view that judges should strive to interpret legal materials "to make them the best they can be."[21]

Judge Posner offers pragmatic policy reasons for dismissing Dworkin's approach, but like Dworkin, Posner has adopted an almost mythical faith in the power of what he calls "cogent policy" analysis. For example, Judge Posner criticizes Duncan Kennedy's book *A Critique of Adjudication {fin de siècle}* for failing to appreciate the power of "cogent policy analysis." He never defines what he means by "cogent policy" and instead assumes that the uttering of those words had some magic meaning that Kennedy has failed to grasp. Posner's critique of Kennedy's work is quite remarkable for he never justifies the leaps of unjustified faith required by his pragmatic view of policy.[22]

Judge Posner is aware of the enormous empirical and theoretical difficulties of *cogent policy* analysis; he has, for example, acknowledged that economic analysis lacks a certain exactness when rigorously pursued in adjudication.[23] Despite his considerable reputation as a skilled law and economics analyst, Judge Posner practices a sort of *as if* jurisprudence that proceeds on the belief that judges should act as if policy analysis has a certain exactness that other methods are said to lack. For all the grandiloquent talk by judges of "reason" and "policy," the fact remains that adjudication is a contingent product of fallible human choices that are more imaginary than real. I think most people in our culture, after watching the O. J. Simpson murder trial on prime-time television, would regard Judge Posner's claims about what judges do to be quite ridiculous.

Not everyone follows the conventional view of judges. More recently, a pair of legal scholars, Edward Rubin and Malcolm Feeley, have argued that adjudication requires a deeper inquiry into the institution of judging. In focusing on the institution of adjudication, Rubin and Feeley, who regard themselves as "new legal process" scholars or the "new institutional" scholars, have investigated the relation between the judges' methods of analysis, the institutional setting, and the psychological motivation in which adjudication takes place. The approach of these scholars has led to some interesting new ideas about the nature of adjudication. Rubin and Feeley conclude that what judges regard as legal reason and policy is but a subset of methods that are in fact used by them to decide cases.[24]

The institutional inquiry has led Rubin and Feeley to wonder whether we are missing something important about adjudication in ignoring the role of the judge's subjective motivation and imagination, including metaphor, that enables judges to expand their perspective to contemplate new ideas for creating new doctrine.[25] In viewing adjudication as a psychological and metaphoric forum, Rubin and Feeley are beginning to develop a new framework for studying adjudication as an institution of individual human beings, with human psychological impulses, shaped by a human imagination and background ideology. Rubin and Feeley insist that psychological phenomena and metaphoric reasoning should be thought of as a form of "legal reason" that shapes what judges actually do when they decide cases.[26]

An unescapable conclusion drawn from the new learning from the fields of cognitive theory and cognitive psychology is that the conventional understanding about the nature of adjudication is flawed. In the following sections, I will attempt to explain why and how cognitive theory offers a better way of understanding what judges do when they adjudicate disputes like those found in this book: group boycotts. Specifically, I am interested in exploring how cognitive theory offers a deeper understanding of what judges do when they are doing law in cases involving high ideological stakes. When judges "roll up their sleeves," as Judge Posner has put it, what is it that they really do?[27] There are four important activities of adjudication: finding the facts, law application, policy analysis, and subjective motivation. The last factor, subjective motivation, will require extensive examination since it provides insight for understanding the relationship between metaphor and ideology in adjudication.

FINDING THE FACTS

One of the lessons of the boycott cases is that boycott metaphors perform a conceptual function in framing a judge's understanding of complex phenomena. As we have seen in chapter 2, default metaphors performed a basic conceptual role, often unconscious, in shaping the way judges saw the facts of labor boycott at early common law. As I argued in chapter 3, the metaphor "corporation is a person" influenced the way judges viewed the nature of labor boycotts. Because the corporation was conceptualized as an individual person, the boycott was seen to involve the inherent coercive force of a group of workers against a single individual.

The point is that the factual phenomena judges must interpret in adjudication (either as finders of fact at the trial court level or as law interpreters at the appellate court level) are never objectively certifiable independent of the psychological or imaginative motivation of the person interpreting them. In giving meaning to factual phenomena, such as a boycott, judges make factual conclusions about the nature of the phenomena, but the facts are always selectively reached to support the conclusion the judge wishes to reach. By understanding the imaginative process used by the judge's mental mind-set, we can come to see why certain facts are heavily weighed and others are not, and why certain goals are favored and others are not. In contested cases, where factual phenomena must be interpreted as they are in the boycott cases, who is to say that the facts selected by the judge are the actual objective facts for understanding the meaning of some perplexing phenomena?

Consider, for example, how the image of the tiger shaped the judge's understanding of the labor boycott in the *Glidden* case. The tiger, metaphorically understood in light of the *Great Chain of Being* proverb, motivated the judge to see an otherwise peaceful labor boycott as something akin to murder. The factual conclusions reached ("boycott is many against one;" "boycott is murder") were hardly the innocent conclusions of the facts in the record of the case. There were facts to be found, but the way the judges found the facts was based on a highly imaginative mode of inquiry. At some point the pursuit of the facts becomes not merely contestable, but highly selective. Just as surely as facts are always the product of a selective observation, the mental process a judge uses to reason and interpret is also influenced by a highly selective legal imagination.

Of course, sometimes the mental images invoked by the judge's cognitive thoughts enables the judge to create a new rule that has highly useful features for analyzing legal problems in a doctrinal field. Justice Holmes's "marketplace of ideas" notion, for example, has been quite effective in rationalizing the law of free speech under the First Amendment. However, the rational effect of the marketplace-of-ideas metaphor has also created distortions in legal thinking. Judges who rely on the marketplace-of-ideas metaphor find it difficult to square campaign-spending legislation with the First Amendment.[28]

The lesson to be drawn is that imagination is central to the cognitive process because the judge's view of the world of "facts" is very much influenced by the judge's imaginative form of reason. If cognitive thought in adjudication is imaginative, and if imagination shapes the way judges evaluate the facts of a case, then imagination and metaphor are the basic cognitive tools that judges in fact use when they do law. Hence, when judges say they are pragmatic policy decision makers and do the best they can, they are not telling us what is really going on when they decide a factual issue relevant to a case.

Conclusions of Law

The relevance and significance of cognitive theory should also give judges and lawyers pause when they apply the law to the facts of complicated phenomena. As we have seen, judges and lawyers categorize legal problems and then develop legal principles for deciding boycott cases that fall in the relevant legal categories they have constructed. Hence, labor boycotts were categorized under rules of labor law, and civil rights boycotts were categorized under different rules applicable to civil rights boycotts. As we have seen in the preceding chapters, judges apply the rules of the legal categories they create in just the same way that they find and evaluate the facts. Legal categories constructed from radial categories based on idealized models are imaginatively created to identify the relevant legal categories and rules. Default metaphors, sometimes chained to two or more radial categories, define the boundary lines between the legal categories that determine the relevant rules to be applied to a given case. What passes as law application turns out to be a product of the metaphoric form of reason that structures the way judges understand and give meaning to factual phenomena.[29]

The rules work not in the usual rational way that judges and lawyers imagine (i.e., in terms of categorical deductions from the relevant category), but rather in light of the prototypical effects of radial categories based on idealized models of phenomena. For example, if judges were truly rational in adjudication, then the rules of criminal conspiracy they applied to some of the first labor boycotts in American law would be based on an obvious category mistake. Peaceful labor boycotts were not criminal conspiracies any more than collective activities of the National Association of Manufacturers were criminal conspiracies.

What made peaceful labor boycotts criminal conspiracies was a radial category of boycott shaped by metaphors that had the default consequence of treating labor boycotts as rioting mobs, exploding bombs, and acts of murder and violence. The rationalization of the judges' opinions made sense only because the default metaphors applicable to labor boycotts were presumed to be factually correct representations of the boycott phenomenon. Instead, each judge's opinion was motivated by a historical and cultural context. Hence, the Haymarket Riot, the violence attributed to Irish-American mine workers known as the Mollies, the anarchist activities of the Industrial Workers of the World, and other highly sensationalized events involving labor, provided the metaphoric source for each judge's conclusion of law in each case.

POLICY

How is it that judges and lawyers entirely overlook the important role of imagination and metaphoric reason in adjudication? And what permits judges to say without any queasiness that they do policy when they decide hard cases? When judges are presented with a hard case and when the law provides no answers or conflicting answers (indeterminate law), then how do judges evaluate the instrumental goal to be achieved, and how do they decide if the instrumental goal they choose makes sense for the case at hand? In turning to policy analysis, judges assume that they can both gain access to the relevant information needed to evaluate instrumental goals and make reasonable guesses about the effects of particular decisional outcome. These assumptions frequently require empirical sorts of information that are not available to the judge. So what do judges really do? They make intuitive, pragmatic hunches and do the best they can with whatever information has been provided to them by the litigating lawyers.

The pragmatic hunches that are made are never free of subjective motivation and influence. Policy presumptions, like factual findings and legal conclusions, are based on a set of starting points that are fixed by the way the judge views the facts, law, and instrumental goals. If judges rely upon a radial or family resemblance category that defines labor boycotts as coercive activity, then the imaginative nature of the category will shape the way the judge evaluates and accesses instrumental goals. Policy analysis will thus be motivated by cognitive metaphors that frame the way the judge views policy, facts, and law.

The judicial resolution of hard cases will always require judges to apply policy with a certain open texture and fuzziness because what makes cases hard is that they do not easily fit into the existing categories that have been established for the central or common case. The fuzziness of policy analysis produces the experience of indeterminacy that frustrates most law students when they commence their law studies. It is only after they learn the imaginative categories of the law and learn to intuitively apply the metaphoric structures of the relevant legal categories that they become comfortable with dealing with the initial experience of rule indeterminacy. Conceptual inconsistency soon disappears as the law student becomes trained to manipulate and apply the relevant radial categories of a given doctrinal field.

Experienced judges and lawyers, like seasoned graduating law students, do not even find indeterminacy to be much of a problem in law. What is surprising is how easy it becomes for the seasoned legal analyst to gloss over the chaotic complexity of policy analysis. When judges use what they regard as cogent policy analysis, they rely upon a set of cognitive tools that shape policy in ways that are never really examined by the judge. When judges resort to policy as an explanation of what they do when they do law, they are either acting in bad faith (because they know that policy is just another word for discretion or ideology), or they are simply deluding themselves in thinking that there is something really cogent in what they regard as policy.

Judges are human beings, and as such, they are influenced by complex subjective motivations, as all people are. A general theory of adjudication would seem to require an examination of the ways the legal mind establishes the mental machinery for adjudication. There have been others who have examined such things. Interest in the nature of subjective motivation in adjudication framed the legal realist critique by Judge Jerome Frank of the 1930s as well as the more recent critique of adjudication by Duncan Kennedy. In the next section, I will summarize how Frank and Kennedy view the link between adjudication and subjective motivation, and then I will explore how metaphor figures into these critiques. My goal in the concluding section of this chapter will be to develop a general theory for understanding the link between metaphoric reason, ideology, and legal imagination in adjudication.

Reason Versus Imagination: What Judges Really Do

Jerome Frank, a New York attorney who was appointed to the Second Circuit Federal Court of Appeals, was one of the leading legal realist thinkers of the 1930s and 1940s. The legal realist movement was marked from the beginning by a deep skepticism about the possibility of decision making according to rule.[30] In arguing that judges made law as they adjudicated cases, the legal realist insisted that judges clung to the myth that law was objective and predictable. Frank was interested in finding out what was behind this myth. He wanted to know "Why this obstinate denial of the juristic realities?"[31] For Frank, the answer could be found in the psychological motivation of judges. As Frank explained, "[the myth] is a direct outgrowth of a subjective need for believing in a stable, approximately unalterable legal world—in effect, a child's world."[32]

A hallmark of Jerome Frank's psychological examination of adjudication was premised upon his own psychoanalysis and his interest in the child psychology of Jean Piaget.[33] Frank's pioneering work *Law and the Modern Mind* relied upon such sources to debunk the myth of legal predictability and judicial neutrality in adjudication by showing that judges were psychologically motivated to relate to the law the way a child relates to a father figure. The omniscient and omnipotent father figure of the law became for Frank a psychological frame for the "father-as-Infallible-Judge." As Frank explained:

> The Law—a body of rules apparently devised for infallibly determining what is right and what is wrong and for deciding who should be punished for misdeed—inevitably becomes a partial substitute for the father-as-Infallible-Judge. That is, the desire persists in grown men to recapture through a rediscovery of a father, a childish, completely controllable universe, and that desire seeks satisfaction in a partial, unconscious, anthropo-

morphizing of Law, in ascribing to the Law some of the characteristics of the child's Father-Judge.[34]

Frank thus drew from Freudian psychoanalytic theory and Piaget's
theory of child development to explain a *myth* about adjudication—the
myth that adjudication can be entirely predictable and that judges refrain
from lawmaking in deciding cases. This myth, according to Frank, was
the product of self-deception made "without complete knowledge of its
falsity."[35] As Frank explained:

> The self-deception, of course, varies in degree; many judges and
> lawyers are half-aware that the denial of the existence of judicial
> legislation is what [has been] called a "form of words to hide the
> truth." And yet most of the profession insists that the judiciary
> cannot properly change the law, and more or less believes that
> myth. When judges and lawyers announce that judges can never
> validly make law, they are not engaged in fooling the public; they
> have successfully fooled themselves.[36]

Frank assumed that if we looked behind the official texts of law to
judicial temperament and childhood experience of the judge, we could
explain the judicial choice under a rule. Frank, like other legal realists
of his time, believed that rationalism in adjudication concealed the true
psychological motivations of the judge by perpetuating the myth of
objective and predictable law. For Frank, subjectivity was inevitable in
adjudication because facts are always selectively formed, and the desired
legal conclusion is always a product of nonrational psychological motivation. For Frank, the opinions reached by judges are always the product of deep-lying postulates motivated by the judge's psychological
mind-set.

Jerome Frank's psychological concept of "father-as-infallible-judge"
was based on what Freudian psychotherapists would now understand to
be "the relations of anxiety to consciousness;" that is the idea that
"[a]nxiety is always present somewhere or other behind every symptom."[37] In the psychoanalytic context, infant sexuality and the Oedipus
complex are important analytical realms for understanding how individuals invent themselves from the past relations of their childhood.
Frank used the infant psychoanalytic realm to investigate why judges
might engage in acts of self-deception. Frank apparently believed that

judges are motivated to deny a messy internal drama about their own childhood, an imaginary relation that they have projected onto law to avoid facing the pain of their individual past. In Frank's mind, judges show fidelity to the Law because they repeat in the performance of their role the early experiences of their childhood.

One could thus say that for Jerome Frank, denial and self-deception were defense mechanisms of psychological repression. Such repressed feelings permitted judges to avoid the anxiety of admitting that they were lawmakers and that the law they made was not predictable in the usual ways. According to Frank, when judges and lawyers denied the lawmaking activity of the bench, they were only fooling themselves since the public has always known that judges make law in adjudication. Frank's concept of denial (repression) thus rendered judges innocent of the charge of bad faith, since they had, according to Frank, "successfully fooled themselves" about their ideological role.

In Freudian theory, however, repression operates as a sort of malaise that in the individual triggers neurotic symptoms of guilt and dissatisfaction. Freud's talking cure aims to get the individual to recognize the source of anxiety so that the psychological symptom could be cured. Frank apparently believed that judicial anxiety produced symptoms of unpredictable and uncertain law, and these symptoms were the psychological manifestation of the myth that judges do not make law. Frank's book *Law and the Modern Mind* could be read as Frank's attempt at a talking cure. The problem, of course, was that the people in Frank's audience were unwilling participants. The vast majority of judges and lawyers quickly rejected Frank's effort as the worst example of what was wrong with legal realism. Frank soon became associated with *gastronomy jurisprudence*—the view that a judge's eating habits might be a more fruitful predictor of the law then the printed precedent found in the library.

Duncan Kennedy's critique attempts to explain why adjudication is an ideological activity that most (not all) judges are motivated to deny.[38] Kennedy's notion of denial is developed from eclectic sources found in popular culture as well as from the ideas of Sigmund and Anna Freud, whose theories are now widely accepted in popular culture. As Kennedy has explained, Freud's theory of psychological denial shows up in "daytime talk shows and twelve-step programs ('he's been in denial about his drinking for years'; 'she's been in denial about his cheating for years')."[39]

Kennedy's theory of judicial denial is adopted from these sources and from "related ideas of bad faith and cognitive dissonance."[40] Kennedy claims that judges act in bad faith when they deny their ideological role in adjudication because they know at some level that they are, as many people instinctively realize, ideological decision makers. The charge of bad faith, in part derived from Sartre's notion of bad faith,[41] is based on the idea that judges exercise a degree of free will in denying something they know. According to Kennedy, the collective exercise of bad faith by most judges is a response to a role conflict that they are motivated to deny.

It is important to note how Kennedy's critique differs from that of Jerome Frank. Kennedy's notion of denial is a psychological defense mechanism that has to be brought into operation by the actor. Denial in adjudication, according to Kennedy, is based on the idea that judges are really conscious of their role conflict because they act strategically and collectively in adjudication to deny their role conflict. Judges know that interpretation is an ideological activity, but their obligation to maintain fidelity to the law motivates them to deny the true nature of their role. Jerome Frank assumed that judges were in complete denial of their law-making role; they were unaware of the subjective motivations influencing their decisions.

Kennedy offers a topology of judicial postures that he claims judges use strategically in adjudication to deny their role conflict: (1) a constrained, activist strategy aimed at bringing about "just" outcomes, (2) a difference-splitting strategy aimed at bringing about the moderate or middle-of-the-road view, and (3) a bipolar strategy aimed at alternating between two or more ideologies or philosophies over time.[42] These strategies, according to Kennedy, enable judges to accept much of what legal realists like Frank claim to be true about adjudication (judges perform a legislative function in deciding cases without having to acknowledge that they were ideological [i.e., policy] decision makers). Judges are conscious that they are policy makers, but they depict their policy analysis as a pragmatic form of nonideological policy making. Over time, strategic behavior and denial transform law into the judge's ideology—hence, the ideology of the bench.

Kennedy argues that no matter how sophisticated the judicial strategy, judges are inevitably motivated to deny their ideological role in adjudication. Kennedy claims that the motivation of judges to deny their ideological role is in fact a bad-faith response to the anxiety caused by their role conflict. As Kennedy explains, "[T]he motive for denial is not guilt at deviance but the anxiety produced by the dilemma of not being able to do the right thing no matter how hard [the judge] tr[ies], because [the judge] is being told to do two things at the same time [i.e., decide ideological group conflict by remaining nonideological]."[43]

Kennedy asserts that "[t]he denial of the ideological resolves the conflict by making it appear that their role definition is coherent rather than contradictory."[44] In other words, neutrality in policy making is maintained in order to legitimate the role of the judge so as to avoid exposing an aspect of the job that would disqualify the office holder from the job. Judges are motivated to deny their ideological role because to do otherwise would be an admission that might require that they quit judging. Judges are psychologically motivated by their office to deny that they are translating law into their ideological positions. "The neutral judge is an ideological performer in this sense: He or she develops the solution to a legal problem and then justifies it in a legal language that is also an ideological language."[45] What is missing in Kennedy's account of psychological denial in adjudication is an explanation of the cognitive dimension of denial. How does the mechanism of psychological denial work, and what triggers it in adjudication? What is the anatomy of psychological denial? These are the critical questions that can be answered by examining the role of imagination and metaphoric reason in adjudication.

LEGAL IDEOLOGY, COGNITIVE THOUGHT, AND ADJUDICATION

The ideology of the world that judges must deal with is not just there for the knowing but has to be grasped and mediated with "suitable mental machinery."[46] Judges must be able to process and mediate what they deny to be true. The mind is the thinking machine that processes information and permits (and constrains) ideology and the experience of denial.[47] The workings of the mind cannot be understood without appreciating the pivotal role of metaphor. Metaphoric reason is what enables the thinking mind to make correlations, to create ideologies, and to deny the truth of things. Metaphoric reason allows judges to process information by translating what is known about the physical world to gain information about the abstract intellectual domain of the law. The cognitive engine of metaphor is the language of thought that enables the thinking mind to make perceptions and draw inferences for processing complex information.[48]

If we were to consider full and complete information about external phenomena—in other words, if we were to consider the vast metaphoric universe applicable—we would be flooded with metaphors, calling up categories of information, some of which would create serious conflicts and contradictions in the process of information gathering. The conflict and contradiction posed by the complexity of the world creates the anxiety that motivates us, consciously and unconsciously, to use the partial frames of metaphors in adjudication to deal with information complexity. Judges, like everyone else, use metaphors to selectively process complex information about the world.

Judges, however, are only required to consider a subset of relevant information applicable to a set of facts involved in a controversy, and the particular law relevant to the legal issues. In interpreting and processing this information, judges still need to define terms, ascertain the meanings of things, and process other legal information as they interpret law and facts. In the conventional view of adjudication, as Duncan Kennedy argues, judges are supposed to "categorically exclude their ideological preferences and 'stick to law,'" or "first interpret the law." The law is thus "not [only] a constraint . . . but a source of guidance."[49] The law, signified by the ideal of the Rule of Law, defines the role judges assume in adjudication, and it is thought that the law provides guidance for what judges can and cannot do. The reality is that judges rely upon metaphor, radial categories, and image schemata in analyzing and classifying phenomena under rules, and the partiality of the metaphoric structure of their models and categories are what permit judges to act as if they were merely following the command of the law, when in fact they are very much implicated in its construction.

Metaphoric reason permits the exercise of ideological power, and that power motivates judges, as Duncan Kennedy insists, to deny that they act ideologically in adjudication. Kennedy claims that judges are nonetheless half conscious of the conflict between their perceived role as a neutral-decision maker and what everyone else knows to be ideology.

Because judges are half conscious of this conflict, Kennedy argues that judges are really acting in bad faith when they deny their ideological role in adjudication.[50] Kennedy's notion is that someone can both experience psychological denial and still have some awareness (viz., be half conscious) of the thing that is denied. This is how most people cope with anxiety. On a good day, we deny the anxiety of living in a dangerous and frightful world. A person who is in psychological denial, however, is unlikely to be aware of the source of the conflict causing them painful anxiety, as Jerome Frank clearly recognized.[51]

Consider Kennedy's example of the alcoholic who is in denial of his alcoholism. Such individuals would not regard themselves as being alcoholic; indeed, their defense mechanisms of *ego* would prevent them from even recognizing their own alcoholism. The awareness of it would raise for them the necessity of ending their drinking career, a very painful possibility for an active alcoholic. Psychological denial would thus permit the active alcoholic to remain unconscious of the fact that his or her drinking was even a problem. Applying the analogy to judges and adjudication, one might argue that the judge, like the alcoholic, has a psychological motivation to deny his or her ideological role in adjudication. Awareness of the ideological role may well mean an end to the judge's career, just as awareness of alcoholism would require the active alcoholic to come to grips with the necessity of ending a life-long career of drinking. The pain of this awareness, for both the alcoholic and the judge, would not be something that either wish to face, so they deny it. The active alcoholic denies that he or she is an alcoholic, and the judge denies that he or she is an ideological decision maker. Both remain aware of their behavior: the alcoholic is aware that he drinks, and the judge is aware that she is a policy maker. What both deny is what would be dangerous to their self-images and their life-long careers.

If judges are in psychological denial about their ideological role in adjudication, can it still be said that they are acting in bad faith as Kennedy claims? Bad faith, even as defined by Sartre, would require that the judge be somewhat conscious of his or her ideological role conflict. The psychological defense mechanism of ego that may support Kennedy's claim of bad faith may be a metaphoric-induced defense mechanism of *suppression*. Psychological suppression involves the conscious and deliberate avoidance of a disturbing matter.[52] An example would be when Scarlett O'Hara in the movie *Gone with the Wind* said, "I'll think of it tomorrow."[53] Another example would be an active alcoholic, who knows he or she is an alcoholic, saying "I'll do something about my drinking next year when I can take time off from work for a few days."

A judge who is conscious of her ideological role would be psychologically motivated to suppress the disturbing thought of her ideological role in order to remain on the bench. Because psychological suppression is a conscious defense mechanism, the individual is nonetheless quite aware of the disturbing matter that is suppressed. The charge of bad faith would thus seem to make more sense in terms of the psychological experience of suppression. When we suppress the true facts, there is a part of our psyche that is aware of what we are doing. To be sure, the person who suppresses the truth practices a form of bad faith in hiding a displeasing truth. In suppressing the truth, the person also hides it by rationalizing its existence or importance. The person is thus half conscious of this, as Duncan Kennedy has claimed about his notion of denial. The ideology of the bench is therefore suppressed by judges as they collectively intellectualize and rationalize their legal conclusions in reaching decisions. The act of opinion writing in the law with its pragmatic stance motivates judges to commit their minds to a form of *as if* thinking that is self-serving to the judge's purpose of maintaining a neutral policy-making position in adjudication.

Hence, judges complain that they are too busy deciding cases to think about their ideological role; what they do think about is how to pragmatically decide complex legal problems. Judges intellectualize and rationalize their role as busy pragmatic problem solvers, and when pressed to confront their own lawmaking activity, judges evade the ideology of their work by suppressing the thought from their daily tasks much in the same way that Scarlett O'Hara did in the concluding scene of *Gone with the Wind.*

Intellectualization and rationalization may be a more realistic way of understanding how ideology of the bench actually operates in practice. Metaphor is the cognitive mechanism that conceals ideology in adjudication. It is metaphor that provides judges with a mechanism for intellectualizing and rationalizing. It helps judges to knowingly conceal their ideological role and provides them with a normatively loaded tool to rationalize their true role as ideological decision makers. The explanation for this can be understood in terms of the concept of *metaphoric transference*.

Ideology and Metaphoric Transference

When judges use a metaphor to translate the meaning of some event, the metaphor carries with it a particular normative orientation. Metaphor is a transference device that enables judges to repeat normative patterns from the past in adjudication. Metaphoric reason relies upon knowledge about one kind of thing to name or define another kind of thing. When metaphors of the past are used to name things in the present, the metaphor carries with it meaning from the past and repeats the past meaning in the present to give meaning to some new event. Metaphor thus performs an ideological transference reaction by bringing out in the present, information and normative meaning created in the past by the source domain of the metaphor. If the metaphor's source domain is normatively loaded, the transference of the metaphor carries with it normatively loaded meaning.

Metaphor is thus not only a default device used to narrow the relevant field so that information gathering and processing can be done, but also a framing concept that repeats normative patterns embedded within the prototypical cognitive effects of the metaphor. The transference reaction of the metaphor repeats in the present a normative orientation of a domain that was used as the source for defining the meaning about some present phenomena. Unlike the psychological transference reaction of repression in Freudian theory that is hidden in the internal world of the individual, metaphoric transference is externally concealed in the source domain of a metaphor used in discourse, and as such, it can be accessed by examination of that domain. The relation between metaphor and psychological phenomena can therefore be explained in terms of a cognitive mechanism triggered by a metaphoric transference that enables judges to intellectualize (i.e., rationalize) their normative role in adjudication.

For example, when the judge in the *Glidden* case translated the story of Captain Boycott to define the meaning of a labor boycott, the story had certain prototypical effects that were shaped by a highly ideological metaphoric background. Captain Boycott was interpreted as an innocent victim, and the boycott was viewed to be an example of unruly and wild crowd violence. The image of boycott as violence, and even murder, became the metaphoric property of the central case, and peaceful protest became the exception. The central case defined the metaphoric territory such that an otherwise peaceful labor boycott was imaginatively interpreted, at another time and in a different legal culture, as animalistic and murderous behavior of a wild tiger. The default metaphor "boycott as murder" was thus chained to metaphors that had historically characterized Irish boycotters as "bloodthirsty Zulus."

A judge is never completely unaware of the transference reaction of metaphor because the metaphor is chosen by the judge and used in the judge's analysis of the legal controversy. The judge may not be totally aware of the full normative background embedded in the metaphor, but a judge would certainly be aware of the impact of using a metaphor like "tiger" to define the meaning of peaceful boycott activity. Awareness of this is what establishes the awareness of the judge's ideological role in adjudication. The unawareness of the normative orientations of the cognitive models and radial categories created by metaphor remain, however, concealed within the judge's discourse, so even well-versed judges such as Justice Stevens, Judge Cardozo, or even Justice Holmes might be unaware of the full normative implications of the metaphoric systems they use to analyze phenomena.

Metaphoric transference, like Kennedy's idea of psychological denial, is never absolute or complete because the partiality of the conceptual frame of metaphor is always a subject of debate and controversy and because the common case of the radial category cannot be constrained by a single metaphor. Duncan Kennedy is right in concluding that many (but not all) judges are conscious and unconscious at the same time of the ideology of their imagination, and this half consciousness provides support for Kennedy's charge that some (but not all) judges act in bad faith when they rationalize their ideological role.[54] There are, however, two levels of ideology at work in adjudication: there is the *ideology of the bench* that motivates judges to act strategically as neutral policy makers, and there is the *cognitive ideology of metaphoric transference* that enables judges to use normatively loaded tools of analysis to decide highly ideological litigation. These two levels of ideology (one external, the other internal) trigger the psychological motivation of a judge to deny (Kennedy's term) or rationalize (my term) their ideological function.

What is dangerous about metaphoric transference in adjudication is that it enables judges to exercise a type of authority and power independent of their official role. The exercise of this power is troubling because its consequences have never been fully recognized. In shaping the legal meaning of boycott, for example, metaphor has operated to perpetuate a form of violence in the law. As the late Robert Cover has explained, "Legal interpretive acts signal and occasion the imposition of violence upon others: A judge articulates her understanding of a text, and as a result, somebody loses his freedom, his property, his children, even his life."[55]

THE BACKGROUND/FOREGROUND SHIFT

Judges, of course, inhabit their own normative worlds, and thus, we cannot expect that they can easily free themselves from the metaphors they use in legal decision making. Judges may be incapable of evaluating nonlegal norms that may be central to deciding a particular legal case. However, it ought to be possible to influence the way judges use metaphor in the law by exposing the normative background that metaphors hide and conceal.

One strategy involves an ideologically motivated "background/foreground shift."[56] The methods of legal reasoning (law, deduction, policy, statutory analysis) are in the foreground, and metaphor and ideology are in the background. The foreground/background shift would aim at reversing the hierarchy so that attention would be focused on what is in the background. In consciously bringing about a shift from foreground to background, the legal critic seeks to make an intervention for purposes of bringing out the normative and political orientations and assumptions in the background of the materials judges use in making their legal arguments and in rendering their decisions.

The intervention brought by the background/foreground shift creates an opportunity to consider what is missing in legal decision making in a particular doctrinal field. For example, in the boycott case law, the intervention of such a shift would be helpful for identifying the normative character of the metaphors judges have used in creating the various radial categories of group boycotts. In doing so, an opportunity would then be created for considering other normative metaphors for creating new radial categories or for giving new meaning to the existing categories. Using metaphor against metaphor can enable one to see that it is more plausible to change the status quo than what previously appeared possible.

In making the background/foreground shift, it is important to distinguish two fundamental types of cognitive metaphors: *conventional* and *imaginative*. Conventional metaphors structure the ordinary conceptual system of our culture reflected in our everyday language. These metaphors operate to organize systems of ideas so that we can make sense of statements like "Happy is up." Conventional metaphors such as "Up is happy" are so embedded in our thoughts that we use them without reflection. In the law, these metaphors simply seize the judge such that the judge's decision flows from these metaphors. We don't consciously choose to think of "up" as "happy or upbeat," and yet we do in everyday conversations. Similarly, judges don't choose or select these metaphors; they are simply there in the commonly accepted modes of discourse we all use in communication.

Imaginative metaphors are created by judges in the course of writing an opinion or announcing a ruling from the bench. They are created in the sense that a judge consciously chooses to use them in advancing an argument or making a point. An example of this would be the tiger metaphor used in the *Glidden* decision. These metaphors have conventional entailments, which in the case of the tiger metaphor in *Glidden* included the *Great Chain of Being* proverb.

When used in legal analysis, *conventional* and *imaginative* metaphors work together to establish the idealized cognitive models judges use in adjudicating legal controversies. One might think that critiques of conventional metaphors entail critiques of reason and that critiques of imaginative metaphors entail critiques of imagination, but since reason is itself imaginatively structured by conventional and imaginative metaphors, reason in the law operates on both imaginative levels.

An analogy could be drawn to the relation between doctrinal and policy modes of analysis. The doctrinal mode of analysis is largely based on logic, but doctrine and logic are also features of policy analysis in the law. Although the doctrinal mode of analysis is largely logical, policy and normative value play a role in doctrinal analysis. Therefore, because boycott adjudication in the law involves both doctrine and policy, imaginative metaphors used by judges involve both conventional and imaginative metaphors. Conventional and imaginative metaphors found in the law thus work together to create the cognitive engines driving the logic of doctrinal and policy analysis.

Once metaphor is used in a legal opinion, it becomes part of the common law, and other judges under the doctrine of stare decisis are encouraged to use the same metaphor over and over. Imaginative and conventional metaphors thereby get embedded in the law through the process of case-by-case decision making. However, because even stare decisis can be ignored, gradual change in the law is possible, and new arguments using new imaginative metaphors might overcome the old metaphors embedded in the law. Eventually an old metaphor will die for lack of use or lack of fit. New metaphors can thus replace dead metaphors. It is possible then that legal advocates can use new metaphors to bring about surprising changes in legal analysis.[57] Even conventional metaphors, such as "up is happy," that are embedded in our language can be made less influential in our thoughts simply by bringing out the ideological effect they perform in context.

What metaphor will not do is provide judges, or anybody else, with an objective ground for evaluating the merits of a particular normative position. At the level of normative evaluation, metaphor will do no better than the cool reason of rational analysis. But what metaphoric reason can do, and what the cool reason of the law cannot, is to provide judges with a more informed understanding of the ideological orientation of the tools they use in adjudication. Such knowledge should be critically useful for dampening the violence of law.

Part Two

RADIAL CATEGORIES OF BOYCOTT

CHAPTER 5

RADIAL CATEGORY OF
SECONDARY LABOR BOYCOTTS

AS WE HAVE seen in chapter 2, the official legal discourse of labor boycotts at early common law was dominated by images that were quickly associated with ideas of force, violence, disorder, and insurgency. It is as if judges visualized an unruly mob every time they saw the collective action of a labor group. Violence and class conflict, vividly highlighted by the Haymarket Riot, influenced the way judges interpreted the legal meaning of boycott. These negative images of boycott led judges to conclude that labor boycott publicity had a propensity for violence, and this perception justified opinions finding that otherwise peaceful boycott publicity was unprotected under law. In this chapter, we will see how boycott metaphors at common law continue to influence the way secondary labor boycotts are regulated under the Taft-Hartley amendments to the National Labor Relations Act.

Oddly enough, the National Labor Relations Act does not even mention the term *secondary boycott*; the Act only proscribes specific unlawful means and objectives and leaves unregulated consumer publicity, other than picketing.[1] In interpreting the meaning of secondary labor boycotts under the labor statute, judges have used a disease metaphor to extend the radial category of boycott to secondary labor boycotts. The metaphor of this radial category equates the spreading effects of secondary labor boycotts with the idea of metastasis. Because this metaphor highlights the widening effects of secondary boycott activity and purports to distinguish such activity from primary activity, I will first turn to the distinction in labor law between primary and secondary boycott effects.

THE PRIMARY/SECONDARY DISTINCTION

Every labor dispute involves the application of collective economic pressure by workers against the person or entity with which they have a dispute regarding their own terms and conditions of employment. Thus, whenever workers picket the employer's place of business, a labor boycott ensues. The resulting boycott, if successful, has two important effects: First, there is the primary effect of turning away employees from working for the employer. Second, there is also the effect of the refusal of customers and suppliers to continue doing business with the employer. This latter effect is what labor lawyers refer to as a *secondary boycott*. The former is called a strike or concerted refusal to work.

Figure 5.1 maps the primary effects of a labor dispute. The union having a dispute with an employer asserts economic pressure through a picket line for purposes of advancing its dispute over wages, hours, and working conditions. The *primary* effects of a labor dispute can be identified as those flowing from an ordinary strike: workers refuse to work for an employer with whom they have a dispute or grievance. Additionally, there can be secondary effects from such a boycott: other employees may refuse to work for the primary employer, and customers and suppliers of the employer may refuse to patronize with the employer during the course of the labor dispute.

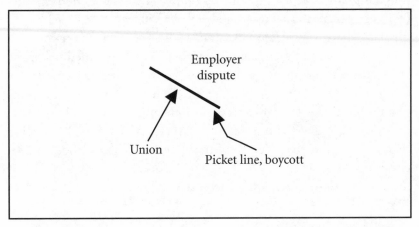

Figure 5.1
Primary Labor Effects

Figure 5.2 maps the nature of the secondary effects of a labor dispute. The union having a dispute with the primary employer asserts pressure against other (secondary) employers (suppliers) and other secondary employees, as well as customers, for purposes of persuading them to cease doing business with the primary employer. The *secondary* effects are those involving secondary parties who are persuaded to cease from doing business with the primary employer, against whom the workers have a dispute or grievance. A labor dispute becomes a secondary boycott when picketers try to get people not to patronize or work for those who do business with the primary employer or when they try to get consumers to boycott the primary employer.

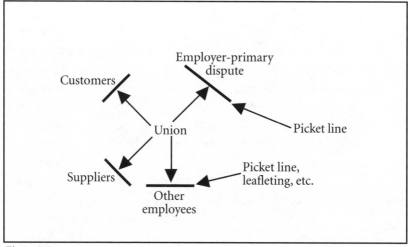

Figure 5.2
Secondary Labor Effects

The primary effects of the boycott were initially deemed unlawful at early common law, but by the turn of the century, judges began to recognize that primary picketing was lawful so long as it did not involve elements of force, violence, or coercion. Judges, however, soon condemned the secondary effects of labor boycotts as an unjustified extension of boycott coercion against neutral parties.

Under federal labor legislation, the primary effects of a labor dispute are called a strike, and they are generally protected under the labor statute, but secondary effects are not. The primary/secondary distinction has been justified as a basic analytical device to avoid constitutional questions that would be raised by an all-encompassing ban on labor boycotts, especially those boycotts involving the expressive conduct necessary for the exercise of labor's collective rights.

The primary/secondary distinction of federal labor legislation has brought about curious results. In *NLRB v. International Rice Milling Co.*,[2] for example, the Supreme Court held that union picketing at the situs of the struck employers' premises was lawful even though the picketers had urged the drivers of suppliers' trucks not to cross the picket line, thereby engaging in an activity of a clearly secondary nature. The Court found that the secondary effects of the picketing were mere incidental effects of an otherwise lawful primary activity.[3] Had the picketing occurred at the situs of suppliers' premises, however, it would have been banned as a secondary labor boycott, even though the same effects were incidental to the primary strike. Why situs should be the controlling factor in distinguishing lawful primary from unlawful secondary boycotts is far from clear.

When workers strike and picket, they hope that everyone (other employees, customers, suppliers) will honor their picket line and cease doing business with the employer with whom they have a dispute. If the effort is successful, parties not immediately involved in the labor dispute will be affected by the strike and picketing. A primary strike called against a nationally distributed product that is assembled from component parts produced by other suppliers and distributors would, for example, have precisely the same effect as a secondary boycott of component manufacturers.

The prohibition against secondary boycotts is thought to be justified in order to protect so-called "neutrals" ("innocent bystanders," "unoffending employers," or "noncombatants") from being drawn into a labor dispute not of their own making. Yet, in the postindustrial business environment, the primary/secondary distinction no longer makes sense. The problem is that in the current global marketplaces, linked by complex business relationships of interrelated technology and organizational structure, it is difficult to separate the "combatants" from the "noncombatants."[4]

For example, General Motors Corporation has discovered that it can save considerable labor costs by outsourcing as much production as possible to smaller, independent producers located throughout the world. By buying more of its parts from small producers, G.M. hopes to save money and keep its business competitive, as it subcontracts work to nonunion and low-wage firms. During the 1970s, before contract outsourcing, more than two-thirds of the hourly work force in the automobile industry belonged to the United Automobile Workers Union (UAW). By 1996, with manufacturing outsourcing, only one-quarter of the workforce were UAW members. This growth in the nonunion work force means that today whenever the UAW calls a national strike against General Motors, or any of the other big three (Ford or Chrysler), a substantial number of secondary workers will be affected by the strike, even though they do not work directly for G.M. If G.M. workers directly picketed these other employers, their actions would have obvious secondary effects.

THE CANCER METAPHOR AND THE TAFT-HARTLEY AMENDMENTS

The traditional policy qualifications for restricting the use of secondary labor boycotts have been the protection of neutrals, the importance of limiting the disruptive effects of the labor dispute, and the fear that secondary boycotts would spread labor disputes to other sectors of the economy. As Howard Lesnick's study of labor law's secondary boycott legislation indicates, a disease metaphor of cancer animated much of the legislative thinking about secondary labor boycotts.[5]

Describing the understanding of secondary boycotts in the congressional materials leading up to the Taft-Hartley amendments, Professor Lesnick graphically identified the underlying metaphor animating the legislative concern as the "metastasis of labor disputes."[6] The metaphor is structured by the image of invisible organisms attacking the body. The image creates a powerful emotional appeal for legal regulation of all secondary boycotts.

If a secondary labor boycott is like cancer cells spreading throughout an otherwise healthy body, the appropriate legal response would be analogous to the medical response: the cancer cells should be surgically removed from the body. The drafters of the Taft-Hartley amendments, establishing the secondary labor boycotts prohibition, apparently assumed that secondary boycotts should be thus prohibited in order to protect innocent "healthy" parties, and to limit the demonic "cancerous" rot of otherwise healthy economic activity.[7] The image of boycott as a *metastasis* projects an image of the secondary labor boycott as a nonspecific disease to be surgically excised, contained, or quarantined.

By encouraging judges to think of secondary labor boycotts as a spreading disease, or abnormal growth, disease and illness become powerful domains for defining the meaning of boycott activity much in the same way that the tiger metaphor became a powerful default metaphor in *Glidden*. In using the image of cancer to describe the meaning of secondary labor boycotts, judges and legislators associated a human activity with a lower-order being, thus placing boycott on a metaphoric level with cancer cells. The disease metaphor reinforces the judicial call for national regulation to contain the spreading of abnormal growth. Judges are encouraged to overlook the fact that federal labor legislation was enacted to protect the right of workers to engage in peaceful concerted collective activities, including the historical right of employees to engage in picketing, leafleting, and boycott, because the *Great Chain of Being* proverb places secondary boycott in a radial category defined by images of lower life forms having the properties of abnormality and violence.

The metaphor, "secondary boycott is metastasis," establishes a metaphoric system in which the domain of a disease is the source of metaphors for regulating all secondary labor boycotts. Secondary labor boycotts are thus treated as Susan Sontag has described in the plight of cancer patients in the 1950s and 1960s: they are "shunned" and treated as the "objects of practices of decontamination by members of a household, as if cancer, like TB, were an infectious disease."[8] As Sontag's compelling prose described how the metaphor of illness animates and shapes our thinking of cancer, similar metaphors of illness animate and shape the way the drafters of the 1947 Taft-Hartley amendments to the National Labor Relations Act thought about secondary labor boycotts.

The cognitive insight gleaned from the cancer metaphor, however, came at a high cognitive price. In using the metaphor to understand the effect of secondary labor boycotts, judges have focused their attention on the need to protect neutrals from being drawn into a labor dispute the union has with the primary employer. However, in using the cancer metaphor to rationalize the need to protect neutrals from the effects of a labor dispute, judges have used a normatively loaded metaphor that has historically portrayed cancer patients as social leopards, much in the same way many HIV patients are treated in the current AIDS epidemic. Sontag's work explains how the cancer metaphor actually killed people in the 1950s, and so it is no wonder that the legislative drafters of the 1947 Taft-Hartley amendments to the labor statute would be captured by the cognitive sway of this same metaphor in regulating secondary labor boycotts. During much of the postwar era, cancer was viewed the way TB was viewed in the nineteenth century: it was an evil and invisible predator, more than just a disease; it was an incitement to violence.

The disease metaphor motivates judges to adopt a distinct normative position about this form of boycott activity; it is a deadly disease that, like the wild bloodthirsty tiger, must be constrained and eliminated in a civilized society. The metaphor thus commits judges to a normative view of secondary labor boycott that is hard to justify in light of the way the law has regulated other collective activities of labor.

As Clyde Summers and Harry Wellington explained in 1968:

> [the metaphor misleads because it] focuses on the union's actions rather than on the conflict's economic repercussions. A draymen's strike may be felt by every business man in the city, and the effects of a steel strike may radiate to remote parts of the economy, but the union's action is neither curbed nor tailored to quarantine the impact of the strike. More important, the metaphors misrepresent the function of secondary action. No matter how widely the union spreads the dispute, the purpose remains the same—to prevent the primary employer from continuing operations until he has reached an agreement with the union. Normally, all a union seeks to achieve by secondary action is the equivalent of a fully effective strike of the primary employer; and all the union asks of the "neutral" is that he act as if the primary employer were in fact closed by a strike.[9]

If courts are to preserve the right to strike and to encourage collective bargaining, as they are required to do by federal labor legislation,[10] then they must recognize that even peaceful secondary boycotts aimed at coercing noncomplying employers to bargain collectively may be a necessary and beneficial practice of federal labor policy.

Rather than perceiving secondary labor boycotts as a disease, judges could have perceived the secondary boycott as a remedial practice, a cure, or a preventive therapy for upholding federal collective bargaining policy. The fear of cancer, like the fear of class conflict, provided judges with a rather powerful way to understand some aspects of secondary boycotts, but in the process of mapping the meaning of labor boycotts with the images of disease and class conflict, the metaphors carried with them all the normative baggage of the way judges thought about cancer and class conflict in America. The default consequences of these metaphors created prototypical cognitive effects for associating the meaning of labor boycotts with the negative consequences of disease and violence, imaginative realms that were powerful myths of boycott in 1947.[11]

SECONDARY LABOR BOYCOTT AS RADIAL CATEGORY EXTENSION

The prototype that defines the legal meaning of secondary labor boycotts is an extension of a radial category from the central case of boycott, chained to a different radial category of disease. The prototypical effect of this *chaining* transfers the idea of metastasis to define the legal meaning of secondary labor boycott. This new radial category encourages judges to stray farther and farther away from other prototypical properties of boycott, such as boycott as a legitimate concerted response to employer behavior. Alternative metaphors, and other prototypical effects, never get considered because they are ruled out of the imaginative territory by a default metaphor that associates labor boycott with the consequence of a dreaded disease.

The cognitive meaning of secondary labor boycotts is thus created from the merger of two radial category extensions; one extension from

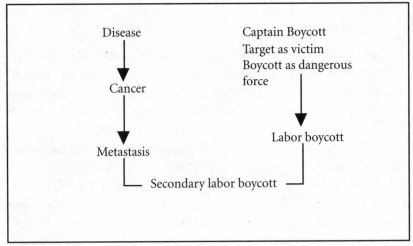

Figure 5.3
Radial Category of Secondary Labor Boycott

the radial category of disease, the other from the radial category of boycott. A metaphor chains the two radial categories to create legal meaning of secondary labor boycotts. The metaphor encourages judges to view secondary labor boycotts as a disease that must be surgically removed from the body of the economy. Figure 5.3 maps secondary labor boycott as a category extension of two radial categories.

Of course, secondary boycotts are neither a disease nor a metastasis. Instead, they sometimes are a legitimate tactic that labor organizations rely upon to counter the superior bargaining power of their employers. If we invoke different metaphors, say for example, "body is machine,"[12] we might imagine a system of labor law doctrine that provides affirmative protection for secondary labor boycotts. For example, the prevalent legislative goal of advancing industrial peace might be achieved if courts conceive of boycotts as a means of repairing injuries and resolving labor-management disputes, as a way of restoring the machinelike functions of the body.

Boycotts might also be understood as a social mechanism for influencing social and economic decision making. Rather than viewing boycotts as a threat to the balance of the body, lawmakers might come to understand boycott phenomena as an important connective force for maintenance of a civic process, for example, the democratic process. Lawmakers, legislative as well as judicial, might then imagine the legitimacy of a new system of labor law that provides affirmative protection for secondary boycott activity as an essential and legitimate "lubricant" for bringing resolution to labor disputes.

Legalizing secondary boycotts would not necessarily increase the spreading effects of labor disputes. No-strike clauses in collective bargaining agreements limit the vast majority of incumbent unions from engaging in secondary strikes and boycotts. Moreover, in the railway and transportation industries, unlike other industries covered by the National Labor Relations Act, federal legislation does not bar the use of secondary boycotts by labor unions, and there is no evidence that boycotts in those industries have had "cancerous" consequences.[13]

The historical origins of the word *boycott* offer alternative imaginative ideas for understanding the legal meaning of secondary labor boycotts. The tenants' boycott against Captain Boycott, as we have seen, had a positive meaning defined by the social perception of Captain Boycott as predatory. If we think of the meaning of the word *boycott* as it was understood by Irish tenants boycotting Captain Boycott, we could see how boycott was not a disease, but rather a remedy for predatory behavior of the target of the boycott. "Boycott is justice" and "target is predator" were alternative default metaphors for defining the meaning of secondary labor boycotts in the law. The normative sway of the disease metaphor, however, like the Zulu and tiger metaphors, motivated judges to a normative orientation that was biased against boycott in all of its manifestations. The ideology of secondary labor boycotts was rendered invisible by the imaginative tools judges used to evaluate the meaning of boycott phenomena.

THE SPEECH/CONDUCT DISTINCTION AND THE SPEECH THEORY OF MODERN LABOR LEGISLATION

Another perplexing question posed by federal labor law legislation of secondary labor union activity is why such legislation does not offend the First Amendment guarantee of freedom of speech? Surely, freedom of speech is not limited to the linguistic activity of speaking, for if it were, flag burning and civil rights demonstrations would be unprotected.[14] The Supreme Court has thus recognized "that the Free Speech Clause is not limited to the literal meaning of 'speech,' or even to language in spoken and written form, but extends to other types of nonverbal communication as well, sometimes referred to as symbolic speech or expressive conduct."[15]

In the 1940 decision in *Thornhill v. Alabama*,[16] for example, the Supreme Court recognized that peaceful labor picketing was protected as a form of expression and could not therefore be banned in the absence of compelling state interest. In *Milk Wagon Drivers' Union v. Meadowmoor Dairies, Inc.*, the Court recognized that "[p]eaceful picketing is the workingman's means of communication."[17] While the Court has recognized that peaceful picketing and leafleting are forms of nonverbal communication to which the Free Speech Clause applies,[18] the Court has never extended the Free Speech Clause to protect the effects of peaceful secondary boycotts.

The Supreme Court, however, has treated secondary labor boycotts as a type of illegal action or conduct that falls outside of the protective zone created for the expressive activities of picketing and leafleting. Unfortunately, no clear reason has ever been given for denying labor boycotts legal protection as a speech act covered by the Free Speech clause of the First Amendment. Although the Supreme Court has determined that peaceful labor picketing is protected by the First Amendment, the Court has also recognized in a series of cases following *Thornhill* that labor union picketing can be constitutionally restricted whenever a valid state purpose has been found.[19]

The Court has concluded that because picketing involves both conduct and expression, picketing is "speech plus," such that a state could regulate the "plus" elements without violating the First Amendment. The Court has assumed that because labor picketing involves elements of conduct (pickets walk back and forth, carry signs, yell slogans, etc.), the conduct element of picketing can be regulated. The speech/conduct distinction, however, fails to explain why peaceful secondary labor boycotts are excluded from First Amendment *coverage* altogether. Secondary labor boycotts, unlike peaceful picketing or leafleting, have been perceived to be activity without any communicative elements worthy of First Amendment *coverage* or *protection*.[20]

It is difficult to justify the prohibition against secondary boycotts established by the Landrum-Griffin Amendment to the National Labor Relations Act.[21] Section 8(b)(4) of the Act outlaws secondary labor boycotts that have the effect of inducing employees of a neutral or secondary employer to engage in a work stoppage. The provision also forbids a union "to threaten, coerce, or restrain any person" who is a neutral or secondary employer. A proviso to the section, however, shelters "publicity other than picketing, for the purpose of truthfully advising the public, including consumers . . . that a product or products are produced by an employer with whom the labor organization has a primary dispute and are distributed by another employer."[22] It is generally thought that this proviso was necessary to insulate the section from a serious First Amendment challenge.

The courts, however, have interpreted the Act as prohibiting *all* secondary labor boycotts, because the prototypical effects of every secondary labor boycott fall within the statutory prohibition. Even though the statute recognizes an exception for truthful publicity picketing, the statutory exception is limited to publicity of the primary dispute with the struck employer. Proviso publicity picketing is *covered* and *protected* by the Act, but only if it does not have the secondary effect of inducing anyone other than an employee of the primary employer to refuse to make pickups or deliveries or perform services at the establishment of the secondary employer. In other words, the statutory exception protecting for truthful publicity picketing is limited if the publicity results in the prototypical effects of a secondary boycott.

Consequently, the means and objectives of the statute are defined judicially by the prototypical effects of the forbidden labor boycott radial category. The exception created for truthful publicity advising the public that a secondary employer is handling the products of a struck employer is defined by a different radial category for First Amendment activity. The *effects* of secondary labor boycotts are thus rendered illegal, while the publicity of the underlying dispute is protected because it is assumed that publicity as distinguished from illegal effects are covered by the First Amendment.

The leading labor law precedent attempting to justify the legislative prohibition against secondary boycotts in light of the First Amendment is the 1964 decision in *NLRB v. Fruit & Vegetable Packers Local 760 (Tree Fruits).*[23] In *Tree Fruits,* the Supreme Court held that consumer product picketing (picketing for purposes of encouraging the public not to purchase the products of a struck employer) was protected by the publicity proviso to Section 8(b)(4). The Court reached this result by reasoning that the First Amendment would be implicated if the statute were construed as prohibiting all forms of secondary consumer picketing. As a result of *Tree Fruits,* the Court was able to avoid deciding a constitutional question that would have been raised if the Court had broadly construed the secondary boycott prohibition to ban secondary consumer picketing. If it had done that, the Court would have contradicted its precedent in *Thornhill,* and would have consequently called into question the idea that peaceful labor picketing is covered by the protection of the Free Speech clause.

The Supreme Court's decision in the *Tree Fruits* case accepts the idea that expression can be distinguished from conduct and that the effects of conduct can be constitutionally regulated. The problem is that boycott publicity can have the same effects of otherwise prohibited secondary labor boycott activity. The problem is that the speech/conduct distinction assumes that there is such a thing as pure speech or pure conduct, when there is not.[24] All verbal communication can be understood as a form of action.[25] As nearly every legal scholar recognizes, communicative behavior is "100% action, and 100% expression."[26]

The call for a boycott can involve conduct like marching and parading with picket signs, which carry a verbal message. Every secondary labor boycott will also have collateral consequences independent of the communicative message of boycott publicity. One might argue that boycott publicity is like throwing a rock at someone as a way to express a message about that person. We would not regard the rock throwing as a communicative activity worthy of legal protection. Boycotts could be analyzed as rock throwing; the message communicated by the refusal to deal is incidental to the serious potential danger posed by the disruptive effects of the boycott.

The problem is that the same can be said of picketing or mass assemblies. All of these activities can have serious disruptive consequences, and yet we do not deny these activities coverage under the First Amendment. First Amendment coverage does not necessarily mean an activity will be protected under the First Amendment. The actual harm of the boycott can be prohibited without removing First Amendment coverage. No one is arguing that acts of violence should be covered or protected under the First Amendment, or any other law for that matter.

A peaceful group boycott may result in concerted action against the target of the boycott, or it may result in action taken against the boycotter; those requested to boycott may laugh in the boycotter's face. In either event, the activities of the boycott can help to create the possibility of shared understanding among all of the actors through the messages that each communicates. Thus, the nature of every peaceful group boycott ultimately depends on speech acts that seek to persuade others to do something, or to agree with something.

The communication of a boycott, like most forms of speech, requires action—direction, incitement, persuasion, disagreement. In other contexts, the Supreme Court has recognized that "[s]peech does not lose its protected character . . . simply because it may embarrass others or coerce them into action."[27] Because speech solicits action from an intended audience, every secondary labor boycott will also involve, to use Justice Lamar's words, "a force not inhering in the words themselves."[28]

The fact that secondary parties would be pressured or influenced is, in and of itself, neither a reason to deny either First Amendment coverage *or* protection to communication action.[29] If pressuring others is the reason for denying secondary labor boycotts First Amendment protection, then why do we tolerate mass assemblies or other forms of offensive expression now covered and protected by the First Amendment? The answer is that judges have placed mass assemblies and group boycotts in different metaphoric categories. The default consequences of the boycott metaphors place labor boycotts in a legal category defined by images of violence, and the "marketplace of ideas" metaphor places mass assemblies in a legal category covered by the First Amendment. The metaphor "actions are motion" motivates judges to forget that the First Amendment applies to mass assemblies and expressive conduct when they decide boycott issues in the law, and this forgetting of an important constitutional value has prevented labor groups from receiving the full benefit of First Amendment coverage.

LABOR LEAFLETING AND THE SIGNAL THEORY

Peaceful boycott activity frequently involves leafleting and picketing, both of which have been held to be inextricably intertwined with free speech for First Amendment purposes. In the case of leafleting and picketing, the courts have been willing to recognize that the communicative aspect of such activity involves important free speech values. A "signal theory"[30] has been developed to allow judges to distinguish protected speech from unprotected conduct in this context. Under this theory, judges must distinguish between activity intended as pure expression and that intended as a signal for conduct. Pure expression is protected, while signals are not.

The signal theory in labor law is the likely fallout from the bomb that exploded in Chicago during the famous Haymarket Riot. The bomb that exploded created in the legal mind a picture of labor violence that continues to influence the development of modern labor law regulations. The idea of the signal of boycott publicity has been understood as the fuse of a bomb waiting to explode. The bomb consists of the pre-existing union organization and the loyalty of union members. The threat of the signal is the underlying concerted agreement of the union, waiting for the signal to unite a collective explosion. The courts cannot do anything about the bomb, so judges try to keep its fuse unlit. Once the signal is given and the fuse is lit, judges imagine that the automatic response will be an explosion.

The Supreme Court has carved out an exception to this signal rule that expands boycott protections, albeit slightly. In its 1964 decision in *NLRB v. Fruit & Vegetable Packers Local 760 (Tree Fruits),*[31] the Supreme Court held that labor picketing that follows the product[32] is protected even if the picketing is meant to signal customers not to buy the struck product, so long as the union's appeal is closely confined to the primary dispute.

The *Tree Fruits* Court found that picketing limited to the struck product was not coercive of neutral employers even though the appeal of such picketing had the effect of signaling consumers not to buy the product from such employers. Interestingly, on the one hand, *Tree Fruits* can be read as implicitly rejecting the signaling justification used by the *Gompers* Court to enjoin boycott publicity. On the other hand, the same Court also indicated that the product boycott *would* violate the secondary boycott provision of federal labor law if the appeal to consumers sought to persuade them to stop doing business with a neutral employer altogether.

Seven years later, the Court reversed course in *NLRB v. Retail Store Employees Union, Local 1001 (Safeco),*[33] holding that product picketing that reasonably can be expected to threaten neutral parties with ruin or substantial loss is not protected by the *Tree Fruits* exception to federal labor regulation of secondary boycotts. The approach taken in *Tree Fruits* and *Safeco* for analyzing the legality of product picketing cannot be reconciled.[34] For example, as a result of *Safeco*, labor union picketing found to signal a secondary boycott is normally to be declared unlawful even though only speech may be involved. Yet *Tree Fruits* held that such speech, directed at consumers, has value that should be constitutionally protected. *Safeco* therefore infringes on the right of consumers to boycott.

In its 1988 decision in *Edward J. DeBartolo Corp. v. Florida Gulf Coast Bldg. & Const. Trade Council (DeBartolo II),*[35] the Supreme Court refused to extend the signal theory of *Safeco* to peaceful leafleting publicizing a boycott and labor dispute. In doing so, the Court found that peaceful leafleting, unlike peaceful picketing, involves protected First Amendment activity and cannot lawfully be curtailed on the basis of speculative fears that it might incite others to act against a neutral secondary employer. Hence, what is coercion in the case of peaceful picketing becomes legitimate free expression in the case of leafleting.

Thus, concerted activity loses its constitutional protection when it is understood as a signal. Yet, *Tree Fruits* and *DeBartolo II* recognize that concerted activity such as boycotting may also involve protected First

Amendment expression, thus raising a serious question about the legitimacy of the current federal regulation of secondary boycotts under federal labor legislation. The real problem with the signal theory is that it fails to appreciate the subtle expressive value of signals between group members as a communicative medium for solving coordination problems and for publicizing group identity. Those studying the behavior of groups have found that "signaling" is an important means for engaging the collective action of groups.[36]

The Supreme Court has yet to explain why the signal of a handbill should be considered less coercive or threatening than the signal of peaceful picketing or boycotting. Judges simply assume that a picket calls for an automatic response to the signal rather than a reasoned response to an idea. Picketing and boycotting are thought to go beyond mere persuasion because they may signal the obedience of others to a pre-existing agreement to boycott, perhaps backed up by the threat of group sanction, and perhaps because picketing and boycotting trigger deeply held class tensions captured by the union principle that union men or women do not cross picket lines. As a signal, picketing is thought to be an act that lights the fuse of the labor bomb, the force being the uncontrollable appeal of an imaginary crowd and the bomb being the collective action requested. Leafleting is thus imagined to be something that can be individualistic in nature, whereas picketing and boycotting are imagined to always involve a crowd or mob.

The words *handbill* and *leaflet* encourage judges to think in these terms. According to the *Oxford English Dictionary*, a handbill is "[a] printed notice or advertisement on a single page, intended to be delivered or circulated by hand."[37] A leaflet is defined as a "small or young foliage leaf" or a "folded printed sheet intended for free distribution."[38] The concept of a handbill is thus defined in terms of parts that belong to a larger whole—the hand is only part of the body; the leaf is only part of the tree.

The word *handbill* is in fact a *metonymy*. A metonymy consists of the use of the name of one thing for defining the meaning of another thing. In cognitive theory, a metonymy is a conceptual map that relies on information derived from the part-whole *image schema* to designate the knowledge about an entity by reference to some other entity to which it is conceptually related. The word *handbill* like expressions such as "all hands on deck" or "lend a hand" are all metonymies that are experientially motivated extensions of a common model or central meaning of hand. The linguistic category *hand* is thus a radial category.

The legal anomaly created by *DeBartolo II* has linguistic roots in the radial category *hand* and the *part-whole* schema. The metonymy *hand* is experientially motivated as a form of individual action. In focusing on the individual nature of handing out handbills, judges are less prone to find that even group distribution of handbills presents the same coercive dangers as picketing. Thus, in *DeBartolo II*, the Supreme Court drew an all-or-nothing distinction between picketing and giving out handbills because the language the judges used to describe the leafleting evoked the embedded conceptual mapping of an imaginary structure that uses knowledge of part-whole relations to designate the legal meaning of handbill activity.

THE HANDBILL EXCEPTION

The collective dissemination of handbills and consumer product picketing has been accorded different legal treatment because judges do not perceive such activity to pose the potential toxic force attributed to boycotts. Judges do not view leafleting or picketing as being as coercive as boycotts. Leafleting is thought to depend only on the "persuasive force" of an idea; whereas the persuasive appeal of picketing is thought to depend on physical coercion of a crowd or mob.[39] In *DeBartolo II*, for example, the Supreme Court assumed that the secondary effects of leafleting are not coercive because consumers can turn away after they read a handbill; they are not "intimidated by a line of picketers" as they would be if they had to choose between crossing a picket line or moving away.[40]

Leafleting is thought to be less coercive than picketing because it is a force that comes from within the receiver, rather than a force conveyed from outside. Consumers who choose to go along with the request of a handbill are considered to do so freely, because the Court has assumed that there is no outside force intimidating them to take action, as is the case in picketing. This is because the legal meaning of picketing, structured by the *Actions Are Motions* metaphor, conjures up an image of idea-objects being thrown by a group to an intended audience of receivers. The receivers are then induced (i.e., compelled) to take action by the force of the message thrown at them. The force originates outside the hearer and is thought to be different in kind from the internal force of the written handbills, which recipients can always throw away or ignore.

It is true, of course, that handbills are also packaged in word-containers. This would suggest that handbills are like the picketer's oral solicitations to boycott. Both involve word-containers that can be thrown at an intended audience. However, because handbills involve a written message, they are not like the oral stones thrown by picketers. The reader of the handbill can choose not to receive the message of the handbill, but the person within earshot of oral boycott publicity has to hear the message. Judges assume that the message of a boycott, however, once received, has the dangerous potential of inciting riot.

The notion of internal self-regulation is thus a matter of degree. The persuasive effect of picketing solicitations on the intended audience is something the individual may find hard to resist. The reason for this is that when judges think of handbills, they think of individuals, and when they think of pickets, they think of groups. As the number of participants increases, as it does when one moves from leafleting to picketing, verbal acts are seen as posing an increased threat such that external legal intervention is warranted. Thus, judges' decisions accord leafleting greater First Amendment protection.

As for peaceful consumer picketing, judges have understood that picketing is a way of expressing ideas and communicating a message because they are experientially motivated to conceptualize this form of picketing as a radial category of human speech covered by the First Amendment. Cultural metaphors from our revolution, associated with colonial protests and mass assemblies, and embodied experiences of physical force, shape the defining prototype characteristics for characterizing the meaning of mass picketing as a category of speech. Even though consumer and labor picketing is not literally speech, the linguistic category *speech* is a radial category for associating this form of picketing with the free speech clause of the First Amendment.

Judges have come to understand boycott as metaphoric stone-throwing by a group rather than as an expressive activity. The reason for this is that boycotting resides in a different radial category. Individuals who join a boycott, however, do so because they identify with the goal and message of the boycott as well as the identity of the boycott group. A boycott serves to create and disseminate information about the identity of a group, and this information is what gives boycott an expressive and communicative value. The nature of group action is essential to communicate effectively a message about a group. Boycott can thus be a way for groups to express their solidarity and to collectively assert their dignity.

The fact that labor boycotts also involve physical action and have secondary effects should not distract from the communicative nature of the practice. Every labor boycott conveys a message that is intended to elicit a response from an audience. In the case of picketing and leafleting, the courts have recognized the importance of extending constitutional coverage to protect the communicative conduct of groups. The different legal meanings of picketing, leafleting, and boycotting are the consequences of the different conceptual models used for extending the radial categories of these phenomena. Each of the usages of these words is related to different metaphoric understandings of group activity. The different metaphoric understandings have default consequences for determining coverage and protection under the First Amendment.

The fact that judges have taken sides with the interest of capital is not surprising given the history of labor in the courts. What is surprising is that judges have been able to do this while at the same time they deny that they are ideological in adjudicating labor disputes. Metaphor is what has enabled judges to suppress and deny the ideological in labor law for much of the postwar era. Imagination and ideology have thus shaped the legal mind to see entrepreneurial control and managerial prerogatives to lie outside the regulatory process of federal collective bargaining law and to treat concerted activity of workers as either a disease or an incitement to violence.

The way judges have used boycott metaphor to interpret the meaning of secondary boycott regulation is thus consistent with the "deradicalization" thesis advanced by Karl Klare and Katherine Stone in their germinal work on the National Labor Relations Act.[41] According to Klare's thesis, adjudication under the statute has had the effect of deradicalizing the original understanding of collective bargaining because judges were hostile to the idea of labor militancy and protest. In developing metaphors of collective bargaining based on market values and managerial interests, Klare argued that judges naturalized a concept of collective bargaining that has since become a process that places more importance on protecting the rights and interests of capital, and ignoring those of labor.

The irony of this is that the judicial interpretations of the National Labor Relations Act have worked to favor the very interests that had necessitated the enactment of the Act. Katherine Stone has subsequently shown how the ideology of judges created an "industrial pluralist paradigm" hostile to worker control and participation in the workplace.[42] In restricting the right of workers and their unions to engage in secondary boycotts, judges have taken sides in the ideological stakes of the conflict between labor and capital. The way secondary labor boycott legislation has been framed by a disease metaphor is a powerful example of what critical legal studies scholars have claimed: that federal labor legislation has been interpreted by judges in a distinct ideological direction.

CHAPTER 6
RADIAL CATEGORY OF CIVIL RIGHTS BOYCOTTS

WHEN CIVIL RIGHTS groups began boycotting to protest racial discrimination, judges turned to new conceptual metaphors to define the meaning of boycott. The linguistic category *boycott* was extended by a categorization process that generated a new conventionalized meaning of boycott in the law applicable to civil rights groups. Judges analyzed civil rights groups under the central model of boycotts created for labor groups. As a result, civil rights groups were condemned as destructive forces. A different imaginative meaning of boycott subsequently developed, however, from new cultural assumptions about the meaning of civil rights demonstrations brought to protest racial discrimination. The new radial category was recognized in an important civil rights case decided by the Supreme Court in 1982. This chapter will examine how imagination and ideology helped to shape the radial category extension created for protest boycotts by civil rights groups.

Initially, civil rights boycotts were condemned in the courts for the same reasons labor boycotts were condemned: the boycott was perceived to be an inherently destructive force, threatening to civil society. The linguistic category for the term *labor boycott* became a barrier to confine the meaning of civil rights boycotts. The logic for this linguistic category developed from cases involving civil rights picketing regulated under antilabor picketing statutes. In *Hughes v. Superior Court of California,*[1] for example, the United States Supreme Court upheld a state court injunction forbidding civil rights protesters from picketing a retail store accused of racial discrimination in hiring. The injunction had been justified in state court on the ground that picketing to bring about "proportional racial hiring" violated, ironically, the state's public policy forbidding racial discrimination.[2] The Supreme Court upheld the injunction even though picketing had been found to involve First

Amendment protection in *Thornhill v. Alabama*.[3] In *Hughes,* Justice Frankfurter concluded that "[p]icketing is not beyond the control of a State if the manner in which picketing is conducted or the purpose which it seeks to effectuate gives ground for its disallowance."[4] The decision gave legal legitimacy to state antiunion statutes that had been applied to prohibit picketing and boycotting by labor groups in the South.[5]

As we have seen, judges in the labor boycott cases understood the law as necessary to restrain the irrational forces of labor groups. The Rule of Law was thus invoked to require participants of boycott activity to conform their irrational conduct to the civil rules of society, rules guided by reason, objectivity, and dispassion. During the 1950s, civil rights boycotts were thus subjected to the same rigid limitations and the same imaginative and conventional metaphors that were applied to stifle labor boycotts at early common law. But then, in 1982, a metaphoric shift occurred in an important civil rights case.

Reptiles Hidden in the Weeds and Freestanding Trees

In the landmark civil rights boycott case, *NAACP v. Claiborne Hardware,*[6] decided in 1982, the Supreme Court reversed course: it associated a civil rights boycott with a new metaphor that was more in keeping with the way boycott was understood by the Irish during the Irish Land Wars, and with the way American Colonists understood mass protest during our revolution. This new civil rights boycott metaphor stemmed from the Court's willingness to imagine boycott as a law-enforcing practice necessary to defeat racial segregation. This metaphor analogized boycott to law enforcement, and associated the target of the boycott with violence, disorder, and insurgency. Apparently, the metaphor, like others used in the law of boycotts, is capable of invoking different meanings in the law, and for that reason, it too has chameleon-like qualities.

The Supreme Court invoked this different legal meaning of boycott for determining whether a civil rights group boycotting the racially discriminatory practices of white merchants and civic leaders in Claiborne County, Mississippi, could be held civilly liable in state tort law for the damages caused by the boycott. The local branch of the NAACP, attempting to transform an entrenched cultural regime of racism in Claiborne County, called for a boycott of private merchants and governmental offices. The boycott was supported by several hundred citizens and a number of religious leaders, including Martin Luther King, who brought with him the political clout of the NAACP. The NAACP-sponsored boycott was successfully organized by a group known as the Deacons or Black Hats. Violators of the boycott were characterized as "traitors" to the African-American community and were socially ostracized; in a few isolated incidents, "traitors" were physically attacked. Many white-owned businesses suffered considerable financial loss as a result of the boycott.

The Supreme Court unanimously held in *Claiborne Hardware* that the courts of Mississippi could not constitutionally enforce tort judgments for recovery of economic losses by businesses that lost customers as a result of the boycott. Justice Stevens, writing for the majority, concluded that the civil rights boycott constituted a political form of expression that was constitutionally protected by the speech, assembly, association, and petition clauses of the First Amendment.[7] Justice Stevens's decision was also influenced by a very real concern: a contrary decision would sustain a state tort damage judgment that might have bankrupted the NAACP. Indeed, a legal realist explanation of *Claiborne Hardware* is that the Supreme Court concluded that the boycott was constitutionally protected because a civil rights group was boycotting. The decision could thus be explained as the policy result of the Court's historical treatment and commitment to the civil rights movement, the significance of which I shall consider more fully later.

What enabled Justice Stevens to justify his conclusion, however, was an imaginative conceptual structure involving a number of basic conceptual metaphors such as "Ideas are objects," "Words are containers," "Communication is seeing," and a source-path-goal image schemata. Recognizing that the *Claiborne Hardware* boycott involved more than peaceful assembly, Justice Stevens emphasized that the boycott involved ideas that were like containers that were communicated by action of a group that moved through space for achieving a purpose or goal protected by the First Amendment. Justice Stevens depicted the civil rights boycott as a political act involving the assertion of collective economic power to achieve a political objective. As Justice Stevens explained,

> The boycott of white merchants at issue in this case took many forms. The boycott was launched at a meeting of a local branch of the NAACP attended by several hundred persons. Its

acknowledged purpose was to secure compliance by both civic and business leaders of a lengthy list of demands for equality and racial justice. The boycott was supported by speeches and non-violent picketing. Participants repeatedly encouraged others to join in the cause.

Each of these elements of the boycott is a form of speech or conduct that is ordinarily entitled to protection under the First and Fourteenth Amendments. Speech itself was used to further the aims of the boycott. In sum, the boycott clearly involved constitutionally protected activity. . . . Through speech, assembly, and petition—rather than through riot or revolution—petitioners sought to change a social order that has consistently treated them as second-class citizens.[8]

What Justice Stevens failed to explain was why boycott was not a type of compulsory *force* that in the labor cases had been found to justify the imposition of court injunctions. A labor boycott analogy was arguably relevant given that the state's injunction against the *Claiborne Hardware* boycott was issued under a state statutory prohibition against secondary labor boycotts, enacted specially for regulating labor boycotts. The *Claiborne Hardware* Court, however, unlike the Court in *Gompers,* did not see the force of the boycott as dangerous or unlawful, even though Justice Stevens acknowledged that the trial record contained evidence of physical force.

The trial record, for example, disclosed that the black community in Claiborne County was threatened by the Black Hats or the Deacons. Several incidents, some substantiated by the evidence, some of doubtful credibility, reflected a general attitude of hostility towards violators of the boycott. For instance, the trial record revealed that a brick was thrown through a car windshield of a violator, that in two instances shots were fired at a house, and that one violator was allegedly beaten.[9] One would think that the evidentiary record called for the application of the "force" metaphor used in labor cases to give meaning to the boycott. But this is not what happened in *Claiborne Hardware.*

The Court downplayed evidence of coercion, force, and criminality and focused instead on what Justice Stevens characterized as the "majestic elements" of the boycott's appeal. In finding that the word *boycott* was chameleon-like, Justice Stevens went on to give future courts a warning: *"A court must be wary of a claim that the true color of a forest is better revealed by reptiles hidden in the weeds than by the foliage of countless free-standing trees."*[10]

The Court emphasized the majestic, treelike elements of the boycott in *Claiborne Hardware,* noting that the boycott was aimed at accomplishing civil rights objectives: "Its acknowledged purpose was to secure compliance by both civic and business leaders with a lengthy list of demands for equality and racial justice."[11] In finding that the boycott was "a form of speech or conduct" protected by the First Amendment, Justice Stevens emphasized that the boycotters "banded together and collectively expressed their dissatisfaction with a social structure that had denied them rights to equal treatment and respect."[12]

What permitted Justice Stevens to see the majestic elements of the *Claiborne Hardware* boycott was a new radial category for civil rights boycotts. What enabled Justice Stevens to comprehend the nature and meaning of this category were conceptual metaphors such as "Ideas are objects," "Words are containers," and "Communication is seeing." These metaphors permitted Justice Stevens, and the other justices of the majority, to see boycott action as a constitutionally protected speech. The boycott was a vehicle that transmitted the idea-object of expression, in the container of boycott publicity. The communicative message of the boycott was comprehended by ignoring the metaphor "Actions are motions." Other metaphors were favored in order to explain the outcome reached. Metaphors drawn from the First Amendment enabled Justice Stevens to see how a boycott of a civil rights group would involve the majestic element of a constitutional purpose. What was ignored was the metaphoric reptile hidden in the weeds of Justice Stevens's opinion, a point that I will address in the conclusion of this chapter.

The legal meaning of the boycott was thus analyzed under a new radial category for subordinate groups who boycott to oppose an arbitrary and unjust legal and social regime. In *Claiborne Hardware,* the radial category of boycott was *chained* to images of legality, and it was racist state-sponsored practices that became chained to the central category that normally is used to understand the meaning of labor boycotts. Awareness of the racial hierarchy of white Southern culture, and the illegitimacy of that culture, enabled the Court to downplay the "force" metaphor of labor cases and instead adopt a new "majestic" metaphor aimed at establishing the resemblance between the boycott and the civil rights movement. The "majestic" nature of civil rights was used to evoke affirmative legal values like equality, justice, and fairness to support the Court's decision. Figure 6.1 maps the radial category applicable to the *Claiborne Hardware* boycott.

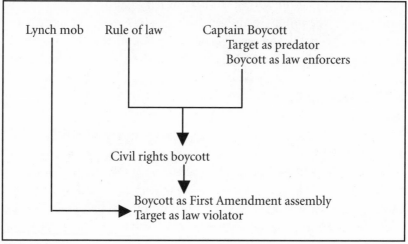

Figure 6.1
Radial Category of Civil Rights Boycott

    Claiborne Hardware offers the pathos of the civil rights movement to define the legal meaning of boycott. The pathos of the civil rights movement was highly influential during the Warren Court era. Indeed, the California Supreme Court, in *Environmental Planning & Info. Council v. Superior Court,*[13] subsequently extended the *Claiborne Hardware* decision to provide protection to a nonprofit environmental organization's boycott against a newspaper publisher's editorial policies on environmental matters. In finding that the boycott could not be enjoined under state law, the California Supreme Court rejected the publisher's argument that only civil rights boycotts should be afforded constitutional protection. The California Supreme Court emphasized that it was "precluded by the First Amendment itself from gauging the degree of Constitutional protection by the content or subject matter of the speech."[14]

    In finding that the meaning attributed to the boycott exhibited elements of "majesty," Justice Stevens downplayed the importance of protecting the freedom of the targets, and the importance of limiting the coercive effects of the boycott. The "force" metaphor was at work in *Claiborne*, since the boycott was understood as a means of political leverage designed to move the legislature to act. What remains unclear is why the civil rights boycott in that case should be viewed as a positive political force deserving constitutional protection.

One explanation for the Supreme Court's decision in *Claiborne Hardware* is that a contrary result might have bankrupted the boycott's principal supporter, the NAACP, a result that would have had serious political implications for the civil rights movement. *Claiborne Hardware* could thus be read as a case that was decided to prevent the bankruptcy of an important civil rights organization. This view of the case has much going for it, but it never comes to grips with the full metaphoric importance of the Court's decision.

The more interesting question to be asked about *Claiborne Hardware* is this: Why did the Supreme Court imagine the civil rights boycott as a majestic act rather than as a reptile, a tiger, or a disease? The answer to this nagging question sheds important light on the metaphoric significance of *Claiborne Hardware* for regulating civil rights boycotts. *Claiborne Hardware* can be seen to be a truly exceptional case when one considers the metaphoric source of the metaphors that have been used to give meaning to civil rights boycotts.

CROWDS, LYNCH MOBS, AND CIVIL RIGHTS

Throughout the 1950s, federal judges were bombarded with picketing and boycott cases that invoked not positive, but negative images of civil rights boycotts as mobs. A general bias against group action and mass protest may have also been colored by prejudices about mob action and racial oppression in the pre–Civil War South. As Gary Peller has noted, "[p]robably the most powerful single image in the American experience is the image of the Southern lynch mob—there, in the common understanding, the mob, ruled by irrational racism against blacks, bypassed the orderly, rational, and judicial means of dispensing justice in favor of the `pragmatic and the expedient.'"[15] The Southern lynch mob predisposed judges to associate group action with law-breaking activity. The picture of a lynch mob brings to mind the awful consequences that can flow from crowds of people who act outside the law.

Further, there has always been a long-standing view that has associated crowd behavior with negative images of irrational, violent, and contagious conduct. C. Edwin Baker, for example, has observed how sociologists and social psychologists have embraced the view that crowd behavior is evil and menacing.[16] Le Bon's classic nineteenth-century book *The Crowd*, for example, uses mob and disease metaphors to explain the sinister qualities of crowd behavior.[17] Le Bon, using a disease metaphor, observed that "[c]rowds are only powerful for destruction. Their rule is always tantamount to a barbarian phase. . . . In consequence of the purely destructive nature of their power crowds act like those microbes which hasten the dissolution of enfeebled or dead bodies."[18] This view of crowd behavior has been deeply ingrained in our culture, and it would be surprising if judges were immune from the influence of cultural images of crowds.

In the case of civil rights, the image of the Southern lynch mob established a limited subset of the prototypical properties of the radial category of boycott. The prototype was then chained to imaginative ideas about crowd behavior to create an extremely powerful default metaphor. The default metaphor defined the fault lines of extension from the common model of boycott to cover the meaning of boycotts by civil rights groups. The central model of labor boycott had thus a new extension, though related to the central case in some fashion, could not be generated by the rules and legal decisions applicable to labor. The radial category extension was shaped by normative orientations and assumptions derived from a cultural context of racial oppression and mob action. The way the default metaphor functions depends on whether one imagines the meaning of lynch mobs and crowd to apply to the boycott or the target.

The meaning generated by the metaphor is thus highly contingent upon context. A particularly poignant illustration of this metaphor was the 1991 United States Senate Judiciary Committee hearings on President Bush's nominee, Clarence Thomas, to the Supreme Court to replace the late Justice Thurgood Marshall, the first African-American to sit on the Supreme Court. Clarence Thomas, an African-American, was a highly controversial nominee since he was known to have opposed many of the liberal positions that Justice Marshall had advanced on the Supreme Court. Thomas was also handicapped by the fact that he was charged with some rather graphic instances of sexual harassment. Anita Hill, a reserved, young African-American woman lawyer who had worked for Thomas at the Department of Education and the Equal Employment Opportunity Commission, claimed that Thomas had made a number of lewd sexual advances toward her, repeatedly used the workplace to discuss his account of pornographic films he had seen, and generally bragged about his sexual prowess.[19]

Hill, however, was never able to effectively pursue her allegations against Thomas, and the Committee members present at the hearings were never able to effectively challenge Thomas's credentials. Thomas silenced all questions concerning his conduct, character, and ability by invoking a metaphor that associated his position with the historical position of all black men who have been literally lynched by white-racist mobs. In his opening statement to the committee, Thomas claimed that he was the victim of "high-tech lynching," in response to Hill and his other critics.

By suggesting that he, an African-American, was being subjected to a "high-tech lynching" at the nomination hearings, Thomas was able to effectively shield himself from criticism and searching inquiry about his past behavior, and his credentials. In facing the all white and male Senatorial committee, Thomas was able to effectively use this default metaphor of a "high-tech lynching" to associate his position with the plight of black men who historically suffered brutal forms of discrimination, including lynching, for asserting their manhood. The metaphor silenced not only Anita Hill, but also the questioning by the white Senators.[20] The charges of sexual harassment and the gender issues those charges raised, as well as questions concerning his credentials and prior employment record, were thus placed in abeyance by the metaphor. That metaphor probably won Thomas a seat on the United States Supreme Court.

Thomas's use of the metaphor of a "high-tech lynch mob" was rhetorically effective because it relied upon information based on a disturbing social practice involving the plight of black men in the South to give a political meaning to confirmation hearings and charges of sexual harassment. The "high-tech lynch mob" metaphor is not unlike the "tiger" metaphor in the *Glidden* case. The imaginary picture of a lynch mob or a wild tiger give new meaning to something that seems to be in a totally different linguistic category (confirmation hearing investigation or boycott publicity). The use of these metaphors illustrates how the chameleon-like quality of metaphoric reasoning permits the author to shift from one conceptual context to a totally different conceptual context in the process of categorizing the meaning of some event or phenomena.

In the case of civil rights boycotts, the cultural background of lynch mobs and civil rights demonstrations creates a highly contingent and con-flicting set of images and pictures for understanding the meaning of a civil rights boycott. The metaphors of lynch mobs and ideas of crowd behav-ior became part of the background assumptions and normative orienta-tions that motivate judges to initially understand civil rights boycotts and picketing as a dangerous group activity, conceptually similar to the forms of activity involving labor groups that are associated with ideas of violence.

Labor and civil rights are thus extensions of the radial category of the words *boycott* and *picket*, but the unique social context of civil rights helps to create two entirely different metaphoric models for analyzing the right of groups to boycott and petition the government. The model adopted by the Court in *Claiborne Hardware* is exceptional because it represents, in the law, a highly unusual category. To understand why this model is exceptional, we must consider how the model differs from the dominant, usual model, the "marketplace of ideas" model.

MARKETPLACE OF IDEAS MODEL

The dominant model of group action was first recognized by the Warren Court in its 1961 landmark decision in *Eastern Railroad Presidents Confer-ence v. Noerr Motor Freight*.[21] As a result of *Noerr*, the courts have inter-preted the constitutional right to petition the government as establishing a near absolute right of groups to lobby the government. In *Noerr*, the Court held that the railroads could use even deceptive lobbying tactics to influence state government to pass road-weight restriction laws that would effectively ban truckers from competition in the interstate freight market. In a sense, the railroads were attempting to use state government as a means for boycotting competition of the truckers. The Supreme Court in an opinion by Justice Black held that so long as the lobbying effort was not a "sham," it was absolutely protected by the First Amendment.[22]

While Justice Black offered several rationales for the Court's decision in *Noerr*, he noted that "[t]he right of petition is one of the freedoms pro-tected by the Bill of Rights," and he thus found it difficult to "lightly impute to Congress an intent to invade these freedoms."[23] What Justice Black was affirming in Noerr were the central tenets of pluralist ideol-ogy,[24] a political conception of democratic society "that denie[s] absolute truths, remain[s] intellectually flexible and critical, value[s] diversity, and [draws] strength from innumerable competing subgroups."[25] Pluralist ideology projects an image of the political process based on a market metaphor. Government is understood to be the result of a no-holds-barred fight between various interest groups. When applied to interest group petitioning, pluralist ideology requires tolerance for direct political action of groups because interest group action is assumed to advance the public interest through a competitive struggle. Interest group pluralism supports the idea that legal neutrality or nonintervention in the political spheres of government advances the public good and guarantees democracy.

The "invisible-hand" of interest group competition encourages judges to analogize the political process to an unregulated private market. Deregulation of interest group competition is encouraged because it is thought that the pursuit of private interests would, like the invisible hand of the market, lead to the greatest aggregate social welfare. Interest groups are presumed to have predetermined, unified desires and to be capable, like people buying and selling products in the market, of engaging in rational decisions.[26] Thus, the market-like interest group competition brings its own form of order to the political sphere.

A number of richly textured metaphors combine to give meaning to the legal theory of interest group pluralism. The "invisible-hand" image is shaped by a homeostasis metaphor, analogous to the body's biological system, to evoke the ideas of balance, self-regulation, and equilibrium. It is the *homeostasis* metaphor that enabled Oliver W. Holmes Jr. to understand the political process as a dialectic struggle between conflicting ideas and values. Holmes believed that judicial meddling into the political process would only undermine the natural process of selection in the search for truth.

In addition, the model of interest group pluralism is structured by another influential metaphor in the law—the "marketplace of ideas." The metaphor comes from Justice Holmes's dissent in *Abrams v. United States*.[27] Justice Holmes asserted in his famous dissent that "the ultimate good desired is better reached by free trade in ideas—that the best test of truth is the power of the thought to get itself accepted in the competition of the market."[28] As constitutional scholars have noted, Holmes's idea of the marketplace as a truth-discovering process has influenced modern constitutional principles defining the nature of free speech guaranteed by the First Amendment.[29] The metaphor of a marketplace enabled a future generation of scholars and judges to understand interest group petitioning as market activity like selling a product, and to understand legislation as a "no-holds-barred fight" between competitors, where truth is the result of that competition. The normative domain of the marketplace thus permits powerful interest groups, like corporations, to use their resources to influence legislative decision makers to boycott competitors through legislation.[30]

In *Noerr*, the image of dangerous conduct, normally associated with labor *boycotts*, was replaced with the image of a naturalistic marketlike process. The image of *force* that supported findings of coercion in labor cases was replaced with a new idea of force as a necessary and beneficial ingredient of the truth-finding process of the marketplace. Special interest groups thus have a constitutional right to ply governmental processes with enormous economic resources to influence governmental action to the detriment of rivals and the public interest. Judges replace the images of rioting mobs or exploding bombs with images that justify collective efforts by competitors to restrain trade by appealing to the invisible hand of the market.

CIVIC REPUBLICAN MODEL

While *Noerr* appears to have established near absolute immunity for special interest group lobbying, the Supreme Court has been less willing to extend the same legal treatment to boycotts, even when they attempt to influence governmental policy by making appeals to the electorate. When it comes to boycotting, a different theoretical model of political activity is used to analyze the legal parameters of group activity. In finding that the civil rights boycott was constitutionally protected in *Claiborne Hardware*, Justice Stevens, for example, found that the boycott exhibited "majestic" elements because the objective sought transcended the self-interest of those boycotting. The boycott represented to the Court a transitory moment in American politics where a group was engaging in the type of social activism practiced by the revolutionary founders of the Republic.[31] An idealized cognitive model structured by civic republican values justified the Court's decision.

In thinking of the deployment of economic power in the market as a surrogate for revolution, civil rights boycotts could be conceptualized as important constitutional moments for the expression of political dissent necessary for constitutional evolution. This understanding of boycott may explain why the Court found the civil rights boycott in *Claiborne Hardware* to be constitutionally protected.[32] The boycott advanced constitutional objectives because it was aimed at pursuing the goal of equality for African-Americans rather than narrow self-interest. By focusing on the altruistic purposes of boycotts, the Court found a constitutional right to boycott. The discovery of this new right was possible because Justice Stevens chose to focus on the majestic goals of the boycott (what he called "the foliage of countless standing trees") rather than immediate, and suspicious, economic interests of those boycotting (the "reptiles hidden in the weeds").

The Supreme Court, however, has not been consistent. Sometimes it has preferred to focus on the reptiles. In the same term that *Claiborne Hardware* was decided, the Court also held in *Allied International* that a boycott called by the longshoremen's union to protest the Russian invasion of Afghanistan could be proscribed as an illegal secondary boycott.[33] In *Allied International,* the labor boycott was aimed at influencing the policies of a foreign government, and the boycott could only be described as political. The Court, however, refused to recognize that the boycott involved constitutionally protected political expression because a different metaphor was involved. Because the boycott in *Allied International* was secondary in nature and hence arguably proscribed by federal labor law, the Court was influenced by the metastasis metaphor of labor cases. The boycott was therefore understood to be a disease spreading throughout an otherwise healthy economic system. The cure was federal proscription of the boycott. The problem is that the model of boycott as civic republican politics fails to instruct the courts as to whether a given boycott is majestic or reptilian.

THE IDEOLOGY OF CLAIBORNE HARDWARE

What, then, caused the Court in *Claiborne Hardware* to view a civil rights boycott not in terms of reptiles and disease, but in terms of majestic and curative powers? As previously explained, one explanation for the Court's decision lies in the need to protect the NAACP from civil tort judgments. According to this view, the Court simply chose "majestic" treelike metaphors in order to justify its outcome in favor of the civil rights organization. I think, however, a deeper explanation can be discovered in the background of the cultural assumptions that enlightened the Court's metaphors.

In *Claiborne Hardware,* the Court recognized a First Amendment defense by envisioning the civil rights boycott as a *conduit* for bringing a message of protest. Even though the boycott had secondary effects,[34] the Court concluded that the boycott was not a disease, but rather a cure for curtailing discriminatory practices that had been sanctioned at one time in society by official state actions. The problem the Court saw was that civil society, not the boycott, represented the threat to law and order. The civil rights boycott of *Claiborne Hardware* arose, after all, out of the historical struggles of the civil rights movement of the 1950s and 1960s, which actively challenged the regime of Jim Crow discrimination in the South, discrimination that had been firmly entrenched by state law. From the cultural experience of the civil rights movement of the 1950s and 1960s, one can come to see why the boycott in *Claiborne Hardware* would be perceived by the Supreme Court in 1982 as an important political event that represented the virtues of popular civic republican values.

Similar examples spring easily to mind. The Montgomery bus boycott involving Rosa Parks's refusal to take a seat at the back of a city bus reserved for blacks in the winter of 1955 illustrates, for example, how boycotts were used during the civil rights movement of the 1950s to desegregate the South.[35] Dr. Martin Luther King organized the African-American community in Montgomery and boycotted the city buses to protest Rosa Parks's arrest. The boycotters created a volunteer car-pool system, eventually raised enough money to sustain a small fleet of vehicles that functioned with military-like precision, and ultimately forced the city to desegregate buses.[36]

The Montgomery bus boycott, aided by favorable court decisions,[37] helped to advance the collective interest of the African-American community in Montgomery, Alabama. The process of boycotting the buses of the city imbued Dr. King and his organization with a sense of solidarity and collective impetus necessary to implement social change.[38] The months of boycott activity in Montgomery also inculcated many community leaders with a sense of political responsibility to represent minority interests in the community.[39] Finally, the mass gatherings and collective effort of the boycott forced the community to come together over class lines and allowed members of the different classes a basis for understanding each others' lives and culture. As Randall Kennedy has explained in his study of the boycott:

> The boycott made black Montgomerians aware of themselves as a community with obligations and capacities to which they and others had previously been blind. On the eve of the boycott, few would have imagined the latent abilities that resided within that community. The protest elicited and clarified those abilities. On the eve of the boycott, few black Montgomerians would have considered themselves as persons with important political duties. The protest inculcated and enlarged their sense of responsibility. Moreover, by publicizing their willingness and ability to mobilize united opposition to Jim Crow practices, the protesters in Montgomery contributed a therapeutic dose of inspiration to dissidents everywhere. Later developments would attest to the influence of the boycott as a role model that encouraged other acts of rebellion. Participants in subsequent protests remember Montgomery as a distinct, encouraging presence.[40]

The *Claiborne Hardware* and Montgomery bus boycotts can be imaginatively aligned with images of law and order, stability, and justice. In contrast, the targets of these boycotts, local governments, represent the image of the unruly mob. Judges can thus associate state action with the cultural images of Southern lynch mobs and the metaphor "boycott is violence." It is, in other words, the image of boycott as a law-enforcement expedient that explains why a civil rights boycott may be legally protected, and why the labor boycotts are imaginatively found to be a completely different legal category.[41] Justice Stevens's "reptile in the weeds" metaphor thus controls the labor boycott cases, and his "majestic" or "freestanding trees" metaphor controls the civil rights boycott cases. The choice of metaphor relates to the Court's perception of the target, but that perception is itself shaped by a highly selective legal imagination that conjures up ideas about how collective behavior of a boycott enhances or hinders important democratic and constitutional values.

The metaphors of *Claiborne Hardware* establish a *conceptual frame* for understanding the relation between boycott and democratic process. The imaginative frame enables us to see the relation between boycott, free assembly, and association that have always been a critical feature of our society. While mass demonstrations and boycotts involve elements of coercion and pressure, they also involve "expressive, value-based conduct, independent of the pressure [or coercion] they impose."[42]

As C. Edwin Baker has explained: "The boycotter affirms that under present conditions she considers purchases from or interactions with the boycotted party to be objectionable. The rally participant considers her participation, the protest symbolized by her presence, to be ethically and personally the right thing to do at this time."[43] In both boycotts and mass demonstrations, there is the same expressive and political value implicated by the participants, the right to freely associate for purposes of participating in the affairs that determine how we live. In *Claiborne Hardware*, a new metaphor of boycott, conceptually framed by civic republican values, enabled the Supreme Court to see the connection between boycotts and mass political activities that have always enjoyed a respectable history in our society.

Justice Stevens was thus able to discover a meaning of boycott that had been concealed by radial extension of boycott in the labor cases. Justice Stevens saw that boycott can serve an important civic function in allowing groups to influence and participate in their community and government. His perception of boycott can be understood in the way the boycott against Captain Boycott was understood by the Irish tenants. The tenants' boycott against Captain Boycott was very much like the civil rights boycott in Claiborne County: they both were forms of liberating moments, representing the effort of a disempowered group to advance and protect the groups' interest. An important meaning of boycott thus lies within the weeds of the prototypical effects of the word *boycott,* and this meaning can be seen to have been discovered by Justice Stevens in the *Claiborne Hardware* case.

To justify the result he wanted, maintaining at the same time his non-ideological role, Justice Stevens used a metaphor to reach the preferred ideological outcome. The imagery of Southern lynch mobs, angry crowds, the marketplace of ideas, which had been used to deny civil rights boycotts legal protection, were metaphorically realigned to give new legal meaning to a boycott the Court believed to be ideologically justified. The metaphors of *Claiborne Hardware* are exceptional, however, because they are embedded within a historical context that involved a federal-state conflict over the meaning of civil rights. Boycott was imagined as law-enforcing activity because boycott became a self-help mechanism for enforcing federal antidiscrimination policies against state segregationist policies. It was metaphor that permitted Justice Stevens to conceal the ideology of his activism in *Claiborne Hardware*. Ideology of the Warren Court thus shaped the law's understanding of civil rights boycotts much in the same way that ideology has historically shaped the way the law has responded to concerted activity of workers in conservative, less activist courts.

CHAPTER 7
RADIAL CATEGORY OF
COMMERCIAL BOYCOTTS

WHEN BOYCOTT HAS involved one business entity against another, judges have reached different conclusions about the legal meaning of boycott. Judges have perceived business boycotts to be different from those of labor and civil rights groups, and this perception has necessitated the use of different imaginative extensions from a radial category derived from the central model of boycott. This radial category extension of boycott emerged from the cultural background of a market economy. The key metaphors shaping the category are embodied metaphors derived from the physical experience of *balance, equilibrium*, and *homeostasis*.

In the commercial context, judges have naturalized the legal meaning of boycotts as a legitimate and normal form of business competition, although they have also acknowledged that boycotts should be condemned when they are found to involve illegitimate forms of competition that threaten the equilibrium of the market system. Commercial boycotts thus reside in a metaphoric position between labor boycotts, which are almost always condemned, and civil rights boycotts, which are sometimes presumed to be constitutionally protected.

A powerful example of the metaphoric position of business boycotts, at early common law, is the Rhode Island Supreme Court case of *Macauley v. Tierney*,[1] decided in 1895. There, a professional plumbers association boycotted plumbing supply distributors that did business with plumbers who were not members of the association. The boycott was challenged on the ground that it interfered with the freedom of the plumbing suppliers to contract with plumbers on their own terms. In finding that the boycott was lawful, the court stated that the goal of the boycott was merely an effort by one business group to compete with another.[2]

The boycotters had done nothing more, as the court explained, "than to pursue to the bitter end a war of competition waged in the interest of their own trade."[3] The court thus associated boycott with natural competitive market forces necessary for maintaining a competitive equilibrium, or balance, in the economy. Instead of regarding the business boycott as a disruptive force, the court relied upon an image schema derived from experiential knowledge about equilibrium, balance, and weight in finding that the pressure of the boycott served a beneficial, competitive effect.

A similar result was reached in an earlier Massachusetts Supreme Court decision in *Bowen v. Matheson*.[4] There, the court concluded that a combination of Boston shipping masters could lawfully boycott new competitors doing business in the Boston harbor by refusing to do business with anyone who did business with these competitors. In finding the boycott lawful, the Massachusetts court concluded that the intention to inflict economic injury on a competitor by boycott was an incident of lawful competition. According to the court: "If the effect [of boycott] was to destroy the business of shipping masters who are not members of the association it is such a result as in the competition of business often follows from a course of proceeding that the law permits."[5]

Three years later in *Carew v. Rutherford*,[6] the same Massachusetts court held, in an opinion by the same judge, that a labor union's refusal to work on a project that included nonunion workers, unless the employer paid the union a five hundred dollar fine, constituted an unfair method of competition. As in *Bowen*, the workers in *Carew* engaged in activity that could be characterized as a boycott. While the *Carew* court emphasized that the workers had attempted to extract an illegal fine by their boycott, it is difficult to see why this fact should serve to distinguish the two cases. Why should the refusal to deal in *Carew* be treated differently from the refusal to deal in *Bowen*, which had the potential consequence of destroying a competitor's business; a far more substantial injury than a fine of $500?[7]

The different result reached in *Carew* can be explained on the basis of different radial categories judges have imaginatively used to characterize business and labor boycotts. When the boycott has involved one business against another business, for example, the courts have tended to associate the word *boycott* with the central case or model developed from prototypical properties of a market. The market thus becomes the common model or *idealized cognitive model* or ICM for structuring the meaning of a group commercial boycott in terms of legitimate commercial activity. The word *boycott* was imaginatively chained to an idealized cognitive model having prototype effects of normal competitive market phenomena.[8]

The body becomes the frame, schema, stock story, or idealized cognitive model for formatting the controlling default metaphors of boycott.[9] The prototypical cognitive effects of the body creates a new extension or *ray* of meaning from the radial category. Boycotts by business groups are described in images that project ideas about the behavior of *homo economicus*: boycotts are found to be lawful when they are seen to promote consumption, efficiency, spending, and all the behavioral properties associated with the radial category of an economic market. However, when the boycott involves a threat to bodily process, then the word *boycott* is associated with images of negative behavior: coercion, force, waste, abnormal growth, refusal to compete. Today, in the law, boycott is described in images that reflect homo economicus (market behavior) of the twentieth century: commercial boycotts are imagined to reside within a radial category extension of the word chained to market metaphors. Figure 7.1 maps the radial category of boycotts.

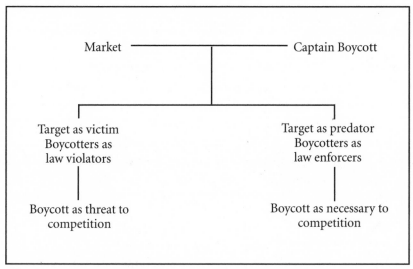

Figure 7.1
Radial Category of Business Boycott

Basic Default Metaphors of
the Business Boycott Radial Category

In the business boycott cases, the body image of *balance* has generated a new metaphoric meaning of boycott force. Business boycotts found to promote competition in the market are imaged as natural forces, much like "our *experience* of systematic processes and states within our bodies."[10] By understanding the nature of these boycotts within the metaphoric image projected by balance, judges conceptualized most business boycotts as legitimate practices necessary for competition.

Judges have understood balance in terms of an image schema of body balance—kinesthetic balance, systemic balance, psychological balance, and so forth. "Despite the different manifestations of balance, there is a single image-schema present in all such experiences; *a symmetrical arrangement of force vectors relative to an axis*."[11] Because the default metaphors are partial representations of reality, however, the legal rules applicable to labor and business boycotts were vulnerable to the objection that judges were applying a double standard in these cases. Indeed, Justice Holmes argued at the turn of the century in his famous dissent in *Vegelahn v. Guntner*[12] that American workers should have the same legal privilege that business groups then had—to boycott for competitive objectives. To get to this result, Holmes had to map with his prose the conceptual relation between labor and commercial boycotts. To do this, Holmes sought to explain why the central case of labor and business boycotts fit the prototypical properties of market competition.

Holmes first recognized the inherent ideological nature of the struggle between labor and capital. He then portrayed the ideological conflict as the central case as unstable and not amenable to rational solution. The only solution was a new conceptual frame, one forged out of the imaginative struggle Holmes attributed to market competition. As Holmes explained in the following famous passage from his dissent in *Vegelahn*,

> One of the eternal conflicts out of which life is made up is that between the effort of every man to get the most he can for his services, and that of society, disguised under the name of capital, to get his services for the least possible return. Combination on the one side is patent and powerful. Combination on the

other is the necessary and desirable counterpart, if the battle is to be carried on in a fair and equal way.[13]

Holmes disagreed with what most other judges thought about labor boycotts because he used in his legal analysis new default metaphors that described the behavior of twentieth-century homo economicus. Holmes was not just making an interesting new analogy, he was shifting the law's boycott categories to take account of the new social meaning of industrial competition. As Mark Tushnet has noted, Holmes "premised his analysis on a fundamental disagreement with the majority's interpretation of social reality."[14] Hence in *Vegelahn*, the majority had adopted images of boycott that described nineteenth-century homo economicus—competition was seen as a threat of violence. In his dissent, Holmes argued that peaceful boycotting could be justified by characterizing labor picketing as a means of competition because he saw how competitive behavior was being redefined by the Industrial Revolution of the twentieth century. As Holmes argued, a combination of workers was "a necessary and desirable counterpart [to a combination of employers], if the battle is to be carried out in a fair and equal way."[15] To Holmes, the majority in *Vegelahn* had adopted an obsolete metaphor for defining the meaning of labor picketing and boycotting, one that interpreted peaceful concerted labor activity as violence.

Holmes's idea of competition can be understood in terms of a homeostasis metaphor that captures the prototypical behavior of twentieth-century homo economicus.[16] For Holmes, labor and business disputes were a natural systematic response. Viewing labor disputes as a free struggle for life, Holmes characterized picketing and boycotting as natural symptoms of a competitive process. The homeostasis metaphor made it possible for Holmes to foresee how a modern system of collective bargaining law might function as an unregulated process of competition. Later, when Holmes was on the Supreme Court, he used the same metaphor to develop his marketplace of ideas theory of the First Amendment.

The likely source of Holmes's homeostasis metaphor was Darwinian theory, which was popular in Holmes's day. Here, one can see how Darwin's notion of a biological process of selection, where struggle between and within biological species leads to the natural selection of the fittest, serves as an imaginative metaphoric system where the domain of biological evolution is the source of metaphors for operations in the intellectual domain. The biological laws of evolution, understood as a homeostatic system where the survival of the fittest ensures the desirable balance of development, established for Holmes an entire metaphoric system for understanding the relations between labor and capital, as well as the meaning of boycott for either group. Instead of viewing labor union activity as animalistic behavior, Holmes saw how labor and capital could be conceptualized as a metaphoric ally by the world of Darwinian evolution: Boycott is homeostatic response. In this important sense, Holmes sought to bring about a paradigmatic shift in the metaphoric and legal meaning of labor disputes and later, free speech, through a type of metaphoric reasoning.

For Holmes, competition between labor and capital was necessary and desirable for the process of evolutionary economic development. He saw a category breakdown caused by the felt social needs of his time. As Holmes explained: "[I]t is plain from the slightest consideration of practical affairs, or the most superficial reading of industrial history, that free competition means combination, and that the organization of the world, now going on so fast, means an ever-increasing might and scope of combination."[17] A new radial category of boycott was needed to make sense of labor-capital competition in the emerging Industrial Era. The point advanced by Holmes was that competition involved a general adaptive process that, if left free of regulation, would serve to ensure that the general problems of injury and justification were resolved fairly.[18]

The homeostasis metaphor reveals the hidden meaning of Holmes's view of competition.[19] Holmes never explicitly referred to this metaphor to explain his ideas about labor and capital competition, but the metaphor was there concealed in his prose and his analysis of the evolutionary process of market competition. Thus, a *parts-whole* schema, and a biologically derived metaphor, "body is homeostatic organism," enabled Justice Holmes to metaphorically argue that labor and capital were engaged in a "struggle for life," and that business combination and labor boycott were but natural tendencies of the same process.[20] In his dissent in *Vegelahn*, Holmes concluded that combination of workers was as natural as combination of capital, and that competition necessarily meant that labor and capital must be free of law's regulations to combine and engage in a common competitive struggle.[21]

Apparently, the dominant labor metaphors, which associated boycotts with violent mobs, had become so entrenched that even Holmes's insight could not change the course of labor law. Labor law boycott cases retained the metaphors of violence, while business boycott cases retained the homeostasis metaphor. It would take several decades before Holmes's homeostasis metaphor would catch on in the secondary labor boycott cases, but when it did, secondary labor boycott would already be imagined as the abnormal growth of negative competitive behavior.

MIXING BOYCOTT METAPHORS

In some cases, the legal characterization of the boycott as "labor" or "business" is ambiguous because the boycott is the product of a nontraditional group.[22] When this occurs, judges mix metaphors. The Supreme Court's decision in *FTC v. Superior Court Trial Lawyers Ass'n (Trial Lawyers)*[23] illustrates this phenomenon. The *Trial Lawyers* case involved an antitrust challenge brought by the Federal Trade Commission against a boycott organized by criminal defense lawyers practicing in the District of Columbia. The lawyers, who represented indigent criminal defendants under the District's Criminal Justice Act, conducted a boycott to get higher hourly fees. The boycott was designed to pressure the legislature to amend the Act to increase the hourly fee schedule paid to legal aid attorneys who were court appointed to represent indigent defendants in the District's courts. The legal aid lawyers thus refused to accept any further court appointments until the fee act was amended, and other lawyers and the public were requested to honor the lawyers' boycott. The District, however, took legal action against the boycott, claiming that it represented an unlawful restraint of trade.

In defending their boycott in court, the trial lawyers argued that their boycott was a constitutionally protected exercise of their First Amendment right to petition government, and their petition was constitutionally necessary to protect the Sixth Amendment rights of their clients, who would be given inadequate representation by underpaid and overworked lawyers. The Supreme Court rejected their arguments, holding six to three that the boycott constituted an illegal price-fixing conspiracy, proscribed *per se* under the Sherman Antitrust Act applicable to commercial boycotts.[24]

Justice Stevens, who authored the opinion for the Court, first distinguished his opinion in *Claiborne Hardware*, concluding that First Amendment protections for civil rights boycotts were different, because they were limited to instances where the boycotters seek no special economic advantage for themselves. He then concluded that the *Trial Lawyers* boycott fell outside *Claiborne Hardware* because it was motivated by an economic incentive to fix the price of the lawyers' services. Justice Stevens thus reinterpreted his own opinion in *Claiborne Hardware* as being limited to the case where the boycott involved objectives that transcended the economic self-interest of those boycotting.[25] *Trial Lawyers* was distinguished because the boycotting lawyers in that case had a direct financial stake in the outcome of the boycott—the success of their boycott determined the amount of fees they would earn in representing criminal defendants.

It may well be that Justice Stevens, who has also authored a number of important antitrust decisions, has come to favor an idealized cognitive model constructed from a market model, animated by a number of conventional metaphors such as "Actions are motions," "Ideas are objects," "speech is conduit." The model is then used to evaluate the legal meaning of boycott expression. He seems to be using this cognitive model to develop the principle that the governmental interest in maintaining competitive markets outweighs the values of self-advancement and collective participation of labor groups.[26]

The imaginative nature of Justice Stevens's *Trial Lawyers* opinion, for example, is revealed by an analogy he drew between the per se rule of antitrust and reckless driving and airplane stunt-flying. Using these imaginative analogies, Justice Stevens depicted a picture of the *Trial Lawyers* boycott as an activity that "pose[d] . . . a threat to the free market."[27] Reckless driving, airplane stunt-flying, monopoly price conspiracies are known to pose dangers to society, and in Justice Stevens's mind "[s]o it is with boycotts and price fixing."[28] The *Trial Lawyers* boycott was thus distinguished from the civil rights boycott in *Claiborne Hardware* by attributing to the lawyers' boycott, prototypical properties of a radial category involving reckless driving and airplane stunt-flying. These prototypical properties are then used to derive the anticompetitive meaning of the boycott extended from the radial category created for a commercial, rather than a labor, boycott.

As a result of Justice Stevens's radial category, the critical factor distinguishing *Trial Lawyers* from *Claiborne Hardware* is financial motivation: if the boycotters are perceived to profit personally from the boycott, then the boycott will be treated as reckless driving and airplane stunt-flying and condemned as potentially dangerous activity. However, if those who boycott do not profit financially, then the boycott will fall within the majestic metaphors of *Claiborne Hardware* and will be protected.

Unfortunately, the metaphors Justice Stevens uses assume that boycott can be easily classified under a motivational criterion. When collective action is involved, however, it is naive to think that a single motivating cause may be isolated. The *Trial Lawyers* boycott, for instance, was conducted to improve the financial interests of legal aid attorneys, but it was also conducted to obtain favorable legislation that would increase representation of the poor and thus ensure effective representation of indigent defendants. The *Trial Lawyers* boycott was therefore a mixed-motive boycott. There were too many participants (lawyers, incarcerated clients, future clients, the general public, etc.) and too many potential motivations and objectives (higher court fees, more effective representations, constitutional requirements to representation, etc.) to justify the Court's finding of unity of purpose. In a mixed-motive boycott, motive becomes an unworkable standard for determining the right to boycott because judges cannot be expected to determine what goes on in a person's heart or mind, and whether those motives are legitimate. Judges who follow Justice Stevens's metaphoric logic are likely to make serious category errors.

Indeed, Justice Stevens's decision in *Trial Lawyers* is difficult to understand in light of the approach he took in *Claiborne Hardware*, where he determined that political expression *may* provide a basis for First Amendment protection. Justice Stevens's attempt to distinguish *Claiborne Hardware* on the factual ground that the civil rights boycotters "sought no special advantage for themselves"[29] ignored the fact that the civil rights boycotters were protesting widespread employment discrimination against African-Americans in Claiborne County. The civil rights boycott in *Claiborne Hardware* involved economic matters in addition to legal principles of antidiscrimination. The African-American boycotters wanted jobs, and they were boycotting because they were denied economic opportunities in the marketplace because of their race. The fact that Justice Stevens, the author of *Claiborne Hardware*, should distinguish that case in *Trial Lawyers* suggests that he has become what Duncan Kennedy has called a "bipolar judge," a judge who exhibits the tendency to alternate between ideologies and radial categories over time.[30] The metaphoric shift in the *Trial Lawyers* decision thus illustrates how metaphor can conceal ideological shifts of judges over time.

Apparently, when boycott activity takes place on the streets, as it did in *Trial Lawyers*, judges are less willing to find constitutional protection for the boycott because metaphoric reason associates the legal meaning of boycott with abnormal behavior. *Claiborne Hardware* represents the rare exception, but that case is now made problematic by *Trial Lawyers*. Because financial motivation was a factor in *Claiborne Hardware* (elimination of racially discriminatory practices would have led to greater economic opportunities for minorities), the logical integrity (*Logos*) of Justice Stevens's "majestic" metaphors of boycott may no longer hold sway in other civil rights cases. It is not just that Justice Stevens has incorrectly mixed his own metaphors, but rather it is that the categories of boycott do not operate in the rigidly defined manner that many lawyers suppose. The categories are fluid, and metaphors can be mixed, because metaphoric reason is shaped by the judge's imaginative understanding of the normative context of a given controversy.

Because the prototypical case is necessarily only a subset of the array of cases that might cover the meaning of a word-category, there is a relative gray area between categories where metaphors of different category types can be mixed. A judge has considerable discretion in deciding whether a new factual situation is more or less within one or another radial category. When prototypical properties are presented in a new and novel configuration, as they were in the *Trial Lawyers* case (lawyers boycotting for labor and business objectives), judges are prone to mix their own metaphors and sometimes, as in *Trial Lawyers*, a new hybrid radial category is created.

When traditional forms of governmental petitioning (e.g., lobbying the legislature) have been involved, it is ironic that the Supreme Court has had little trouble in recognizing that direct political action is protected absolutely by the First Amendment. As we have seen, the Supreme Court in *Eastern Railroad Presidents Conference v. Noerr Motor Freight*[31] held that the lobbying activities of an association of railroads was protected under the First Amendment as government petitioning, even though the petition was aimed at securing state-imposed road-weight restrictions for interstate, over-the-road trucks, legislation that was intended to block—boycott—truckers from the interstate freight-hauling business. Thus, *Noerr* held that the association's lobbying, aimed at instigating a legislatively created boycott, was absolutely protected. The association was analyzed as an entity, and not as a mob of capitalists, and thus the boycott metaphors of labor groups were ignored. In *Trial Lawyers*, however, the lawyers' attempt to petition government through a boycott was found to be absolutely prohibited under the per se rules of antitrust applicable to commercial boycotts. The lawyer group was analyzed as an angry mob, much in the same way labor boycotts are analyzed in the law.

In *Noerr*, the Court emphasized that the defendant's financial motivation in petitioning government was irrelevant. In *Trial Lawyers*, the Court distinguished *Noerr* on the ground that the objective of the lawyers' boycott (a concerted effort to fix lawyers' fees) would be brought about by private rather than governmental action. The immunity afforded to petitioning activity under the First Amendment was thus limited to traditional lobbying campaigns and other political activities seeking to influence governmental decision-making. Petitions by boycott are apparently not accorded the same constitutional status as petitions by other means.

Hence, where a special interest group seeks a state-created boycott, the Court has recognized that lobbying for private economic gain is comparable to constitutionally protected election-like petitioning. Is it practical, or even possible, however, to distinguish between boycotts motivated by political, governmental, and/or economic objectives? What is political or governmental may be collective resistance to economic conditions, and what is economic may be collective interest seeking a right to participate in the larger society. Economic motivations and interests can be, after all, just one subset of political reasons for a boycott.

The legal aid attorneys' boycott in the *Trial Lawyers* case was not all that different from the petitioning in *Noerr*, nor was it all that different from the boycott in *Claiborne Hardware*. In *Trial Lawyers*, boycott was a form of petition used to influence policy. The fact that someone was pressured should not alter the legal analysis of boycott phenomena. As

C. Edwin Baker has explained: "All societies permit some means of exercising power over other people. The use of money or property in exchange transactions, for example, involves an exercise of power that gets others to act in ways that they would not otherwise choose."[32]

In *Trial Lawyers* and *Claiborne Hardware*, the boycotters had an economic stake in the outcome of their boycott and petition. In *Trial Lawyers*, the legal aid attorneys had an obvious economic interest in having the D.C. legislature increase statutory fees for court-appointed lawyers, and in *Claiborne Hardware*, African-American boycotters had an obvious economic interest in ending racial discrimination in employment. Indeed, most civil rights boycotts are about advancing the economic interests of the group. Political objectives are nearly always tied to economic objectives. Boycotts by labor and civil rights groups in *Claiborne Hardware* are thus like the acts of the petition and mass demonstration in *Noerr*, which the Supreme Court has recognized to represent a respectable practice of our constitutional democracy.[33]

THE NAKED/ANCILLARY METAPHORS OF ANTITRUST

Judges have created somewhat different legal distinctions for distinguishing different hybrid categories of boycott under the antitrust laws. Modern antitrust case law condemns as per se illegal concerted refusals to deal with group boycotts by business combinations, but the courts have been inconsistent in their condemnation. In *Eastern States Retail Lumber Dealers' Assn. v. United States*,[34] the Supreme Court held that a boycott by retail lumber dealers against wholesale lumber dealers who sold to competitors was a per se violation of the Sherman Act. Recognizing that a single firm can lawfully boycott anyone, an agreement among competitors not to deal with certain persons acts as blockage or clog on the market competition.[35]

Concerted refusals to deal by commercial entities are not always treated as unlawful boycotts, however, especially when they are found to support efficiencies in marketing or producing a product.[36] As Judge Robert Bork once remarked: "According to conventional wisdom, boycotts . . . are illegal per se. But that proposition is easily shown to be false. . . . The categories of lawful and unlawful boycotts have never been defined, [and] the law makes many mistakes and does much harm."[37]

Indeed, antitrust boycott doctrine, like its labor law counterpart, has exhibited considerable elasticity when it comes to group boycotts. In antitrust law, boycott becomes a term that is used once the court has concluded that the challenged practice is anticompetitive and hence bad.

On one hand, there is little disagreement among antitrust lawyers that boycotts and refusals to deal can be vehicles used by competitors to accomplish illegal conspiracies in restraint of trade—what antitrust experts term "naked" restraints of trade. On the other hand, courts have also recognized that competitors sometimes engage in group boycotts to achieve wholly beneficial objectives such as policing against unethical and shoddy rivals, enhancing operational efficiency, and administering cooperative activities essential to sports, tournaments, and similar activities.[38] Hence, concerted business boycotts are sometimes found to be lawful because they are seen to be "ancillary" to otherwise legitimate activities. An ancillary boycott "is a concerted refusal to deal that contributes to the efficiency or usefulness of a cooperative activity."[39]

Thus, concerted refusals to deal by business entities are distinguished from boycotts and evaluated under a rule of reason analysis. If the "concerted refusal" is found to enhance competition of the group, it is treated as presumptively ancillary and hence lawful.[40] This does not mean concerted refusals to deal are always lawful, but it does mean they will not be presumptively condemned per se. The per se test is reserved for so-called naked boycotts—"concerted refusals of competitors to deal with another competitor, customer or supplier when no case can be made that the refusal is ancillary to any legitimate joint activity."[41]

Boycotts that are seen to be ancillary to some beneficial purpose are thus judged to be reasonable restraints, and hence lawful. Those boycotts found to be lacking such redeeming qualities are struck down per se as naked restraints of trade.[42] Unlike labor law cases, however, where the presumption is that secondary labor boycotts are unprotected forms of conduct, antitrust cases have applied the naked/ancillary restraint distinction in ways that favor the legality of business boycotts.[43]

The courts have on occasion found that a concerted refusal to deal will be exempt from antitrust regulation if it is primarily an expressive activity "operating as a statement to its victims that the boycotters want something."[44] But as the decisions of the Supreme Court in *Claiborne Hardware* and *Trial Lawyers* illustrate, the line between expressive and nonexpressive refusals is difficult to discern. Since nearly every boycott has an expressive component, antitrust judges are ill-equipped to determine how their naked/ancillary restraint analysis should apply to business boycotts.

In antitrust law, the image of nakedness has been used to describe illegal boycotts that restrain trade, and the image of ancillary has come to signify the deployment of collective effort for social progress and development.[45] Restraints of trade that are deemed to be *naked* represent activity that is predatory or pernicious or socially unredeeming. The nakedness of the restraint describes a meaning of boycott as lewd and immoral behavior. Just as the image of the boycott serves to evoke images of disease and illness in secondary labor boycott discourse, the image of nakedness in antitrust boycott doctrine projects ideas about primitive, animal-like passion, abnormal conduct understood to be uncivilized and socially undesirable. The concept of ancillary restraint, in contrast, serves to justify boycotts that have been civilized by a scheme of reason that seeks instrumentally to promote the maximization of private wealth. In other words, ancillary restraints may be necessary in order for vital economic functions to work efficiently. Moreover, the effects of ancillary restraints can be overcome by the general adaptive response of market competition.

In the image of *nakedness*, we can begin to understand how cultural and physical experiences might fuel the belief that commercial boycotts are inherently dangerous practices to be closely regulated, and the belief that boycotts that are ancillary to legitimate objectives should be lawful. Ancillary boycotts are merely conduits for achieving legitimate objectives, while boycotts, as naked restraints of trade, do not wear the mantle of legitimate business function. Naked restraints of trade lack a proper container or conduit of legitimacy, and are thus condemned on a per se basis. The condemnation of naked restraints makes perfectly good sense as a law-generated means of maintaining balance within the economic system.

GATEWAY AND FLOW METAPHORS

While the naked/ancillary restraint distinction has been used in antitrust law mainly for analyzing substantive antitrust violations, other metaphors have influenced jurisdictional issues, as they did in *Summit Health, Ltd. v. Pinhas.*[46] In *Pinhas*, the majority and dissent used the naked/ancillary distinction to bolster different jurisdictional arguments. The majority relied upon the naked restraint strand of the distinction in concluding that the alleged boycott of a merchant substantially affected interstate commerce. The dissent relied upon the ancillary restraint analysis in arguing that the boycott did not substantially affect interstate commerce, without proof of serious obstruction. In the dissent's view, the interstate commerce requirement, which gives a court jurisdiction under the Sherman Act, requires proof that a boycott has the potential to restrict competition and thus substantially affect interstate commerce. At issue in *Pinhas* was the interstate commerce consequences of an alleged conspiracy to boycott a single doctor who had complained about the loss of hospital medical staff privileges. The issue raised a question concerning the proper test for determining the jurisdictional power of the federal courts to decide Sherman Antitrust Act issues raised by commercial boycotts.

Dr. Simon J. Pinhas, a nationally respected corneal eye surgeon, requested that Midway Hospital Medical Center (Midway), the hospital in which he practiced, eliminate a rule that required a second to be in attendance at most eye surgeries. The requirement significantly increased the cost of eye surgery, and Medicare determined the additional services to be unnecessary and refused reimbursement. Midway refused to abolish its practice but instead offered Dr. Pinhas a "sham" contract that provided for monetary payments for services not performed as an apparent effort to compensate him for the loss in Medicare reimbursements.[47] When Dr. Pinhas refused the contract and pressed his demand, Midway initiated a peer review proceeding that resulted in Dr. Pinhas's suspension.[48] The hospital's peer review committee also prepared an unfavorable report regarding Pinhas for distribution to all hospitals to which he might apply for employment, for the alleged purpose of "preclud[ing] him from continued competition in the marketplace, not only at defendant Midway Hospital [but also] in California, if not the United States."[49] Dr. Pinhas claimed that the hospital had illegally conspired to prevent him from practicing medicine, a violation of the Sherman Antitrust Act. A major issue in the case concerned the question of whether a conspiracy to boycott a single person, in this instance Dr. Pinhas, affected interstate commerce so as to establish jurisdiction under the Sherman Antitrust Act.

The Ninth Circuit held that "jurisdiction under the Sherman Act" had been established because Dr. Pinhas satisfied his requirement of showing that "the peer review process in general [had a] 'not insubstantial' [effect on interstate commerce]"—a point which, the court said, "can hardly be disputed."[50] The court's analysis of the jurisdictional standard followed the test set out in *McLain v. Real Estate Board of New Orleans*.[51] In *McLain*, the Supreme Court concluded that the interstate commerce provision of the Sherman Act required a showing that "'respondents' activities which allegedly have been *infected* by a price-fixing conspiracy be shown 'as a matter of practical economics' to have a not insubstantial effect on the interstate commerce involved."[52] While it has never been clear what the Court meant by "infected activities,"[53] it has been assumed that the breadth of the Commerce Clause gave the Sherman Act a sufficiently broad reach to cover most illegal conspiracies, although a minority of appellate courts have disagreed. The Ninth Circuit concluded that the boycott against Dr. Pinhas had a sufficient nexus with interstate commerce to confer jurisdiction.

The Supreme Court agreed that the boycott satisfied interstate commerce jurisdictional requirements, holding that the competitive significance of Dr. Pinhas's exclusion from the market was to be measured "not just by a particularized evaluation of his own practice, but rather, by a general evaluation of the impact of the restraint on other participants and potential participants in the market from which he [had] been excluded."[54] A sufficient nexus with interstate commerce existed, Justice Stevens reasoned for the majority, because the hospital's peer review committee served as the "gateway that control[led] access to the market for [Dr. Pinhas's] services."[55]

The Court measured the effect of the boycott against Dr. Pinhas by considering the potential harm that might ensue if the boycott against a single doctor were successful in closing the gateway to a market. The "gateway" metaphor, signifying the image of a gate blocking passage along a path, enabled the majority to find that peer review by the hospital closed an important passage way for entry into the market. The gateway metaphor also enabled the majority to render its decision without upsetting the *McLain* principle.

The infected activities test of *McLain* seemed to require proof that interstate commerce had in fact been affected by the activities of the defendant, implying that there must be more than one victim involved or one victim capable of infecting the entire stream of commerce. In *Pinhas*, only Dr. Pinhas had been affected by the new rule, and that rule only covered one hospital. It was not clear whether the alleged restraint of his competition was sufficient to be an infected activity for jurisdictional purposes. In shifting to a new metaphor, the majority was able to find that the restraint substantially affected interstate commerce by analogizing the hospital's regulation to a "gate," closing the only passage on the stream of commerce. The metaphor explains how a restraint of a single victim might be infected activity for jurisdictional purposes.

Relying upon *McLain*, but applying its own boycott metaphor, the Court held that the interstate commerce requirement mandated only a showing of some actual or potential connection between the restraint and interstate commerce. While Dr. Pinhas alone had been the victim of the alleged boycott, the majority relied upon the Court's earlier decision in *Klor's, Inc. v. Broadway-Hale Stores, Inc.*,[56] which condemned a merchant boycott as a per se restraint of trade, to find that the single target boycott constituted an illegal activity. As Justice Stevens explained, "[I]f a violation of the Sherman Act occurred, the case is necessarily more significant than the fate of 'just one merchant whose business is so small that his destruction makes little difference to the economy.'"[57] The majority's gateway metaphor thus enabled the Court to broaden the scope of the *McLain* precedent so that it would cover the facts of *Pinhas*.

Justice Scalia, in dissent, complained, that "[t]he Court's suggestion that competition in the entire Los Angeles market was affected by this one surgeon's exclusion from that market simply ignores the 'practical economics' of the matter."[58] According to Justice Scalia, the peer review committee's actions provided "no basis for assuming that this alleged conspiracy's market power—and its consequent effect upon *competition*, as opposed to its effect upon *Dr. Pinhas*—extended throughout Los Angeles."[59] Justice Scalia reached a contrary result by invoking a new metaphor of interstate commerce by analogizing commerce to the "flow" of water on a stream or river.

In Justice Scalia's view the "uncontested facts" of *Pinhas* failed to establish "that [the] peer review process at Midway (hospital) [was] the 'gateway' to the Los Angeles Market in the sense of being the only way (or even one of the few ways) to gain entry."[60] As Justice Scalia argued, the Commerce Clause requires allegations and a preliminary showing that "in its practical economic consequences, the boycott substantially affects interstate commerce by restricting competition or . . . interrupts the flow of interstate commerce."[61] Here, commerce in the market is seen metaphorically as the *flow* of water moving along a river stream. To interfere with this flow, one must obstruct the river. Only a substantial obstruction of the flow would constitute an interference. Since other means were available to Dr. Pinhas to gain entry to the market, such as other hospitals and peer review programs that might grant him access, Justice Scalia rejected the notion that the peer review process at one hospital was in any sense the gateway to the Los Angeles market.[62] Moreover, because the alleged conspiracy was aimed at excluding only Dr. Pinhas, Justice Scalia and the dissent found no basis for finding that interstate commerce, or the *flow* thereof, had been substantially affected.[63]

Pinhas can thus be read as highlighting two different metaphors for understanding the interstate commerce consequences of a group boycott. On the one hand, one advanced by Justice Stevens seeks to evaluate the Interstate Commerce requirement by analogizing a boycott to a door closing a gateway. Boycotts block freedom of access like a door or gate and thus have a potential restraining effect on the gateway to interstate commerce. Under the gate metaphor, every boycott involves restraining market consequences that affect interstate commerce since someone's economic freedom would be actually or potentially restrained. Every boycott would then have an impact on interstate commerce so long as the challenged restraint involves a line of commerce that can be shown to affect interstate commerce in a substantial way.[64]

On the other hand, under Justice Scalia's view, boycotts should be the subject of federal regulation only if those boycotting have sufficient market power to obstruct the *flow* of commerce. Boycotts are not a gate blocking a gateway; they are merely the potential obstructions of the flow of market trade. Under Scalia's view, therefore, proof of market power to obstruct the flow of commerce is necessary to determine the reach of federal antitrust regulation under the Commerce Clause. The Logos of the flow metaphor suggests that the Commerce Clause requirement for jurisdiction is in reality a substantive concern—proof of market power and competitive effects would be, under Scalia's approach, a jurisdictional requirement. The oddity of this is that the Court has also concluded that proof of market power is not relevant for determining whether a group boycott constitutes a substantive antitrust violation.[65]

The *container* metaphor helps to explain the argumentative structure that the justices have advanced in justifying their understanding of the jurisdictional consequences of the commercial boycotts. In the *Pinhas* case, for example, the two different jurisdictional tests advanced by Justice Stevens and Justice Scalia, for the majority and dissent respectively, can be seen to rest on different imaginative ideas about containers and containment. In finding that a price-fixing conspiracy that excluded a single ophthalmological surgeon from the Los Angeles market affected interstate commerce, Justice Stevens and the majority concluded that the boycott was to be judged "not by a particularized evaluation" of a single exclusion, but rather by "a general evaluation of the restraint's impact on other participants and potential participants in the market."[66] In other words, the restraint of the boycott was viewed as being *uncontained* because it could potentially flow outward and have an impact on the whole of the market economy. Justice Scalia, however, dissented because he believed that the boycott was limited to a well-defined container, a hospital. The restraint thus only involved a particularized contained market restraint, and when judged as a part of the market economy, it failed to substantially affect interstate commerce.

THE PROBLEM OF DEFINITION ONCE AGAIN: STRIKES, BOYCOTTS, AND REFUSALS TO DEAL

One might think that judges would resolve some of their doubts about commercial boycotts by simply agreeing to follow the same dictionary definition of the word *boycott*. However one of the most bedeviling problems in the law of boycott has been the problem of definition. Judges and lawyers have been unable to decide how the word should be defined in the law. Sometimes what would appear to be a boycott is not found to be a boycott in strictly legal terms.

Consider, for example, the U.S. Supreme Court's decision in *Hartford Insurance Co. v. California.*[67] There the issue was whether the term *boycott* as used in Section 3(b) of the McCarran-Ferguson Act,[68] which denies antitrust immunity for boycotts by insurance companies, was applicable to a refusal to deal by foreign and domestic insurance companies who were allegedly seeking to restrain trade in the American insurance market. It was alleged that the goal of the conspiracy was to limit the availability of a standard commercial insurance policy for long-term pollution and environmental damage. Nineteen states and a number of private plaintiffs filed thirty-six complaints against the defendants involved in the alleged boycott, charging that the conspiracies violated Section 1 of the Sherman Antitrust Act.

The defendants' principal defense was that the conduct alleged in the various complaints fell within the grant of antitrust immunity contained in Section 2(b) of the McCarran-Ferguson Act, which extended broad antitrust immunity to "the business of insurance . . . regulated by State Law." Section 3(b) of McCarran-Ferguson, expressly exempted "boycott" from the grant of antitrust immunity created by Section 2(b). Hence, at issue was whether the boycott exemption of McCarran-Ferguson applied to deny defendants protection under the antitrust immunity provision of the Act.

Hartford Insurance thus presented the Supreme Court with a deceptively simple question: Was the definition of the word *boycott* as used in Section 3(b) of McCarran-Ferguson applicable to an alleged concerted "refusal to deal" involving the coordinated action of the defendants? This question was deceptively simple because the answer seemed to call for a precise dictionary definition of the word *boycott.* And indeed, because the word was not defined, the justices of the Supreme Court proceeded to decide the statutory question presented by turning to the standard dictionary definition of the word. Sometimes, however, what may appear to fall within the standard dictionary definition of the word *boycott* is not found to be a boycott, as was the case in *Hartford Insurance.*

Justice Scalia, for a slim five-justice majority, ruled that a precise definition of the word *boycott* was limited to the meaning it had in the very first boycott in Ireland. As a result, for Justice Scalia and the majority, the defendants' alleged conspiracy, involving a refusal to deal except on certain terms of their standard domestic insurance policy, was not a boycott because the refusal to deal was limited to specific terms of the proposed insurance agreement. The defendants had not refused to engage in other unrelated transactions as leverage to achieve the terms they desired, and this fact distinguished for Justice Scalia the defendants' refusal from the Irish peasants' actions against Captain Boycott.

Interestingly, Justice Scalia observed that "the verb made from the unfortunate Captain's name has had from the outset the meaning it continues to carry today."[69] What is interesting is that he overlooked the conflicting ways that landlords and tenants had understood the Irish boycott as either a law-enforcing or law-breaking activity. What is even more intriguing is that Justice Scalia failed to even mention the famous statement by Justice Stevens in *Claiborne Hardware* to the effect that boycotts in the law had a chameleon-like nature. It is as if Justice Scalia were writing on a clean slate, defining the term *boycott* for the law for the first time, and ignoring an almost one hundred–year history of conflicting judicial interpretations of this verb. Nevertheless, Justice Scalia proceeded under the assumption that the verb *boycott* had a fixed meaning in the law.

Consulting the *Oxford English Dictionary*, Justice Scalia found that "[t]o 'boycott' means [t]o combine in refusing to hold relations of any kind, social or commercial, public or private, with (a neighbor), on account of political or other differences, so as to punish him for the position he has taken up, or coerce him into abandoning it."[70] In defining the word in this way, Justice Scalia was able to find that it did not apply to the defendants' concerted refusal to deal because the defendants were charged only with refusing to deal on particular terms. This was, according to Justice Scalia, a concerted agreement to seek particular terms, and not a boycott, because the defendants were not seeking to coerce anyone other than the parties to their insurance contracts.

The boycott against Captain Boycott was distinguished because Scalia found that the Irish refusal to deal went beyond a simple dispute over wages and rent, and applied to all other transactions involving the Captain. As Justice Scalia explained,

> Thus, if Captain Boycott's tenants had agreed among themselves that they would refuse to renew their leases unless he reduced his rents, that would have been a concerted agreement on the terms of the leases, but not a boycott. The tenants, of course, did more than that; they refused to engage in other, unrelated transactions with Boycott—e.g., selling him food—unless he agreed to their terms on rents. It is this expansion of the refusal to deal beyond the targeted transaction that gives great coercive force to a commercial boycott. Unrelated transactions are used as leverage to achieve the terms desired.[71]

Justice Scalia also noted that in the sixty-five years between "the coining of the word and enactment of the McCarran-Ferguson Act in 1945,
'boycott' appear[ed] in only seven opinions of [the] Court involving commercial (nonlabor) antitrust matters, and *not once* [was] it used . . . to
describe a concerted refusal to engage in particular transactions until the
terms of those transactions [were] agreeable."[72] However, in the labor boycott cases, Scalia admitted that the term *boycott* was used to describe
protests involving "terms of workers' employment" generally, but he concluded that labor boycotts, as distinguished from labor strikes, involved
matters other than the employment relation.[73] To Justice Scalia, and the
majority, "[a] refusal to work changes from a strike to a boycott only when
it seeks to obtain action from the employer unrelated to the employment
contract,"[74] a distinction that labor union officials would not understand.

Modern labor union officials would not understand Justice Scalia's
distinction between a labor boycott and a strike because in their view
every successful strike will have the intended consequence of affecting
other transactions of the target. For example, if the United Automobile
Workers successfully shuts down a General Motors plant over a contract
dispute, the strike will have the intended effect of affecting other transactions that G.M. has with its vendors, dealers, and retailers. If successful, the union will be able to shut down not only G.M. but all of its major
customers and suppliers. These intended consequences are what Justice
Scalia associates with boycott.

Justice Souter and three other Justices dissented in *Hartford Insurance.* They contended that the majority had adopted an "overly narrow
definition" of the word *boycott.* The dissent argued that because the purpose of a boycott is intended to secure terms in the very transaction that
is the subject of an insurance contract dispute, there was no reason why
a refusal to deal, involving collateral matters related to the underlying
dispute, should be excluded from the statutory term *boycott* under the
McCarran-Ferguson Act.[75] In the dissent's view, the majority's definition
of the word *boycott* "assum[ed] an artificial segmentation of the course
of action, and a false perception of the unimportance of the elements of
that course of action other than the reinsurers' agreement."[76] Justice
Souter went on to complain that the majority's definition of the word
boycott was arbitrarily limited, and contrary to the way boycott has been
understood in the law.

The Supreme Court's decision in *Hartford Insurance* illustrates how debates about the meaning of the word *boycott* continue to provoke controversy about the meaning of boycott. In Justice Scalia's understanding of the word, boycott involves transactions that go beyond the original dispute between the parties. The Irish tenants' boycott against Captain Boycott was used by Justice Scalia to bolster his view. He identified with the position of Captain Boycott. From Captain Boycott's position, the tenants had gone beyond the dispute about rent and had engaged in other illegitimate transactions with third parties for purposes of spreading the effects of the dispute (e.g., refusals to sell food, etc.).[77] From Captain Boycott's view, the boycott was contrary to law because the tenants were engaged in a concerted effort to pressure others to cease doing business with him and his family. In seizing upon a meaning of boycott from the perspective of the target, Justice Scalia defined the statutory term *boycott* in terms of a radial category that in modern-day labor law has been created for secondary labor boycotts. Strikes and boycotts are, according to the majority, in different radial categories distinguished legally on the basis of whether they have primary or secondary effects.

Justice Souter and the dissent in *Hartford Insurance*, however, picked up the meaning of boycott from the perspective of the boycotting group. Hence, for the dissent, it made no difference if the boycott involved "other transactions" since they were related to the underlying source of the contract dispute.[78] Using the tenants boycott against Captain Boycott as the model, one can see how the dissent emphasized the meaning of the boycott from the tenants' perspective. Their boycott was about securing a rent reduction from Captain Boycott. From the boycotting tenants' viewpoint, the rent strike against Captain Boycott necessitated a general refusal to deal in all other transactions of the offending target. Because these "other transactions" enabled the target to continue business during the rent dispute, these other transactions were related to the underlying rent dispute with Captain Boycott, and were consequently critical to winning the dispute over rent.

When analyzed in light of a modern labor dispute over employment terms, one could also see why modern labor union officials would agree with the dissent's view of boycott and disagree with that of the majority. From the perspective of modern labor unions, all successful primary disputes involve secondary effects. Justice Scalia's distinction between a strike and a secondary boycott is a legal fiction that judges have historically used to conceal their bias in favor of employers.

In *Hartford Insurance*, the Court fashioned a rule for the statutory term *boycott* that limits the boycott provision of McCarran-Ferguson to secondary insurance contract disputes. Justice Scalia's approach to statutory meaning of the word *boycott* is an example of his jurisprudential view that rules of law should be analyzed as definitional rules.[79] Many judges and lawyers conceptualize rules of the law this way.[80]

In *Hartford Insurance*, the majority and the dissent relied upon different radial categories of boycott rather than dictionary definitions to get at the legal meaning of the statutory term *boycott*. Hence, the legal rules of boycott categories did not operate categorically under conventional definitions or categorical rules, as Justice Scalia presumed. The rules work, and dictionary definitions seem to project clear operational consequences, but they do not work in the "rule-like way," but rather they operate as a "culturally motivated process"[81] animated by imagination and ideology. The legal distinction between a strike and a boycott, like the distinction between boycott as law-enforcing and law-violating behavior, is the result of legal imagination and ideology, not logical, categorical thought.

Part Three

BOYCOTT, IMAGINATION, AND THE LEGAL MIND

CHAPTER 8

WHY THE BOYCOTT CHAMELEON HAS BEEN MISUNDERSTOOD

MY AIM IN this chapter is to examine the effort of legal scholars to rationalize, through the use of traditional techniques of legal analysis, the law of group boycotts. A number of legal scholars have attempted to clarify the fuzzy chameleon-like character of boycott doctrine by using new analogies and theories of boycott. Some have formulated theories that seek to defend the current state of boycott doctrine under analysis that accepts the necessity of making primary/secondary, naked/ancillary, speech/conduct, and economic/ political distinctions. Others have argued that inconsistency in cases is a consequence of the Supreme Court's commitment to the underlying values or the political causes that some groups seek to advance.[1] Still others argue that legal decision making could be rendered coherent by a new judicial commitment to a process view.[2]

This chapter looks at various scholarly attempts to use analogy and theory to give coherence to the chameleon-like nature of the word *boycott*. What legal scholars have neglected is that metaphoric reason shapes both reasoning by analogy and reasoning by theory. This chapter will then demonstrate why the power of metaphoric reason offers a better explanation of the case law.

THE "ELECTORAL VOTING" ANALOGY AND THE THEORY OF GROUP IDENTITY

Professor Michael C. Harper has approached boycott phenomena from the perspective of labor and civil rights law and has argued that the Supreme Court's creation of a new consumers' right to boycott, in *Claiborne Hardware*, can be constitutionally justified under what Harper calls an "electoral voting" analogy.[3] According to Harper, the consumer right to boycott is "a right in accord with our social and constitutional values" that should be judicially "cast as a broad political right to influence social decision making."[4] In his view, the act of "[j]oining a consumer boycott should be conceived as a constitutionally protected political act by which individuals can influence their society."[5]

In a consumer boycott, for example, Harper notes that the boycotters seek to affect the economy for the purpose of dramatizing grievances or bolstering public support for some cause. In *Claiborne Hardware*, the civil rights boycotters sought to influence private and governmental social decision-making that had denied African-Americans equal employment opportunities. Professor Harper has noted that because it had this objective, the boycott was rightly recognized "as a constitutionally protected political act."[6] In Harper's view, "[r]egistration of the intensity of beliefs in the economic marketplace is no less legitimate than registration of the intensity of beliefs in the political marketplace."[7] He would thus accord the same protection to boycotts aimed at influencing private decision making as to those aimed at influencing governmental decision making, since both can be viewed broadly as means by which citizens can "influence important social decision making."[8]

According to Professor Harper, if the boycotting group is seeking to accomplish a political objective, then the boycott should be analogized to an electoral election. In such a case, Harper reasons that the boycotting group attempts to "vote out," through majority action, the views and actions that the boycotting group rejects. Professor Harper reads the Supreme Court's decision in *Claiborne Hardware* as establishing a constitutional right to consumers and civil rights activists to boycott for political objectives. The thrust of his argument rests on the view that the identity of the boycotting group will reveal whether the boycott is sufficiently like an electoral process to be constitutionally protected. Civil rights and consumer boycotts, unlike labor boycotts, typically seek political objectives, and thus they are presumptively electoral voting activities. In his view, the electoral analogy creates the theoretical case for according boycott constitutional protection.[9]

Professor Harper's argument is quite similar to the view once expressed by Professor Harry Kalven Jr., who, in 1965, argued that group identity helps to explain the way the Warren Court had decided cases dealing with civil rights issues under the First Amendment.[10] Professor Kalven's basic point was that racial minority groups had been historically accorded a unique status under the First Amendment because the Supreme Court was committed to advance the cause of civil rights of racial minorities. Professor Kalven thus provides a reason for why the boycott in *Claiborne Hardware* was treated differently than seemingly similar boycotts of other boycotting groups. The civil rights group was seeking a traditional civil rights objective (to gain equal access to participate in the affairs of the community that had been denied to the group as a result of the electoral process and societal norms of discrimination). Unlike a labor group boycott, which seeks to advance the economic self-interest of workers, a civil rights boycott seeks to achieve altruistic objectives that are relevant to the political rights and liberties of all citizens. Group identity and the boycott's objective are, according to this view of the case law, the critical factors for determining whether a right to boycott will be recognized under the Constitution.

There is reason to question these views. Consider, for example, Professor Harper's electoral voting analogy. Electoral voting is typically thought to be an orderly and highly regularized activity, taking place in the privacy of election booths and regulated by governmental authorities. Voting seeks to influence governmental decision making on the basis of majority will. A boycott, however, does not require majority action, and in fact, boycotts frequently rely on minority action to influence the norms and will of the majority. Electoral voting is supposed to be about giving effect to majority norms, but boycott is frequently about minorities seeking to challenge majority norms. Except in cases like *Claiborne Hardware*, the electoral analogy may not make sense.

Further, the logic underpinning Professor Harper's analogy has been rejected by the Supreme Court in the *Trial Lawyers*'s decision. As we have seen, in *Trial Lawyers*, the Supreme Court viewed a lawyers' boycott to gain higher statutory lawyer fees for representing indigent clients as an attempt to impose a restraint of trade. The *Trial Lawyers* boycott fell outside the constitutional umbrella of political expression because the boycott was found to be more analogous to a labor or business boycott having anticompetitive objectives. And yet in *Trial Lawyers*, the boycott was also seeking a political objective, and the boycott was brought against a state legislative body for the purpose of influencing the electoral process. If there was ever a case that fits the central case of electoral voting, it should have been *Trial Lawyers*.

Professor Harper's electoral voting analogy is persuasive when, as in

Claiborne Hardware, the boycotting group is an insular minority that has suffered as a result of irrational discrimination and has consequently been denied access to the American political process. In such a case, boycott may be the only way for the group to preserve the group's norms from being thwarted by contrary societal norms. On the one hand, it is true that group norms, even those of a minority group, can be quite effective in challenging societal norms if the group is homogeneous and close-knit.[11] The collective action of a boycott, for example, may involve private sanctions that carry considerable force; boycotting can be quite effective in shunning or shaming norm violators with the ultimate sanction being a collective refusal to deal with the norm violator.[12] On the other hand, if the boycotting group is large and heterogeneous, then individuals in the group may not even realize that they share common norms.

Collective action problems will also make it difficult for the group to even identify instances of norm violations by offending individuals. Harper admits that his electoral voting analogy is less persuasive in cases where the boycott involves undefined, diffused, mixed audiences that have diverse goals.[13] He argues nonetheless that "[c]onsumer boycotts have usually targeted businessmen with special political influence" and that "to expand popular participation in social decision making, a democratic society can appropriately deny some citizens economic protection in order to secure all citizens a right to engage in consumer political action."[14] But what if the target of the consumer boycott is a minority business group?

Consider, for example, the Korean grocery store boycott brought by African-Americans in Brooklyn in the early 1990s, known as the "Red Apple Boycott." That boycott involved long-standing resentment between two minority groups: one group that was boycotting had majority standing in the community (African-Americans); the other, the target, did not (Korean-Americans). The boycott was, in fact, found to be bias related by a special report of the Civil Rights Commission.[15] Racial and ethnic stereotypes are likely to be infused with the political objective of the boycotting group, as they did in the Red Apple Boycott, and thus even what may look like a garden-variety political boycott may represent action that is quite opposed to the electoral voting in a society committed to democratic values.

To complicate matters, consumer boycotts, like all boycotts, get defined in light of background assumptions about the meaning of the boycott. In the Red Apple Boycott in Brooklyn, African-Americans understood their boycott in terms of background assumptions about discriminatory pricing practices of Korean-American-owned grocery stores in their neighborhood, and Korean-Americans probably understood their position in light of background assumptions about discrimination they felt from the African-American community. The meaning of the boycott has to be understood in light of background assumptions that are imaginatively constructed from a highly ideological context.

Finally, one lesson from the proceeding chapters is that much of what goes under the legal rubric of "reasoning by analogy" is in fact a metaphoric form of reason that relies upon radial categories, default metaphors, and idealized cognitive models to classify the legal meaning of different types of boycotts in the law. In the early labor boycott cases, for example, we saw how boycott was understood as a coercive force that had the effect of sweeping away individuals who might object to or not support the goals of the boycott. Boycotts were analogized to criminal acts such as murder because judges used a metaphoric system of reason that transferred information about one domain (e.g., the domain of animalistic behavior of a tiger in *Glidden*) to describe another domain (e.g., a nonviolent labor boycott). The tiger analogy worked because the comparison made sense to judges in view of metaphors that associated labor boycotts with animalistic behavior and mass riots. This form of reason manifested knowledge about a particular analogy drawn from a radical category extension of an idealized cognitive model of boycott. The analogy was itself shaped by the underlying normative orientation of boycott metaphors, radial categories, and idealized cognitive models.

In *Claiborne Hardware*, a different analogy, boycott as soap-box oratory, was used to associate the civil rights boycott of that case with First Amendment expression. In that case, the Court grounded its analogy in a radial category of boycott that viewed boycott action as expressive political conduct. The Supreme Court's "soap-box oratory" analogy made sense in light of the "majestic" metaphors used to characterize the meaning of the boycott and a set of background assumptions about the meaning of social interactions between in-groups and out-groups in society. In this way, the analogy and theory of the decision was shaped by prototypical properties of a contingent radial category constructed for dealing with a subset of civil rights boycotts. Hence, not all civil rights boycotts will enjoy a favored status under the First Amendment, and not all political boycotts are protected as First Amendment expression.

In our multicultural society, simple analogies and theories of group identity fail to tell us much about how the courts will define the meaning of a group boycott. Coalitions will depend on specific political exigencies; for example, a boycott over immigration or English-only restrictions may involve Asian-Americans and Latinos boycotting the views of whites and African-Americans. Alternatively, a boycott against affirmative action policies may involve Asian-Americans and whites boycotting the views of African-Americans and Latinos.

Professor Kalven's theory of "group identity," though never pressed by him to describe cases like *Claiborne Hardware*, falls prey to the same problematic. The theory of group identity is no longer helpful given the political and social changes that have taken place since Kalven advanced his ideas about the unique status of racial minority groups in constitutional law. While the Supreme Court's commitment to the civil rights movement may have seemed strong when Harry Kalven was writing in 1965, there is now a new conservative Supreme Court that no longer can be said to be strongly in favor of according racial minorities special status under the First Amendment. There is a profound critique here, but it is not one based on changes in Supreme Court personnel as such. Rather, changes in the larger society have restructured the radial categories judges have used to analyze minority interests under the constitutional standards. New radial categories of *reverse discrimination* and *race neutrality* have restructured the First Amendment frame of analysis of race under the constitution, and these changes have totally disrupted the validity of Kalven's theory explaining the special status of civil rights groups in the constitutional law.

The "Difference in Kind" Test and the Theory of Secondary Labor Boycott

Several years ago, in a highly influential pair of law review articles, Professor Howard Lesnick argued that secondary labor boycotts could be understood in light of a "difference in kind" test derived from his theory of the legislative history of the secondary boycott provision of federal labor law.[16] Under Lesnick's test, the secondary boycott proscription of federal labor law would permit boycott pressure upon secondary employers only if the pressure is no *different in kind* from that generated and applied to these employers by a successful primary strike (against the primary employer). In Lesnick's view, federal judges understand that the legislative purpose underlying the secondary boycott provision was containment of labor disputes, "the legislative desire to discourage what may be called the metastasis of labor disputes: the fanning out of unrest from the struck plant to those doing business with it."[17] Lesnick's "difference in kind" test offers a functional standard for understanding how the legislative metaphor of secondary boycott as cancerous metastasis has in fact influenced the way labor distinguishes between primary and secondary labor disputes.

Unfortunately, the question whether pressure brought against a secondary employer in a secondary boycott is different in kind from that exerted by a primary action is a question not easily answered in most boycott cases. In Professor Lesnick's scheme, the key question is whether the union intends to cause secondary impacts broader than would be caused by a primary strike.[18] The problem with the "difference in kind" theory is that it fails to demonstrate *how* the line between secondary and primary activity should be drawn when the union intends to boycott a national manufacturer that produces a product assembled from other products.

For example, a successful primary strike of such a manufacturer will cut off the flow of the primary employer's goods just as surely as it would cause the loss of services of the primary's employees.[19] The cut-off flow of goods will, of course, affect the manufacturer's dealers and suppliers in the same way that a secondary boycott against these same dealers and supplies would. The difference in kind distinction, therefore, fails to explain why secondary boycotts brought against the national manufacturer's dealers and suppliers would be unlawful, when the pressure used against these parties would not differ in kind from the pressure against them resulting from a primary boycott against the manufacturer. It is this weakness in Lesnick's test that renders it unable to explain the primary/secondary distinction in the law of labor union boycotts.

The "difference in kind" theory seeks to enforce the purpose of the secondary boycotts provision by limiting the proscription of secondary boycotts to those that broaden the effects of a primary economic dispute. The test, however, allows the secondary boycott provision of federal labor law to mean different things to different employers, and thus allows economic disputes to spread in some industries and not others. This result is odd in light of the attempt of Congress to forbid secondary boycotts in labor union disputes. This result is also difficult to justify when a weak union is embroiled in a labor dispute with a much more powerful conglomerate that enjoys the benefit of economic relations with other employers.

Why secondary boycotts should be judged illegal has never been adequately explained. The primary/secondary distinction simply does not hold up in cases involving a target in a national or international market. Every primary strike against such a target, if successful, will have both primary and secondary consequences. If primary strikes are protected as First Amendment activity (when peaceful), then there is no reason why the same protection should not be accorded to otherwise peaceful secondary boycott activity. Both primary and secondary boycotts should be accorded First Amendment protection analogous to that accorded to the right to picket; otherwise, the right to picket and to engage in primary activity remains in doubt. The problem is that peaceful secondary labor boycotts can be more like primary strike or picketing or general refusals to deal (which federal labor law and the Constitution protect) than they are like the metastasis of cancer, an image that judges have called upon to justify a general ban against all secondary labor boycotts.

THE PROCESS-ORIENTED THEORY

Professor Eisner R. Elhauge approached boycott phenomena from the perspective of antitrust law and has argued that the puzzles posed by the Supreme Court's antitrust boycott cases could be solved by what he calls "an objective process approach."[20] By an "objective process," Professor Elhauge means an approach that objectively sets boundaries between the competitive and governmental processes.[21] Under process theory, antitrust liability for business boycotts depends on whether such boycotts were found to serve a valid governmental purpose.[22]

Elhauge claims that his approach is "process oriented" because it is said to turn on "objective indicia" about the incentives of boycotting activities. He argues that financially motivated boycotts should be subject to antitrust liability because such boycotts are not likely to be politically accountable, and because competitive markets "[should] provide a mechanism for harnessing that financial interest in the public inter-est."[23] Under his process framework, *private* boycotts and *public* boycotts can be distinguished on the basis of whether those boycotting are seek-ing a purely private rather than public purpose.

Elhauge attempts to reconcile the inconsistency in antitrust boycott cases by relying upon a basic precept of legal process theory—the idea that an objective legal process can be developed to evaluate boycott incentives on the basis of whether or not they seek to interfere with a competitive or governmental process. When a boycott is found to inter-fere with market competition, antitrust immunity is unwarranted because the competitive process is the better mechanism for protecting the public interest. When a group boycott is directed at persons without financial interest and with public accountability, antitrust immunity is warranted even if those actors making the decisions "act [out] of finan-cial motivations."[24] The "operative factor" in either case is "whether the objective incentives of those making decisions provide some realistic assurances that the decisions will further the public interest."[25]

According to Elhauge, "[f]rom an objective process perspective, courts adjudicating antitrust immunity issues emerge as the switchmen of democratic capitalism: guiding decision makers down the tracks of either the competitive or governmental process depending on which is most appropriate, but not substituting a track or judicial decision mak-ing for either process."[26] Professor Elhauge's metaphor of courts as "switchmen" guiding "decision makers down the tracks" assumes that judges can objectively evaluate the incentives of boycotts and classify them as either public or private.

There are a number of problems with Elhauge's metaphor. First, boy-cotts seeking to influence governmental decisions are likely to be moti-vated by a mix of factors; some may involve competition policy, others may not. In *Trial Lawyers*, for example, the boycotters attempted to assert the constitutional rights of their clients in addition to protecting their own financial interests. The *Trial Lawyers* boycotters were advised to do "something dramatic to attract attention" since they lacked a political constituency to lobby on their behalf.[27] From the perspective of the boy-cotting lawyers, the boycott was merely a means to gain public support for their cause.[28] The lawyers' boycott may have been the only effective way to influence governmental action. If the public supported their boycott, District of Columbia officials would learn that voters supported the lawyers' cause. The boycott had political objectives, even though the boycotters were also seeking private interests.

Professor Elhauge accepts the Court's characterization of the *Trial Lawyers* boycott as anticompetitive. According to Elhauge, the "record [in *Trial Lawyers*] contained clear evidence of anticompetitive effect: severe shortages of lawyers willing to take indigent defendants."[29] However, the lawyer shortage during the boycott was really caused by the extremely low attorney fees set by legislation.[30] The District of Columbia could have purchased legal services by offering lawyers the prevailing market fee to work during the boycott. The District of Columbia, not the lawyers, had the advantages of market power. Thus, the price of legal services was effectively set by a single customer, the government, making the market for court-appointed attorneys essentially a buyer's market controlled by monopoly power.

There is also a problem presented by Elhauge's belief that boycotts can be classified in terms of whether or not they affect a market or governmental process. In *Claiborne Hardware*, the boycott was ostensibly aimed at shutting down local businesses that had discriminated against minorities, but the real targets were governmental officials who had failed to do anything about negative racial attitudes in the community. It is conceivable that this group of official decision makers, seeing themselves as the target of the civil rights boycott, realized they had an economic stake in putting down the boycott since a successful boycott would mean they might lose their jobs in the next election.

Elhauge's framework of analysis incorporates the basic process filter of 1950's legal process ideology[31] that the private economic world and the public political world are separate because the private world of markets is ruled by the objective invisible hand rather than by subjectively chosen policies. Elhauge apparently believes that the invisible hand of the competitive process establishes the basic structure of antitrust law, thereby justifying an objective antitrust process approach to antitrust petitioning and boycott problems. In Elhauge's understanding, federal regulation is something added to the objective realm, in which the invisible hand operates as an objective process. Elhauge thus argues that "as with state action immunity, petitioning immunity reflects the Court's implicit functional process views about how best to set the boundaries between the competitive and governmental process."[32] The invisible hand theory of competitive markets assumes, however, that an objective baseline of property, liberty, and exchange rules exists. These baselines are themselves the result of contingent policy decisions about the exercise of public, social power.[33]

The metaphor of the invisible hand is illusory; there is no such thing as an objective competitive process. Any regulation of boycott activity invariably requires judicial determinations to be made about the exercise of social power. Judicial acceptance of the values of the competitive process cannot occur independent of the judge's regulation. The notion that the competitive process has a pure, apolitical starting-point ignores the contingent nature of power exercised in the day-to-day relations of social culture. There is no objective way to engage in what Elhauge calls an "objective-process oriented" approach.

Finally, Elhauge's metaphor of the judge as a switchman assumes that judges can distinguish between public and private decision making. But these categories, public and private, are metaphoric constructs; they do not exist independent of a particular social or political understanding of the proper role of federal regulation, of the importance of respecting the competitive market process, and of what does and does not affect the public interest. The public/private distinction thus permits judges to make fundamental ideological determinations about the legitimacy of different forms of governmental petitioning in the guise of following an objective process.

LABOR/COMMUNITY BOYCOTTS AND CIVIC REPUBLICAN THEORY

Professor James Pope has developed a novel constitutional theory from the civic republican tradition of constitutional law and history to explain the Court's civil rights boycott decisions.[34] Professor Pope argues that political boycotts have traditionally been protected by the First Amendment only when they are found by the Court to involve what he calls "republican moments"—that is, moments of social activism that involve purely political objectives aimed at securing the "virtues of popular republicanism: namely, the pursuit of interests broader than immediate pecuniary gain, and an appeal to fundamental ideals."[35]

According to Professor Pope, decisions such as *Claiborne Hardware*, *Allied International*, and *Trial Lawyers* can be understood as extending First Amendment protection only to those boycotts that represent freely chosen expression of popular dissent and political aspiration. *Claiborne Hardware*, in his view, exemplifies what he calls a "republican moment" because the civil rights boycotters sought to achieve constitutional objectives that transcended their immediate economic interests. The boycotts in *Allied International* and *Trial Lawyers*, in contrast, lost First Amendment protection; in *Allied International* because workers were ordered by their union president to boycott,[36] and in *Trial Lawyers* because the boycotters had a direct economic interest at stake.[37] The boycotts in *Allied International* and *Trial Lawyers* were denied constitutional protection because they were motivated out of private economic interests that failed to reflect the democratic and communitarian values associated with a republican moment.

The emergence of labor-community boycotts, however, illustrates how boycotts involving an alliance between labor unions and consumer groups attempt to displace marketplace power by utilizing boycott to accomplish economic *and* political objectives. Labor-community boycotts call into question the dichotomous public/private thinking. The notion that labor and community issues can be distinguished in terms of economic and political matters fails to reflect the realities of labor and consumer groups who experience political and economic concerns as interrelated and dependent issues. Professor Pope nonetheless argues that the results reached in *Allied International* and *Trial Lawyers* can be justified because in each case the boycott failed to foster broader political goals.

In *Allied International*, Pope regards the longshoremen's boycott as the product of the coercive power of the union's leadership, which "ordered ILA members to stop handling cargoes."[38] The boycott was not regarded in his view as an exercise of popular republican politics, "[g]iven the long history of autocracy in the ILA, the coercive power [the Union President] Gleason held over individual workers, and the workers' inability to leave the union's jurisdiction."[39] According to Pope, the longshoremen in *Allied International* were not engaged in constitutional political activity because "[f]ar from engaging in an exercise of positive freedom, the longshoremen acted '[i]n obedience to' Gleason's order."[40] The *Trial Lawyers* boycott was found not to be a republican moment because the lawyers' immediate objective was to increase their own hourly fees, an objective that failed to transcend the "day-to-day conduct of business as usual."[41]

While it is true that the union members in *Allied International* were ordered by their leadership to boycott ships trading with Russia, it is also true that the Deacons and Black Hats who organized the civil rights boycott in *Claiborne Hardware* ordered their members to honor their boycott. While the longshoremen's union in *Allied International* was autocratic, so was the civil rights leadership responsible for organizing the *Claiborne Hardware* boycott. If boycotts are to be denied constitutional protection because they are organized under a military-type structure of leadership, then *every* effectively organized union boycott would fail to qualify for constitutional protection under Pope's theory since all unions are, out of political necessity, organized in this way. Autocratic leadership is necessary because corporations are organized autocratically. In order to respond effectively to corporate organizations, unions need strong leaders. The fact that the longshoremen were ordered to obey their association's boycott, and the fact that the union leadership was autocratic, as distinguished from undemocratic, fails to explain why that boycott was treated differently than the boycott in *Claiborne Hardware*.

As for Pope's explanation of *Trial Lawyers*, the boycott in that case was analogous to the type of labor strikes found during the New Deal era, one of the few moments in United States history that Professor Pope sees as the closest approximation to his "ideal type" of republican moments.[42] If labor unions and their members are to enjoy the civic republican values advocated by Professor Pope, they must have the freedom to organize their own organizations to counter the corporate economic decisions that affect their memberships. Concerted activity designed to advance a common-wage demand involves more than mere selfish economic interests; such activity is also aimed at advancing worker control at the workplace. Such activity is intrinsically political activity. But Professor Pope would not extend First Amendment protection to such a case since the boycott sought economic objectives that would advance the self-interest of those boycotting.

Hence, Justice Brennan in his partial dissent in *Trial Lawyers* stated that he was "surprised" by Justice Stevens's majority opinion finding that the lawyers' boycott was not protected speech, given what Justice Stevens had said in *Claiborne Hardware* about the importance of protecting the "established elements of speech, assembly, association, and petition" of expressive boycotts.[43] Professor Pope, however, assumes that judges can identify those boycotts whose motives are immediately related to political, as distinguished from economic, objectives.

As Professor Pope recognizes, the economics/politics distinction like the public/private distinction is problematic in many respects.[44] The distinction fails to address how language and cognitive imagination socially construct the very categories that the distinction seeks to recognize. Legal categories of economic and political activity are assumed to establish an objective empirical baseline for legal analysis, but the categories themselves reflect contingent, highly contestable, and metaphorically constructed ideas about the nature of markets and politics. *Trial Lawyers* and *Claiborne Hardware* are simply too chameleon-like to be color coded by either legal distinctions such as public/private or the economic/political distinction of civic republican theory. What Professor Pope and other legal scholars have failed to discover is that their tool of analysis—language—is itself responsible for the problems they have attempted to resolve through their scholarly evaluations of the boycott case law.

WHY SCHOLARLY EXPLANATIONS HAVE FAILED

Efforts to reconcile boycott cases have faltered because commentators, like the judges they criticize, have assumed that the problem of incoherence in the law can be solved by some chain of reasoning that can be discovered and articulated categorically by simply applying a new analogy or theory to the problem at hand. The inconsistency in the boycott case law cannot be explained in terms of categorical or rational logic. Instead, it stems from a more basic problem involving the manipulability of the language used for distinguishing categories. Language is not a distortion-free vehicle for describing what has gone wrong in the law of boycotts; language is itself socially constructed and is implicated in the process of producing different legal meanings of boycotts. What is needed are not simply new metaphors and analogies, but an understanding of how cognitive metaphors and ideology shape the legal imagination and how imagination is itself limited by an institutional ideology of adjudication. What is needed is a better understanding of how imagination and ideology shape the legal meaning of boycott for our culture.

Like the color of a chameleon, which fades and changes as context changes, the word *boycott* invokes different legal meanings in different specific contexts. The problem is that alternate understandings of boycott are never considered. These excluded understandings of boycott, left outside the borders of legal analysis, however, continually seek to challenge the dominant images of boycott by calling forth the telling of counterfactual boycott narratives. These alternative boycott images appeal to the normative values of the diverse identities of different boycotting groups.[45] These alternative meanings of boycott are not considered in the law because they are not included in the official language of the law. Judges acknowledge that boycott phenomena are chameleon-like, but when they do, they approach boycott problems in a surprisingly unreflective manner; they assume that they can resolve boycott cases under nonideological and objectivist standards. In some cases, judges ignore the inconsistency of boycott cases decided in different doctrinal fields. In still others, judges use the word *boycott* as an epithet for characterizing group activity as illegal when that activity in legal contexts would be perfectly legal. Judges rationalize the inconsistency in the case law in terms of radial categories that attempt to limit, separate, and contain boycott phenomena in different imaginative legal fields.

The prototypical extensions of the radial category of boycott are not merely the identification mechanism judges use to distinguish between boycott categories, but instead are part of the cognitive core of the central model used to give meaning to boycott. Reasoning from the central core of a central case is integral to the cognitive process judges use to decide the ideological stakes of boycott adjudications. The subcategories of boycott, the extensions from the basic radial category, are chained to normatively loaded metaphors that frame and configure legal thinking in terms of the law's dominant understandings of boycott phenomena.[46] The categorization process in adjudication is thus shaped by the judge's understanding of a radial category based on an idealized model of boycott. The underlying assumptions and values that frame the categories and models of boycott inhere not in the word itself, but rather in particular social practices and normative orientations of the metaphors used to give meaning to the word. The legal meaning of boycott is not "hand wired" in language but is rather dependent upon cultural context and the ideology of judges.

The social and historical context shapes the way judges perceive the meaning of boycott, but the ideology of the legal culture creates its own imaginative spin on the way imagination functions in adjudication. The "ideology of adjudication," as Duncan Kennedy has described it, projects an image of a judge as a "mythic figure," a figure embroiled in an ongoing "struggle, much like a religious or monastic struggle, to renounce what is natural and also corrupt and banal in human conduct, to depersonalize him- (or her) self."[47] As we saw in chapter 4, to maintain this self-image, the mythic self-image of the judge encourages judges to pursue, consciously and unconsciously, a number of evasion strategies to deny their ideological role.

These evasion strategies have been quite successful because the legal categories of boycott are conceptualized by a metaphoric container. The idea of *containment* helps to erect an imaginary mental space in legal reasoning between boycotts of different groups so that legal decision making can classify and distinguish different boycott phenomena in a manner that is seemingly nonideological. Legal categories are the containers used in the law to hold ideas about boycott. Thus, in some categories, the word *boycott* is used to signify a threat or menace, or an ominous foreboding of mob violence, or blacklisting and social ostracism, or even murder. In others, boycott is associated with the freedom to abstain or to dissent. In some legal categories, boycott is as American as apple pie; in others, boycott signifies activity that is subversive, a threat to the very fabric of the American way of life. The prototype effect of the imagined containers of boycott categories fit the central model of boycott more-or-less well.

Scholarly explanations of the boycott case law have failed because scholars have attempted to explain the inconsistencies of the case law under the same conceptual models judges use to evade and deny the ideological nature of their work. These models attempt to rationalize legal categories of boycott by utilizing methods of analogical reasoning and policy analysis for measuring definitional fit of the category to a particular case. The scholarly models in the literature offer new ideas and theories of boycott, but the theories and ideas are used as they are in traditional legal analysis, to provide definitional support for the logic of some analytical solution offering a better fit to boycott problems. The problem is the metaphors, rather than the theoretical models they support, cognitively shape the chameleon-like nature of boycott decisions.

It is the cognitive power of metaphoric reason operating as a transference mechanism between different conceptual domains of knowledge that permits judges to maintain their faith in the myth of nonideological decision making. What is missing in the scholarly literature is an explanation of how the legal mind uses metaphoric reason to build-up meaning from the background of innumerable normative assumptions of a dynamic, ever changing cultural setting and practice, and how the legal mind keeps those highly charged political assumptions a secret.

The most plausible account of boycott doctrine is that there exists a stock set of basic default metaphors of boycott that have prototypical effects for defining the legal meaning of boycott, and these effects are regarded as correct by the great majority of judges because they seem to cohere best with the normative and cultural assumptions of legal culture. Boycott metaphors, idealized cognitive models, and prototypical effects strike judges as compelled, and in that sense, the metaphors are capable of seizing the judge in legal decision making. The law of boycott therefore appears to be a self-describing, self-reproducing, imaginative system capable of generating multiple conflicting meanings of social, cultural, and legal practices to support or deny the cultural norms and values of our society.

Consensus in adjudication is reached because the basic default metaphors become what Owen Fiss calls the "disciplining rules" of the legal system.[48] However, because the prototypical effects of the basic default metaphors change over time as new boycott decisions are reached, and new imaginative metaphors of boycott are created, the case law exhibits an evolutionary development that enables commentators to see changes in the law. However, because the basic default metaphors are also deeply embedded in legal and popular culture, the same images and the same legal meaning of boycott is projected for boycotts, and in an important sense, the law adheres to a stable set of normative orientations in each of the different doctrinal fields of boycott. The basic default metaphors have remained relatively constant even though new prototypical properties of these metaphors are in a constant state of flux.

The legal mind, however, is constantly struggling to renounce counterfactual examples from cultural practices of an ever changing society. For example, new coalitions of consumers and labor groups boycotting for political and economic purposes create cognitive models of boycott that do not easily fit within the prototypical properties of the boycott categories used by judges in the law. Should a consumer boycott composed of labor and nonlabor groups be classified as a labor or nonlabor boycott? If the boycott seeks to change the politics of the Adolph Coors Company, is it a political boycott? If, however, the boycott also questions the antiunion policies of the company, does that make it a commercial or labor boycott? What if the boycott is conducted in cyberspace? Should a *cyberboycott* be treated as a boycott conducted on the streets? These questions can become the step toward either the development of new idealized cognitive models to cognize the world of boycott, or they can become bases for new radial categories of the existing idealized cognitive models currently used by judges to decide group boycott cases. In either event, new cultural practices establishing new forms of boycott have potential for shaping the legal imagination.

CHAPTER 9

CHANGING SOCIAL
CONCEPTIONS OF BOYCOTT

IN THIS CHAPTER, I will explore how new forms of boycott
practice fail to fit the radial categories of boycott created by judges.
While the word *boycott* is relatively new, there have been profound
changes in the nature of boycotts since the first such incident involving
Captain Boycott occurred in 1880. The verb made from the unfortunate
Captain's name has come to describe a remarkable diverse social practice. Boycotts have come to represent an important new group practice
for organizing and soliciting popular dissent in *postmodernist* culture.

BOYCOTT IN POSTMODERNIST CULTURE

By *postmodernist culture*, I mean the culmination of social, political, and
economic forces now transforming world economies and social practices
into global markets linked by new informational technologies and mass-
consumer advertising. The postmodernist era signifies the emergence of
a new type of social life and a new economic order, which social theorists
have called the "postindustrial" or "consumer" society of late capitalism.[1]
Key features of postmodernist culture include the following: the increas-
ing importance of multinational corporations and institutions in the
economy; the development of an information economy rather than one
based on old notions of production; economic power resulting from the
ability to manipulate and process information electronically rather than
from the fact of ownership; the erosion of the distinction between so-
called high culture and mass or popular culture; and the decreasing relevance of the nation-state as the source of power and influence.

Today, all has changed. The Berlin Wall has come crashing down, and
the Cold War has given way to new political alliances based on transna-
tional forms of corporate power. Communism and socialism have col-

lapsed and been replaced by a global market paradigm. The integrated World-Wide Web of the Internet has, in turn, shrunk the world and has created a new planetary cyberspace for the interplay of economic and social activity. The emerging new global social space of internationally linked markets has been further enhanced by governmental policies of privatization and deregulation that have transferred governmental functions to the global marketplace. These changes have resulted in a fundamental shift in power and activity from governmental to private nongovernmental global organizations.[2] The process of economic integration and internationalization of governmental and economic activities have posed new challenges. Environmental dangers of climate change due to global corporate activities, for example, have gone unchallenged because of the lack of an effective regulator body to deal with the damage caused by global polluters.[3]

In the midst of globalization, local initiatives of citizen groups have engaged citizen boycott actions to change the behavior of global corporations responsible for the activities that damage the environment and cause human misery.[4] Boycott initiatives of various citizen groups have been effective in redirecting corporate responsibility, forcing corporate boards to adopt codes of conduct, and have attempted, with some success, to redirect corporate behavior. Group boycotts by organizations such as Greenpeace, Amnesty International, Human Rights Watch, the Lawyers Committee for Human Rights, and others, have thus sought to regulate corporate norms and behavior. While boycotts by citizen action groups do not always succeed in achieving their goals, boycotts have been generally effective in raising issues of corporate irresponsibility with the public.[5] Boycott has thus become an important new mechanism for performing the traditional regulatory function of nation-states necessary for human rights and environmental responsibility.

In the postindustrial world order, more and more citizens are feeling alienated from the political decision-making process and are turning to less traditional forms of political and social activity to advance their identity and interests. There are many reasons for this. Money in politics has created a serious barrier to citizen participation in the political process. Political action committees and lobbyists representing organized interests now dominate political decision making. Deregulatory policies of the Reagan-Bush era have in turn precipitated the disappearance of public interest organizations at all levels of government and have brought about a fundamental alteration in the relationship between government and the market.

In postmodernist culture, boycotts fill the void created by governmental deregulation. Boycotts are becoming a commonplace occurrence, as various groups (labor, business, social, political) use new information technologies, including the Internet, to advance a myriad of economic morals to express norms that lack a social consensus in society. Boycotts enforce the informal norm-based regulation of the group, and this new group enforcement mechanism is offering nongovernmental organizations new leverage with governments and corporations.[6] What is different today is that boycotts have proliferated as a result of new information technologies that make it much easier to disseminate the images, messages, and representations of political power.

CYBERBOYCOTT

There is now a Web page on the Internet where one can find announcements and inducements for boycotts involving a variety of groups and causes. Labor unions have in turn created their own Web pages for publicizing a new form of boycott—*cyberboycott*. Cyberboycotts are advertised on the Internet much in the same way that a corporation advertises a new product like dish soap or toothpaste. In electronic publicity on the Internet, the boycott appeal is based on claims about justice, goodness, rightness, truth, fairness, progress, and other bedrock values of contemporary American society. The target is held out to be an enemy of these values, representing a sinister antihero. In postmodernist culture, the conflicting images of boycott are advertised as a commodity for sale in the media marketplaces of America.

With little capital, lots of imagination, and some luck, anyone can organize a cyberboycott. The boycott can be initiated without speakers and listeners revealing their identities. Cyberboycotts can be conducted in chat rooms and on Web sites without anyone knowing who may be boycotting. In such a context, the cyberboycott has taken on a fundamentally expressive nature that may give it new prototypical properties that align it in the eyes of judges with mass demonstrations and political speeches. Cyberboycotts are consequently becoming a new outlet for expressing the social, economic, and political division of American society. The courts may soon discover that cyberboycott is a new means of participating in the political and legal discourse of postmodernist culture.

In the *hypertext* of the cyberboycott messages on the Net, one can "click on" to retrieve the background ideology of the boycotting group. The computer has thus enabled the reader/audience to shift from foreground to background to better understand the normative content of the boycott appeal. Unlike the law, where background assumptions are concealed within the imaginative pictures and images of a metaphor, computers and hypertext enable the reader/audience to easily shift from figure to ground to gain access to the normative orientation of the boycotting group.

Hypertext is a technological domain for understanding how metaphoric reason in the law actually works to conceal ideology in the text of the law. The normative background of text is hidden by an imaginative form of reason that operates to hide from the reader the ideology of the author. The reader reads the text, and the discourse and analysis in the foreground relies upon default metaphors, radial categories, and framing concepts to hide the ideological perspective of the author. Even the author may not be aware of how his or her discourse and analysis conceals ideological choices. A shift from foreground to background reveals the political orientation of the author's text. The shift from figure to ground operates as hypertext functions in the text of the cyberboycott message on the Net: the underlying background ideology is clicked on by highlighting the background normative orientations of the metaphors used by judges to give meaning, and to categorize phenomena. Hypertext of cyberspace thus provides a new source domain for understanding how background information influences foreground information.

Indeed, if there ever was a model that explains how ideology should function in legal texts, it is the model of cyberboycott. Cyberboycott publicity is structured by a figurative language based not on cognitive, logical, or rational reasoning, but rather on the aesthetics of what Greek and Roman rhetoricians understood as the emotional appeal (*pathos*) and the authorial credibility (*ethos*).[7] Unlike judges and lawyers, who tend to conceal the ideology of the logic of their texts, cyberboycott publicists use hypertext in their electronic text to permit readers to "click on" the normative values of their message.

The Internet has also made cyberboycotts a lot easier to organize and manage. By clicking on the proper Web page, one can find information, pictures, and prepared literature for hundreds of boycotts now occurring across America. Clicking on the Boycott Board of the Web, for example, one can find the Industrial Workers of the World (IWW) boycott against Borders Book Stores. Clicking the hypertext to the IWW: "Borders Cyberpicket," one can find a picture of IWW boycotters in front of a Borders store talking to customers. From a flyer at the Borders's Philadelphia Picket on the Web, one learns that IWW has called a boycott of Borders, Inc., to force it to give up "its union-busting practices." The Web user is encouraged to "click on" to the Borders's home page and to sound off by mailing a prepaid letter addressed to Borders, Inc., which can be downloaded from the Boycott Board.[8]

Another boycotting group calling itself the Hispanic American Union is conducting a cyberboycott of American Airlines for allegedly preparing a standard operating manual that purportedly characterizes Hispanic customers as "inferior in mentality," as being "prone to alcoholism," and for being "disruptive and untrustworthy." Another boycotting group, the Muslim Student Body, has called a cyberboycott against Nike, Inc., for using a logo on its Air Basin shoes that duplicates the Arabic script for Allah. The Muslim Student Body claims that the use of Allah on Nike's products is sacrilegious and culturally insensitive. The African-Americans Against Disney (AAAD) has called a cyberboycott against Walt Disney Company/Walt Disney Pictures for its alleged failure to create animated films featuring African-American characters (other than portraying them as animals). And, even a single individual, Evan R. Edwards, has a Web page for a cyberboycott of Wendy's International, Inc., for withdrawing its regular broadcast advertising from the ABC-TV show *Ellen* soon after the starring character, Ellen Degeneres, portrayed herself as being gay.

Cambridge University Press found itself as a target of a cyberboycott by university professors when it refused to publish a political ethnography of the Macedonian region of Greece, entitled *Fields of Wheat, Rivers of Blood*.[9] *Fields of Wheat, Rivers of Blood* is a three-hundred-page study of three villages that details, among other things, how the region's residents speak Slavic dialects and consider themselves Slav-Macedonian, not Greek. The manuscript challenged the Greek government's official position that denies the existence of any Slavic ethnic minority in its borders, an opinion that a number of Greek citizens share. Cambridge University Press decided not to publish the book based on its perception that the book's controversial subject matter would place its staff in Greece at risk of physical harm. The publisher reached this conclusion after consulting with the British Embassy in Athens, which sent a short letter back to the publisher, stating that although none of its staff had read the book, the topic was potentially controversial and that reaction to the book could take the form of "protest and demonstrations . . . or violence against the author or publishers."[10]

The decision by the press, which held onto the manuscript for a year and a half, caused a firestorm of criticism from the publisher's own editorial advisers, three of whom resigned in protest. Two of the resigned advisers called for an academic boycott of the press by urging scholars not to submit manuscripts to or review books from Cambridge. Michael Herzfeld, a professor of anthropology at the University of Minnesota and one of the sponsors of the campaign, stated on the Internet, "By hindering the production and reviewing of new manuscripts, . . . we hope to demonstrate the academic world's collective dismay."[11] Cambridge University Press has also taken criticism from Greek officials like the ambassador to England, Elias Gounaris, who resented the notion that "barbaric" Greeks would attack members of a publishing house due to the content of a recent book. Gounaris stated that although intolerant voices do exist in Greece, as they do in most countries, "they have always dismally failed to silence anyone."[12]

The legal status of cyberboycotts has never been determined, but in the 1997 decision of the United States Supreme Court in *Reno v. ACLU,*[13] the Court accepted the view that Internet communication is generally protected by the First Amendment. The Court thus struck down the Communications Decency Act (the Act attempted to regulate pornographic communications on the Internet) on the ground that such regulation interfered with the constitutionally protected right of speech. In a separate opinion, Justice Sandra O'Connor set out reasons for the need for new judicial metaphors to define the meaning of cyberboycotts.

Concurring in part and dissenting in part, Justice O'Connor noted that the "electronic world is fundamentally different" in that it "is no more than the interconnection of electronic pathways [that enables] speakers and listeners to mask their identities."[14] Cyberboycotts were found to be different from traditional boycotts because Internet technology allows those joining a boycott to "mask their identities." As Justice O'Connor explained, "Since users can transmit and receive messages on the Internet without revealing anything about their identities or ages, . . . it is not currently possible to exclude persons from accessing certain messages on the basis of their identity."[15]

Justice O'Connor's opinion in *Reno* may work to extend the legal meaning of cyberboycotts to a new radial category that is chained to new imaginative metaphors that would justify the law's treatment of cyberboycott as a protected First Amendment activity. Since cyberboycott is no longer associated with the identity of those choosing to be part of a mass group, the radial category applicable to labor boycotts would seem to be inappropriate. The labor boycott metaphors that associated labor boycotts with mob action make little sense in the context of a cyberboycott communicated without the true presence of the boycotting group. Hence, the electronic transmission of the boycott may render cyberboycotts more like speech than action. Here, the cognitive metaphors "Ideas are objects" and "communication is container" may chain with the image schemata source-path-goal to create a radial category for cyberboycott as constitutionally protected expression.

Cyberboycott is thus a prime candidate for a new radial category of boycott. The new cultural space of cyberspace establishes a new domain that may enable judges to see cyberboycotts as being within a substantively different legal category that is culturally relevant to cyberspace. Cyberspace, after all, enables boycotters to transmit and receive messages without picketing or doing all the other forms of conduct that has heretofore distinguished boycotts from expression. One can simply click on or click off the cyberboycott Web page or cyberboycott chat room in deciding to either accept or reject the boycott message. There is no longer any need to confront a group of people or be subject to the pressures of a mob. The sharp-edged legal concepts of boycott coercion and intimidation would seem to have less applicability to the world of cyberspace.

If the Internet is a legitimate First Amendment medium, as the Court in *Reno* suggests, then users who access information can freely utilize all information in cyberspace, including that which may incite or call for placing pressure on others. The cyberspace of the Net permits individuals and groups to boycott without exposing their individual identities and without having to physically participate in group activity. The audience of the cyberboycott can either read the message or surf to another Web page. Like a handbill, the message of the cyberboycott can be easily ignored. Like a handbill, the pressure of cyberboycotts on individuals may not be as significant as picketing or boycotting on the streets. Finally, like a handbill, a written text is the only medium for communicating the message of the boycott. Cyberboycotts may therefore be defined by a radial category applicable to the collective dissemination of handbills and may enjoy greater First Amendment protection as a result of being associated with legal metaphors of individual expression.

DISINTEGRATION OF THE
RADIAL CATEGORIES OF LABOR BOYCOTT

Postmodernist culture poses a serious challenge to the way judges have come to understand boycotts in the law because the groups boycotting are no longer representative of one group (labor, civil rights, or business) but are frequently the result of alliances between different groups. Labor groups, for example, have combined with consumer and community groups to create new alliances for *labor-community boycotts*.[16] Labor-community boycotts do not have the same prototypical characteristics of a traditional labor boycott. Consider, for example, the Coors Beer boycott that was brought by labor and consumer groups in the 1980s to change corporate policy of the Coors Beer Company. The boycott was fueled by the opposition of various groups to the political views of the founder of the Coors company who was instrumental in founding the Heritage Foundation,[17] a conservative think tank that supported and helped to shape Reagan administration policies. The boycott was joined by feminist and gay organizations, as well as by black, Hispanic, and other ethnic communities who believed that Coors represented political causes that were adverse to their interests.[18] The boycott was initiated by the AFL-CIO, which had been attempting unsuccessfully to unionize Coors's breweries.[19]

The Coors Beer boycott had both political and economic objectives. Some groups boycotted Coors because they did not want to support political causes that were perceived to be contrary to their political interests. Other groups protested because they perceived Coors as supporting governmental policies that worked to undermine their economic interests. Finally, labor union groups boycotted to pressure Coors to assume collective bargaining responsibilities under federal labor law. The combined effect of the boycott over several years worked substantially to diminish Coors's market share, a factor that ultimately contributed to the success of the boycott.[20]

In advancing their boycott against Coors, boycotters sought to persuade consumers that their purchases of Coors beer would contribute to corporate policies that were unjust, unfair, and simply un-American. Within the Coors boycott itself, Coors's corporate character was challenged by publicity metaphors that characterized the boycott as an affirmative, just, and democratic act, and Coors's character was associated with images that projected an ethos of Coors as an evil, bad actor. Boycott slogans thus encouraged consumers to see the boycott as inherently good, as a consumer's friend, and as a working-class ally. Coors was associated with shaming metaphors that encouraged people to see the corporation as an enemy, an evil force, and an un-American entity.

Boycotts like the one involving Coors beer illustrate how the cultural practice of boycott now provides new prototypical characteristics for characterizing boycotts under new radial categories. The Coors boycott, for example, illustrates that the radial categories for labor and business used by judges in deciding boycott cases fail to explain the meaning of labor-community boycotts or cyberboycotts. In the postindustrial era, boycotts advance political causes by the use of advertising and dollars in the marketplaces of real places or in the marketplaces of cyberspace. In using dollars as a voice in these spaces, groups gain access to the political discourse by identifying their members with the message of a boycott. Boycott is thus becoming an important supplement to the official political process, where many Americans have been unable to participate as a result of the domination of interest group politics.

Boycotts as Agents of Social Change

In postmodernist culture, boycotts may play an important role in social movement practice. Union-initiated consumer boycotts, for example, such as the one brought by grape pickers in California, represent attempts to transform a traditional labor dispute into a broader political one so that the underlying issues may be expressed in a language that the general consuming public can understand. New boycott practices can interject into the political discourse new symbols and a new language that may serve to provide new prototypical characteristics for the meaning of boycott in the law.

In the postindustrial era, boycotts have been brought by diverse and fragmentary groups reacting to the complex issues of a mass consumer culture. Today, increasingly, the traditional forms of labor, business, and civil rights boycotts are giving way to new technological and social forms of boycotts that mimic the older forms of boycott phenomena. Labor and consumer boycotts have thus been used as a means for organizing new alliances between workers and consumers in an effort to develop new forms of collective action.

Labor-initiated community boycotts, for example, have been based on an attempt to recreate a "new labor institution" built on a new unionism of "decentralized, highly democratic, responsive, and communitarian" values.[21] The Union of Needle Trades, Industrial, and Textile Employees (UNITE), a merger of the International Ladies' Garments Workers' Union and the Amalgamated Clothing and Textile Workers Union, is attempting to expand this approach to an international level in its educational campaign aimed at the Gap clothing store. The unions are protesting the Gap's use of factories in El Salvador that exploit their workers. The success of UNITE's unofficial boycott can be judged from the fact that shoppers turned away from the Gap. The Gap itself allowed an inspection of its factory, and then pulled out of El Salvador altogether.

THE COMPLEX UNFOLDING SOCIAL PRACTICE OF BOYCOTT

One could easily view UNITE's activities as being about jobs and wages for its own workers. If workers can force the Gap out of foreign countries, perhaps the company will return its foreign manufacturing contracts to the United States, where UNITE workers could be employed. However, UNITE recognizes that some degree of global production is inevitable and instead called for an international movement toward higher standards and wages. When UNITE called for this consumer protest of the Gap, the union attracted political leaders, community leaders, and students as well; all of these participants recognize that this movement for international workers rights is effectively a second civil rights movement.

Further, for some, the idea of fighting for a higher wage is in itself a transcendent political value. Consider, for example, the actions of local community/economic empowerment groups that have used the boycott as a knife to cut a larger slice of a city's economic pie. African-American leaders in Miami led a successful boycott of the entire city that led to joint economic ventures and the entrance of African-American leaders into exclusive financial leadership circles.[22]

The boycott, which began in 1990, was provoked by the city leadership's refusal to honor Nelson Mandela's visit to the city due to his alleged support of Fidel Castro. The African-American community was outraged by the snub and decided that the city's decision, besides being offensive, showed how little political power the African-American community had in Miami. The leaders of the boycott began advertising on television and writing to national groups advising them to boycott Miami.

The city lost an estimated $67 million in convention bookings over the next few years. Eventually, Miami's elite began to bend and allowed African-Americans into its exclusive circles. Since the boycott, African-American leaders have emerged in various positions ranging from the head of the Orange Bowl Committee to the leader of the prestigious Beacon Group, an economic development committee. In addition, the boycott has led to certain joint productions such as the $20 million renovation of the Royal Palm hotel, the largest African-American owned hotel in Miami, and the establishment of a $2.6 million equity fund for start-up businesses.

This boycott was about both money and politics. It was instituted by a group of business people and lawyers who were demanding that the doors of economic opportunity be opened. It was coercive, in that it forced financial and political leaders to make political and economic decisions that they probably didn't want to, and it led some consumers away from a choice they had already made. Were these goals less than transcendent? Did the leaders of the boycott have another choice? The further the analysis goes, the more one begins to question the Supreme Court's view that a boycott must have purely political motives in order to be legally protected.

Political Action Committees, too, have jumped on the boycott band-wagon in their attempts to assert various agendas. The American Family Association, a national conservative Christian group, has been on a campaign to end the consumer's access to pornographic magazines like *Playboy* and *Penthouse*. The Association has called a national boycott on Circle K mini-marts for their refusal to remove pornographic magazines from their shelves, and the boycott is on until the chain stops selling them.[23]

Another example of the recent wave of consumer boycotts is the action taken by INFACT, a national consumer activist organization that, during the recent congressional hearings on the tobacco industry, called for a boycott against Phillip Morris, the cigarette company. The theory behind the boycott was simple; since Phillip Morris received 56 percent of its revenues from food and beverage products, a direct consumer boycott might force them to, among other things, stop deceiving the public about the effects of smoking; stop marketing and promoting tobacco products to children; and stop influencing public policy on issues of tobacco and health.[24]

The NAACP also has threatened to use a boycott to support African-Americans in a company that has apparently prevented them from attaining leadership roles. The NAACP threatened Dr. Pepper with a national boycott after determining that although 22 percent of the company's consumer base was black, the company had no black vice-presidents, corporate officers, or bottling plant owners.[25] Here, if one categorizes the promoters and the beneficiaries of the boycott as members of the African-American community, one could argue that the promoters of the boycott had an economic stake in the outcome. Once again, the action is a motivated mixture of political and economic goals.

Political action committees dedicated either to restricting or protecting the right to choose an abortion have also used the boycott as an expressive tool. For example, a local chapter of the Girl Scouts of America was recently boycotted by a large pro-life group, claiming that one of the Girl Scouts's programs allegedly discussed the subject of abortion. Pro-choice activists, meanwhile, threatened Idaho Governor Cecil Andrus with a national boycott of Idaho potatoes if he did not veto what would have been the most restrictive abortion law in the nation.

Gay-rights groups launched a boycott of the entire state of Colorado after its voters passed, by a margin 53 percent to 47 percent, Amendment

2 to the state constitution, forbidding states and local governments from adopting measures that protect homosexuals from discrimination.[26] The boycott, which had run nine months until it was called off pending Supreme Court review of Amendment 2, has cost the city of Denver thirty-one major conventions, amounting to $38 million in lost revenue for the state. Denver's convention chief, Eugene Dilbeck, reported, "In the short term, the boycott had a very negative impact on us."[27] Although the boycott did not seem to dent the state's roaring $340 million ski industry, it did have the unintended result of injuring some gay-owned businesses. As a result, original promoters and supporters are rethinking the use of the boycott. In particular, gay business owners, like Wayne Jackino, whose gay bar suffered a 20 percent drop in business during the boycott, states now that he prefers presence over absence. Frank Whitworth, the executive director of Ground Zero, a Colorado based gay-rights group, supports the need to consider other options like a "gaycott," that would "flood the state with gays and lesbians."[28]

Governments, too, have used the boycott tool to lodge their protests against the acts of nation states and multinational corporations. French president Jacques Chirac's decision to resume nuclear testing in the South Pacific has brought international criticism and lost profits for some French firms. Australia, for example, refused to allow a French aviation company to bid on the purchase of jet fighters that it was selling. In addition, the Australian state of Victoria followed the federal government's lead by refusing to allow French companies to bid on slices of its electricity privatization program, which was worth up to $9.6 billion. In Stockholm, Scandic, a major Scandinavian hotel chain with forty-six hotels in Sweden alone, decided to boycott French wines in retaliation for the nuclear testing.

The European Union (EU), the twelve-nation economic community of Europe, has used a boycott to voice its discontent over the Israeli government's plans to hold a birthday party for the city of Jerusalem. The celebration, Jerusalem 3000, is intended to commemorate the 3,000 years since King David conquered the city and declared it the capital of the Israelites. The EU, however, feels that the celebration is premature and threatens the peace process in its emphasis on Jerusalem as the capital of Israel, as opposed to Palestine.[29] To effectuate its boycott, the EU has withdrawn all financial support from European performers wishing to take part in the program. In addition, it has demanded that the art festivals it has contributed to be removed from the celebration. All of these boycotts illustrate in today's postmodernist culture, the boycott is becoming a popular means for influencing the behavior of individuals, corporations, and nation states.

Contemporary boycotts, however, present some of the same prototypical properties of the central case of the boycott against Captain Boycott. Boycotts requesting consumers to withhold their patronage can be just as coercive as the tenants' boycott against Captain Boycott, and they may be even more coercive.[30] In the Girl Scouts boycott, for example, within forty-eight hours of the announcement of the boycott, the Girl Scouts organization dropped from its programs all references to abortion, apparently because it feared a negative effect on revenues it receives from its annual cookie sales. As a spokesperson for Girl Scouts explained, "The boycott was extremely threatening because we were very vulnerable. A lot of people would not have been sympathetic, and we could not recoup the losses."[31]

A similar result came about with the Idaho potato boycott. The boycott forced the governor of Idaho to effect change in state abortion laws by vetoing legislation he might otherwise have signed. The UNITE boycott of the Gap deterred many shoppers from making purchases at their favorite store and forced the Gap to pull out of El Salvador. In Miami, the African-American boycott led to the establishment of investment projects and the appointment of African-Americans to leadership roles in the city. These boycotts were all successful in their coercion. The new boycott practices, whether done by a labor-community reliance or an individual on the Internet, aim to coerce, and hence, these new forms of boycott practice also involve some of the same prototypical characteristics judges have used to create radial categories for labor, civil rights, and business boycotts.

That boycotts are inherently coercive or damaging to the financial position of their targets does not, of course, detract from their political character.[32] The boycotts against the Girl Scouts and Idaho potatoes were political, and so was the decision of the Girl Scouts's organization to provide instructional programs on abortion, and the political decision of a governor to sign or veto particular legislation. In this respect, one might argue that the right-to-life boycott against the Girl Scouts or the ERA potato boycott were really no different than the product boycotts brought against American corporations doing business in South Africa,[33] UNITE's education campaign against the Gap, or INFACT's campaign against the tobacco industry. UNITE and INFACT understood that an educational campaign embarrassing the target was a more efficient way to stop the inhumane practices of American multinationals than a lobbying campaign in Congress would have been.

One might also see the boycotts against the Girl Scouts, Idaho potatoes, or the GAP as efforts to subvert the normal market and political channels available for citizens to make known their preferences and thus present reasons judges have relied upon for suppressing a boycott. In the case of labor boycotts, for example, we have seen cases such as *Glidden, Gompers,* and *Trial Lawyers* where judicial decision makers have condemned boycotts because they were seen to be a threat to a free market. The Girl Scouts organization, dependent as it was on voluntary contributions and cookie sales, was vulnerable to the pressures of the right-to-life group; the economy of Idaho was similarly dependent upon potato sales throughout the nation; and K-Mart and the Gap, as retail institutions, are susceptible to campaigns that make their consumers feel uncomfortable about purchasing products in their stores. What may be troubling about these boycotts is that boycotters are using consumer appeals to bring about political change without voter or consumer consensus. The fear is that a small boycotting group may intimidate the majority to go along with the boycotters' objective and blackmail the majority to accept minority views, positions, and norms. Of course, the opposite is also probable; the majority may overrule the minority boycott and force the group to accept majoritarian values.

Group boycotts may appear to some as acts of political terrorism. The Girl Scouts organization and the governor of Idaho could be seen to have caved in to the demands of their respective boycott only forty-eight hours after their announcement. Consumers hardly had an opportunity to voice their views about the underlying issues. We don't allow antiabortion demonstrators to engage in acts of political terrorism in other contexts, even if such prohibitions have an incidental impact on their communicative message.

The fear of terrorism is made real by the metaphors of the law such as "tiger," "disease," or "bomb" that seek to persuade us that boycotts are threatening and coercive activities that should be denied legal protection. The metaphors of labor boycotts have the power to shape the imaginative process to conceptualize labor-community boycotts or even cyber-boycotts as being within the same radial category the law has created for secondary labor boycotts. The imagined fear of political terrorism would thus *chain* boycott once again to a picture of boycott as a destructive force. One might see that the Girl Scouts, the governor of Idaho, or the Gap had no choice but to submit to the demands of the right-to-life or pro-choice groups, even though as a factual matter, they had a choice. It takes little imagination to see how almost any protest group could be stigmatized as a political terrorist organization.

The images of boycott in the law may, however, bear little resemblance to the actual practice of boycott. Consider, for a moment, the effects of the Girl Scout boycott. The Girl Scouts organization apparently decided that it was simply more expedient to stop its programs that discussed abortions than to risk a loss of revenue through cookie sales. Its decision, however, may have been wrong; there are some pro-choice consumers who would see the Girl Scouts as siding with the right-to-life group as a result of the organization's response to the boycott. There was also the possibility that cookie sales were lost to consumers who stopped purchasing Girl Scout cookies because the programs were eliminated. Similarly, the governor of Idaho could have stood firm and refused to veto recently enacted legislation if he really believed that it was the will of the majority to do so. Finally, the Gap could have stayed in El Salvador, as was urged by UNITE, and simply enforced its corporate code of responsibility. Yet, if boycott is to be equated with blackmail or political terrorism, then it still would be no more opprobrious than hard bargaining between unequal parties or slum landlordism, both of which enjoy legal protection.[34]

Just as it is a mistake to assume that boycott targets have no choices, it would also be a mistake to automatically equate consumer boycotts with marginalized and powerless groups. Today, everybody feels powerless to some degree; even the right-to-life group that boycotted the Girl Scouts probably felt powerless. Citizen groups of all political persuasions engage in consumer boycotts because every segment of American society has become deeply pessimistic about the capacity of the political process to respond to the needs of various individuals. Some citizens boycott because they believe it may be the only way to gain a voice in the political process. Others boycott because they believe it to be an effective and low cost means of forcing change. Boycotts are simply a popular way to publicize a dispute and garner public support, and they are available to all kinds of groups, large and small, rich and poor.

One commentator has described the market as an amoral vacuum that will only become moral when consumers demand that morals be injected into it.[35] Zachary D. Lyons, publisher of the *Boycott Quarterly*, states that in an economic democracy, every dollar counts as a means of supporting or withholding support from certain companies. "One dollar, one vote," his favorite saying, reminds us that the boycott is imagined by some as a form of political expression.[36]

When individuals assemble together and urge others to join a campaign aimed at changing people's minds about working for or buying from a certain employer, they may rely upon the informal shaming mechanism of group pressure to change behavior. If the group is close-knit, the boycott will likely be an effective shaming mechanism. The fact that a boycott is coercive or may have "shaming" consequences provides boycott its value as a norm-enforcing mechanism. The fact that a group of boycotters, be they teachers, assembly workers, or civil rights activists, has the ability to secure some economic gain through the shaming effects of the boycott may be the only way to enforce societal norms in a world where nation-state authority is being overtaken by nongovernmental global organizations. Boycott may, in the wake of globalization, be the only effective mechanism to motivate private corporate actors to take responsibility for human rights and environmental protection.[37]

The First Amendment significance of boycotts is apparent in the cultural role boycotts may play in American culture, but whether the values of constitutional assembly and free expression will be extended to boycotts will ultimately depend on the imagination and ideology of the legal mind. Mass consumer capitalism and mass politics may depend in part on the availability of boycotts as a means of expressing views on issues as diverse as international labor practices, environmentalism, or the Equal Rights Amendment. Because judges are "enmeshed in and dependent upon the structures of social meaning that make communication possible"[38] they may not be, consciously or unconsciously, capable of appreciating the meaning of new group boycott practices. "If the law is

fused with [its own] narrative, then it seems to face precisely the problem of subjectivity that [it] strives hard to avoid it."[39]

The psychology motivating the suppression of ideology in adjudication, however, prevents the legal mind from understanding the full
complexity of boycott practice now unfolding in postmodern culture.
The imaginative powers of the legal mind are constrained by an ideology that prevents some judges from seeing the diversity and subjectivity
of the subjects the law seeks to regulate. The denial of the ideological in
adjudication has consequently become an evasive strategy used to ignore
the full complexity of boycott phenomena.

CHAPTER 10
ETHOS OF THE LEGAL MIND

IN THIS CHAPTER, I will examine alternative conceptions of group boycott phenomena; conceptions that have been given little attention in the law. My purpose will be to suggest how new metaphors and a new meaning of group boycotts could be reconstructed in legal decision making to create a new legal right to boycott. In other words, I will now attempt to describe aspects of the wholeness of boycotts by bringing to bear ideas and information that the law ignores or marginalizes in its imaginative analysis of boycott phenomena.

Classical rhetoricians used a word, *ethos*, as a way of getting at the wholeness of metaphor.[1] *Pathos* along with ethos and *Logos* represented to them the three means of persuasion of metaphor. So far I have examined how pathos (emotional appeal) and Logos (logical appeal) operate in the law of boycott to provide persuasive appeal to judges' decisions. I will now focus on the ethos of boycott metaphors used in boycott decisions for purposes of uncovering the wholeness in the meaning of boycott. "For Greco-Roman rhetoricians, the advocate's ethos was as important as the logical (Logos) or emotional (pathos) content of what he writes."[2] The ethos appeal of an argument or analysis relates to "the creditability of the person who makes it."[3] This appeal is thus linked to the character of the author as revealed by the metaphor he or she uses in writing and speaking. The advocate's ethos thus depends on carefully selecting good metaphors, avoiding bad metaphors, and never misusing metaphors. The point is that "successful legal arguments depend as much on deliberate stylistic choices as they do on substantive choices."[4] The selection of metaphor is thus an integral part of the ethos, or character, of the legal decision maker.

A basic claim of this book, however, is that metaphor shapes judicial imagination and that most judges are not always conscious of this when they choose the metaphors they use in legal decision making. As explained in chapter 4, judges have the discretion to create imaginative metaphors in writing opinions and announcing rules from the bench, but once these metaphors become part of *stare decisis*, they become embedded in the law and control the future choices of other judges in other cases. The metaphors that appear in judicial opinions thereby take on their own ethos independent of the author. I will thus use the term ethos to assess the character of the author's legal mind, but I will make my assessment on the basis of the boycott metaphors used consciously or unconsciously in legal decision making.

In order to examine the ethos of the legal mind, I will first consider how boycott practices of groups reflect group norms, and how those norms might be imagined differently. In examining how boycott practices represent group norms, we can begin to identify a different ethos for the legal imagination. By comparing boycott practice to the way boycott is currently categorized in the law, we can also learn something about the character of the boycott metaphors judges use in legal decision making. I will begin by examining the relationship between boycott and group norms and the democratic process. I will then examine the relationship between boycotts and the regulation of norms. My overall goal will be to uncover an ethos of boycott that has never been fully imagined in the legal mind.

Boycotts and Group Norms

As an intermediary between the individual and the state, boycotts enable individuals to express their identities, norms, and political orientations. A boycott can offer a valuable medium that permits individuals in society to express their common identities and to shift norms and behavior in new directions. Boycotts can change social norms through the shaming mechanism—a powerful mechanism for identifying unacceptable forms of behavior and for establishing solidarity by holding up to others the pride of adhering to the norms of the group—as well as by the more direct action of a general refusal to deal. As an identity-defining mechanism, boycotts allow individuals to pool their efforts to influence society and to advance the group's identity message. When group norms conflict with societal norms, for example, a boycott may become a way of expressing the conflict, thereby allowing the group norms to get refined and articulated as a result of the struggle and action of the boycott.

Boycotts permit groups not only to express and affirm the identity of the membership, but also to enforce the group's particular normative perspective. Boycott leaders, acting as norm entrepreneurs,[5] use the private social mechanisms of shame, ostracism, pride, and esteem to enforce the group's norms and to challenge norms found offensive to the group. If successful, they can bring about what norm theorists call "norm cascades" (the group using the private mechanism of social control actually shifts the behavior of various groups in society in new directions).[6]

By publicizing identity messages about the group, boycotts also serve as a means for subgroups in society to reach consensus about public issues. Boycotts can become an important rallying event that can enable individuals to represent their group identities in terms of the commonality of pursuits, objectives, and group membership. The collective awareness of the boycott grievance becomes a spark that galvanizes individuals to organize and promote their own interests through collective self-action. In this way, one can understand how marginalized groups might informally regulate behavior and transform existing social structures that ignore the group's norms. Thus, boycotts can serve to advance group norms through a form of *identity-politics*, practiced and enforced by group solidarity, social ostracism, and shame-based sanctions.

Groups, if they are close-knit and homogeneous, enjoy the advantage that results from group consensus. For example, a small group whose members accept the same norms is able to reach a consensus on issues, take collective action, and avoid collective action problems encountered by a large diverse group whose members have competing normative values. A boycott by a well-organized highly homogeneous group could thereby be an effective means for minority tyranny of the majority—the cohesive group, no matter its size, effectively boycotting the much larger majority. A minority group can also find itself the target of a boycott by a much larger group. In such a case, the social mechanisms of shame and pride may be an extremely powerful device for enforcing compliance with majority will. The point is that there is no way of knowing in the absence of an examination of context whether a group boycott may lead to democratic or nondemocratic norms and practices.

Awareness of how a group boycott can serve the identity interests of different groups might allow judges to consider alternative metaphors of boycott or examine new meanings for old metaphors. Boycotts by consumers, environmentalists, pro- and anti-life groups, and others, for example, advance the identity interests of different groups in society. In representing the interests and identity of various groups, these boycotts can bring attention to the particular identity of a group, and they can become the mechanisms for enforcing codes of behavior against powerful corporate interests.

Awareness of the diverse identities of the groups boycotting might also lead to a richer understanding of the identities of individuals in society. Looking at how boycott is practiced thus offers judges an opportunity to examine these different identities and, thereby, to better understand the nature of group conflict. Judges, after all, are implicated in the process of norm regulation when they give meaning to boycott phenomena and evaluate the legal effects of such phenomena. The problem is that judges remain coy about their role in norm regulation; they frequently deny that they are ideological norm enforcers even as they adjudicate norm conflicts.

Racial minorities boycotting discriminatory business practices and Irish tenants and farmers boycotting their landlord's agent are examples of high-stakes ideological group conflicts, each within a particular social and political context. The same can be said of the boycott of the legal-aid lawyers seeking to persuade the District of Columbia to increase legal-aid fees in the *Trial Lawyers* case. Each one of these boycotts is symptomatic of a conflict over norms.

In Ireland, the boycott against Captain Boycott was regarded as both a law-enforcing and law-threatening activity. In *Claiborne Hardware*, the civil rights boycott was both "majestic" and "reptilian" depending on how one analyzed the social and economic effects of the boycott. And, in the *Trial Lawyers* case, the legal aid boycott could be seen as an effort by legal aid workers to either gain self-control over their jobs or to increase the value of their fees via an anticompetitive strategy. Collective self-determination and solidarity of these boycotts was an integral part of the expression of group norms. A new radial category extension of boycott constructed from an understanding of boycott as norm competition might motivate judges to see how group boycotts enable private citizens to compete in norm regulation of a dynamic society that no longer has a strong consensus for identifying societal norms. The metaphor "Boycott is norm competition" may better suit our current multicultural society.

RESOLVING POLICY CONFLICTS

In confronting the normative conflicts posed by group boycotts, judges must choose between competing norms of different ideological camps represented by the boycott group, the targets, and the larger society. In making a choice, the judge renders a decision of policy based on the rational application of background rules and precedents. In evaluating the background rules and relevant cases, the judge will use his or her imagination to cognitively classify the controversy in accordance with the existing categories of relevant law. The judge's official method of classification, however, typically consists of a classification system based on analogy, inductive and deductive inference, and relations between common properties.[7] The similarities between boycotts involving labor groups, for example, becomes a reason for concluding that labor boycotts belong in the category that is different from business boycotts. The conceptual frame that associates labor boycotts with violence has essentially become the legal category of labor boycott. Hence, judges use what they believe to be true about the propensity of labor violence to create a legal category for labor boycotts. This form of reasoning is structured by an analogical structure. "Boycott is to target as violent crowd behavior is to individual."

What is significant about the traditional methods of legal reasoning in the law is that the method, whether it be analogy or inference, invariably comes down to a political conclusion based on a prototypical case, and the merits of the legal controversy gets resolved by the way the prototypical case frames the controversy.[8] Because the policy choice invariably involves reasoning from one case to another, or from one imagined category to another, judges consciously or unconsciously rely upon their imagination to decide how to classify things.

Judges, like all of us, use image schemata and conceptual metaphors of familiar experiences to categorize and analogize new phenomena. Hence, the rational considerations of policy in legal decision making invariably involves an imaginative form of reason that defines the critical categories and domains of an analogy or an inference. In making their policy choice, judges use metaphors, image schemata, and idealized models shaped by a particular normative background to reach a conclusion and decide a controversy. Hence, it is metaphoric reason that enables judges to use policy analysis as a "Trojan horse" to smuggle ideology into legal decision making.[9]

Metaphoric forms of legal analysis would neither deny the intensely political nature of group conflict nor the indeterminacy of the complex policy considerations relevant to legal decision making. What a cognitive and ideological understanding of adjudication offers is a more open examination of the assumptions and normative orientations in the background of adjudication that shape the foreground of legal conclusions. By exploring how imagination structures the perception of the legal mind, we can better understand how the cognitive models of legal decision making have ideological consequences in adjudication. This would provide a way for laying bare the ideological background of the legal meaning of boycott that is currently denied and suppressed by legal decision makers.

Boycotts, Democracy, and Norm Regulation

Some boycotts are called because groups of people decide to associate for purposes of expressing and protecting their interests and values. These boycotts are no different than the mass demonstration where groups of people associate for mutual support and self-protection. Like a mass rally, the boycott is aimed at pressuring a particular target that the group desires to influence. The pressure of the boycott is like that of a rally, since both advance the group's identity for purposes of self-development and self-protection. The fact that boycotts pressure others does not therefore in and of itself provide a reason for their condemnation in the law. As C. Edwin Baker has explained, "although the use [of] instrumental means to apply pressure on others does not justify constitutional protection, it also does not require denying protection. Since pressure that merely results from activities in which people otherwise have a right to engage cannot in itself justify abridging clearly protected freedom, these assemblies and boycotts should be protected."[10]

The distinction in constitutional law between *speech pure* and *speech plus* creates a metaphoric structure that motivates judges to classify labor boycott publicity under a conceptual model that associates boycott activity to ideas about destructive forces. The imagined harm of a labor boycott is analyzed not as a consequence of the content of speech, but rather as the secondary effects of the activity. Regulation of boycott expression is deemed content-neutral even though expressive conduct is in fact regulated. And yet, because the harm is usually attributed to the communicative effects of publicity, the regulation is content-based.[11]

If boycotts are important mediums for realizing collective self-determination, then boycotts may be important social and cultural practices of a democratic society. After all, in such a society agency is located in the people collectively, and that agency is what authorizes governmental officials to govern. The essential problematic of a democracy involves the dilemma of reconciling individual and collective autonomy. If we follow Oliver W. Holmes Jr. and define democracy as a competitive process for collective self-development, then the reconciliation of the problematics of democracy must be allowed to take place in the social spaces of society as situated within particular social practices. Robert Post's conclusion is also helpful here: "[The] First Amendment doctrine will continue to flounder until it focuses clearly on the nature and constitutional significance of such practices."[12]

The social practices of boycotts are not what frame the law of boycotts. What frames group boycott doctrine in the law, however, are *idealized cognitive models* of boycott derived from a limited set of default metaphors. In labor law, boycotts are thought to spread the bad consequences of labor disputes. In civil rights, boycotts are viewed as legitimate forms of political expression but only when the goals of the boycotters transcend their own economic self-interests. In the business setting, market interests color the metaphors used to capture the legal meaning of business boycotts.

The ethos of the *legal mind* would appear to reflect the character of a person who is afraid of groups, who fears mass assemblies, and is anxious about collective protests unless such activity is aimed at upholding the law (either of the state or that of the market). The normative vision of this legal mind motivates judges to think that they are enforcing societal norms, when in reality they are merely enforcing the normative vision of the source-domain of the metaphors they use in giving meaning to phenomena. Judges are motivated to deny the normative orientation of their tools because they are trained to internalize a self-image of constraint. As Duncan Kennedy has explained: "Judges imagine that their duty is to 'rise above' and 'put aside,' to 'resist' and 'transcend' their personal interests, their instinctive or intuitive sympathies, their partisan group affiliations, and their ideological commitments. They act as if they are supposed to 'submit' to something 'bigger' and 'higher' than 'themselves.'"[13] Jerome Frank claimed that "[t]he peculiar traits, dispositions, biases and habits of the particular judge will, then, often determine what he decides to do in the law."[14]

Imagination plays the pivotal role in constraining what judges think they do in legal decision making. If judges were more reflective about how their imagination shapes their cognitive thought, they might be more aware of the normatively loaded nature of the conceptual tools they use in their analysis and more reflective about their choice of metaphor. But this is not what judges have been doing. Instead, the legal metaphors of boycott do the choosing, and it is judges who carry out the authority of the law's metaphors.

As a vehicle for collective action, boycotts can, of course, lead to the enforcement of bad norms. Boycotts can shut down public discourse by bringing economic and social pressure to bear on targets and all others doing business with targets, and they can pressure the individual to do things he or she might prefer not to do. The practical consequences of a boycott can be disruptive of the democratic process. Boycotts are brought by both left and right political groups. Some seek to pressure others to join the boycott through appeals to political solidarity. The fact that boycott may pressure others is not a good reason for treating boycotts differently than mass demonstrations, rallies, and other forms of protest since they too pressure others. Moreover, in pressuring others, boycotts like rallies create an expressive message; the pressure on others is the point of the expression, and it is interrelated with the communicative element of the activity. Absent evidence of physical violence or coercion, boycotts offer prototypical properties that would justify treating boycott as being within the radial category of a mass demonstration, which has always enjoyed a respectable place in our American constitutional system. At the core of this radial category is the idea of group contestability as a necessary predicate of a democratic society.

ETHOS OF BOYCOTT: THE VALUE OF CONTESTABILITY

The ethos of boycott could be understood as the ethos of our revolution: the long-standing right of people to protest and resist injustice. The boycott against Captain Boycott as well as the nonimportation protests of American colonists immediately before our revolution serve to highlight a democratic norm for understanding the social meaning of boycott as a form of democratic contestability.

The norms implicated by group boycotts are thus very much the subject of debate and conflict. In looking to boycott practice in society, we can discover the social facts for understanding the idea of group contestability. Boycott can be useful for discovering new metaphors for defining the social meaning of group contestability, but boycott metaphors cannot tell us how we should deal with problems of group conflict in law or society. The problem is that disagreement and contestability is relative to the choices between competing value judgments and social norms. The ethos of boycott thus raises a basic question: How shall we define the meaning of contestability, and what should the response of the law be? The meaning of contestability will, of course, depend on context.

Consider, for example, the problem of defining the legal meaning of Free Speech. The law's notion of speech has meaning only when evaluated in light of concrete social contexts. As Stanley Fish is fond of saying: "There's no such thing as free speech . . . and it's a good thing too."[15] By this, Fish means there is no meaning of Free Speech independent of the discourse of different ideological communities. This is because the boundaries of ideological communities locate for us different definitions of Free Speech.

The same could be said of boycotts. Judges must look to social context to discover the right definition of boycott. Yet, when they look to context, judges only see what is reflected through the lens of their ideology and imagination. They will never find solace in the reason of the law. The law of reason, as we have seen, is also an ideological discourse structured by normatively loaded metaphors. Judges, however, tend to regard reason as if it were a value-neutral thing to enhance truth-seeking and value-free adjudication. The problem with law's reason is that the courts have blinded themselves by the metaphor of the "Law of Reason" inherent in the legal culture of the organizations and institutions they inhabit.[16]

The most important normative values of the First Amendment jurisprudence are rooted in contestable social practices, not institutions. As Robert Post has explained,

> Democracy is not merely a matter of talking; it also involves all the complicated forms of social interaction by which we govern ourselves. Truth-seeking is not merely a matter of sentences and prepositions; it also involves habits of mind, priorities of reason, intersubjective orientations, and attitudes that, when taken together, make up what we recognize to be rational exchange or a collective search for knowledge. Speech is of course prerequisite for both democracy and truth-seeking, but speech alone, in the absence of other necessary social practices, will not yield the values we seek in either democracy or truth-seeking.[17]

To be sure, boycotts pose problems for democratic discourse by potentially silencing the voice of the target of the boycott as well as many others doing business with or having a relation with the target.[18] Boycotts can, like the law, be a source of violence. Judges may thus seek to protect public discourse from the potential silencing effects of boycott. If, however, boycotts are condemned because they involve only what judges *perceive* to be their silencing effect, or because someone is pressured, then it will be judges who will ultimately determine which objectives are permissible and lawful. Why should peaceful group boycotts be treated as violent activity in the absence of actual violence? The central case of boycott could be a radial category extension based on a stock story of boycott as presumptively peaceful, concerted political activity. The exceptional case of boycott as violence could be regulated under ordinary criminal law and procedure. This imaginative possibility is now concealed, however, by default metaphors that project a strong pathos and Logos appeal for condemning boycott practices as violence.

What better manifestation of legal hegemony than to allow judges to determine from their perspective which boycotts are legitimate and which are illegitimate.[19] The problem is that judges fail to realize that the law they apply is shaped by deeply ingrained metaphors structured by partial cultural understandings of what is acceptable political behavior for groups. The imaginative possibilities, however, are constrained by the normative orientations of a legal culture that exhibits the pathologies of denial, constraint, and suppression.

Because boycotts invariably raise ambivalent feelings about the nature of the activity involved, we will always understand them in different ways. What we can learn to discover is how the cognitive process operates to disguise and permit political choices to be made in legal decision making. The legal meaning of the word *boycott* should require rising above our personal prejudices, idiosyncratic points of view, and dogmatic claims to truth. Objectivity in law should not require taking up God's perspective, which is, after all, unattainable; rather, it should entail an understanding of how shared human perspectives are tied to legal reality by law's embodied cognitive imagination.

Judicial evaluation of group boycotts thus requires a probing analysis of how language and the normative social order interact and function to further democratic norms and practices. But more than enlightened judges and greater judicial discretion are needed. What judges need to know is how the creation of legal meaning takes place through the cultural medium of law's official language. The crux of the problem is that judges and commentators have failed to consider the possibility that their tool of analysis—language—may fail to objectively capture the meaning of the events they seek to describe. In *Gompers*, for example, Justice Lamar sought to describe the legal meaning of a threatened worker boycott by describing how the vast power of a labor group could coerce an individual to take unwanted action. The idea of force provided the legal justification for the Court's conclusions, but the Court's explanation of force depended upon subjective criteria. One could not ascertain the meaning of force without knowing something about the way Justice Lamar understood the problem of force in the *Gompers* case.

If we assume, on the one hand, that reality reflects an objective image of the world like a mirror, then language may be capable of mirroring that reality. If, on the other hand, the words we use to describe reality actually reflect contingent, socially constructed images of that reality, then there is reason for questioning the representative function of language used for the discovery of meaning. The different images of boycott found in the law suggest that there is a mechanism at work that has permitted judges to capture some, but not all, of the reality of boycotts for different doctrinal areas of the law.

To demand more than this is to demand the impossible. It should be enough to show that judges have used imaginative and normatively loaded tools in their opinions as a means of creating legal truth about boycott phenomena. By exploring the nature of imagination and ideology in adjudication, we can discover the keys for unlocking the mystery surrounding the chameleon-like mechanism of boycott doctrine. By discovering what generates the structure of legal interpretation, we can also discover new metaphoric lessons for resolving future boycott issues in the law.

What is needed is better understanding of the relation between reason, imagination, and ideology. Reason in the law has always represented what most lawyers, judges, and legal scholars have focused on in their analysis. It is now time that more attention be given to understanding the role of imagination and ideology in shaping the discourse of law. Reflection and discovery should lead to the development of new metaphors of boycott. New metaphors developed pragmatically from analyzing the actual practice of boycotts in contemporary society may provide opportunities for the development of a new legal imagination.

EPILOGUE

IDEOLOGY AND
THE LEGAL MIND

> We may well want judges with a touch in them of the
> qualities which make poets, who will administer justice
> as an art and feel that the judicial process involves creative
> skill. This means that we want to encourage, not to discount-
> enance, imagination, intuition, insight. But it does not mean
> that we should not frown upon pure phantasy thinking.
> —Jerome Frank, *Law and the Modern Mind*

IS THERE ANOTHER way? Could judges construct different legal categories of boycott that do not rely on some metaphors? I think there is another way. Judicial decision making seems to have been stuck in an imaginative process of thought that is dependent on background assumptions about the social, economic, and political meaning of group boycott practices. These background assumptions have served to establish at least two dominant idealized cognitive models for understanding the meaning of boycott. One model appears to be based on the belief that boycotts represent a dangerous threat to society, to the Rule of Law or the laws of the market. This conception, dominant in labor law, but also influential in civil rights and commercial boycott cases, identifies boycott as a deviant or law-threatening activity. The other model is based on the belief that the public good can be advanced by collective self-determination and discursive citizen participation in public debate. This model pictures group boycott practice as a democratic or law-enforcing activity.

The cognitive models of boycott have given rise to two different conceptions of the right to boycott. One conception, reflected in Justice Stevens's decision in *Trial Lawyers*, has defined the right to boycott in terms of what can be described as the story of interest group pluralism, a story that has assumed that political participation takes place in the official forums of government where special interest groups represent individual interests in an orderly and controlled manner. The other conception, reflected in Justice Stevens's *Claiborne Hardware* narrative, defines the right of democratic participation in terms of a theory of popular sovereignty or civic republicanism, a story that assumes that citizen involvement action, collective self-determination, is essential to a republican form of government.

The meaning of boycott in the law, however, has developed on the basis of imaginative categories structured by a metaphoric form of phantasy thinking, rather than a deductive, categorical, or definitional form of reason as usually assumed. Metaphor, radial categories, chaining within categories, prototype effects, and idealized cognitive models are what have influenced the way the legal mind has categorized boycott phenomena in the law. The compositional structure of the metaphoric narratives of boycott in the cases are thus constrained and enabled by a highly incoherent imaginative process. The fact that the same Justice could author the very different boycott narratives in *Trial Lawyers* and *Claiborne Hardware* is itself testimony to the incoherence of metaphoric thinking on the bench.

The legal mind is thus wedded to a sedimented cultural background ideology. This background ideology has two principle sources. The conception of judge as neutral decision maker enables and constrains the imaginative process of the legal mind. Ideology of the bench constrains the legal mind's ability to contemplate other imaginative possibilities. The legal mind is also sedimented by the ideology of a metaphoric transference that legitimates and conceals ideological preferences as the nonideological effects of neutral decision making.

The tools of legal analysis are used by judges as if they were neutral tools when in fact the tools are skewed by normative assumptions before they are ever even used in legal decision-making. The tools of legal analysis are normatively loaded because they can be shown to reflect cultural bias. Labor secondary boycotts are no more like a violent mob than are civil rights or business boycotts, and yet judges have tended to equate labor boycotts with violence, even when they are peaceful, because they define the legal meaning of boycott with default metaphors that constrain their ability to see the limits and mistakes of their imaginative work.

The right to boycott, crucial to democratic, social, and economic processes, has been recognized in the case law, but the right has been shaped by a legal imagination that has prevented the right from evolving organically. As we have seen, the right to boycott upheld in *Claiborne Hardware* has been limited to those rare instances where groups engage in pure political expression to pursue purely altruistic objectives. It would appear that the metaphors that signified the need for the judicial recognition of a right to boycott in *Claiborne Hardware* are now perceived by judges to be culturally irrelevant to today's corporate-driven mass culture. Thus, while the courts have extended constitutional protection to civil rights boycotts, that protection has come to cover a rather small number of cases, indeed, probably only one case, that of *Claiborne Hardware*.

What may explain the current insignificance of the metaphors of *Claiborne Hardware* is the power of an imaginative legal mind. In the realm of markets, judges imagine that the invisible hand of competition ensures that the system reaches an equilibrium state; in the realm of politics, judges imagine that the free flow of interest groups competing for the favors of government ensures a healthy balance in government. The role of law is thus limited to an imaginary balance or equilibrium state. The law is structured by a basic homeostasis metaphor that seeks to maintain balance between the economic and political power of dominant groups. The homeostasis metaphor may be a symptom of a psychological propensity of law enforcers and bureaucratic managers to see phenomena in the world as a system to be managed and buffered from external disturbances.

What is ignored is the possibility that the legal mind of the judge is the pivotal fact in law administration, and that the ideology of legal culture shapes the way that mind imaginatively constructs meaning of the world. The institutional constraint of judges as neutral adjudicators limits the ability of the legal imagination to contemplate new understandings about the world. Boycotts could be seen as examples of collective political dialogue that create a particular form of political meaning through action. Boycotting could be understood as an activity that is intrinsically necessary for extending political community to all groups in society.

The legal meaning of boycotts could be developed from an understanding of boycott as a dialogic practice necessary for political expression. Instead of analyzing boycott activity in terms of homeostatic functions, the legal meaning of boycotts could be re-imagined in terms of a deliberative politics among persons overcoming, through confrontation, the moral stasis of official power and authority. Thinking of boycotts as a dialogic process of deliberative politics should encourage judges to adopt a new metaphor of boycott; a metaphor traceable to a conception of democracy based on popular will.

Democratic re-enforcing metaphors are given little, if any, effect in the law of boycott because judges have used cognitive metaphors developed from a cultural background and from embodied experience that tend to relate boycott activity to destructive forces, diseases, or coercive activity. Boycott metaphors are constrained by default metaphors that have the ideological consequences of suppressing the recognition of other ways to understand the meaning of a group boycott. The recent wave of consumer and political boycotts, including cyberboycotts, suggests that the idealized cognitive models of judges may no longer be the best models for understanding the meaning of group boycott practice.

It may be that the diversity of boycott practice today will pose a challenge to the validity of the idealized cognitive models used by judges for comprehending the legal meaning of group boycott phenomena. The idea of homeostasis may come to be regarded as a performative act that no longer helps to give meaning to modern boycott practice. It is more likely, however, that the actual social practice of boycott will have changed long before judges ever realize that their boycott metaphors are obsolete. The current metaphors are too deeply embedded in the legal culture to allow a metaphoric paradigm shift.

Judges are, of course, like the rest of us. They, like us, use metaphors and idealized cognitive models in their work for the same reason we use them in our discourses, in our intellectual work, and in our everyday language. The homeostasis metaphor is a highly influential metaphor because it is animated by conceptual metaphors derived from bodily experiences we all share in common. The metaphors of judges may thus be deeply embedded in our cognitive thoughts, and thus the ideology of the metaphors may be an ideology deeply embedded in our society.

But, judges also bring to their imaginative work the unique ideology derived from their legal culture. The ideology of the legal culture creates its own imaginative world for dealing with the complexities of life. The ideology of adjudication creates a performative practice that can be examined by considering how the legal mind creates imaginative structures of thought to justify and legitimate the performative practice of judging. The chameleon-like quality of legal imagination, however, is hidden by the norms of the legal culture that attempts to persuade us that language is a neutral medium, that metaphors are merely interesting rhetorical devices and nothing more, and that law and adjudication is separate from politics.

Justice Stevens's image of boycott as a chameleon is thus apt because the metaphors judges have used to give meaning to group boycotts are not hard wired. Law, culture, and metaphor are inseparably related to imagined understandings of boycotts. Like the color of a chameleon, which fades and changes as context changes, the legal imagination, like the word boycott, relies upon metaphoric images for gaining cognitive meaning of phenomena. The chameleon-like quality of legal imagination, however, seems relatively stable and determinant because judges share a common culture and because they use embodied conceptual metaphors that are shared by all human beings. Understanding how legal imagination and ideology shape the legal mind may provide clues for developing new metaphors or new meanings for old metaphors judges have used in their work to permit the legal recognition of other ideologies of different cultures. The ideology of the legal mind is, as we have seen, the metaphoric reptile that Justice Stevens warned us about. This reptile is hidden in the legal imagination but can be seen if only we look more closely at the way the legal mind functions in adjudication.

Because metaphor performs a constitutive role in structuring the law's understanding of boycott phenomena, it is metaphor and not the cool reason of the law that actually defines the legal meaning of the word boycott. We should therefore want to know more about how metaphor actually works in creating legal meaning. We should want to know whether the law of boycott has become captured by a set of dead metaphors that are no longer capable of responding to the meaning of boycott in today's political and social culture. Metaphors in the law must be able to evolve and change in order to take on new meanings so that future generations can imaginatively express their own identity.

New boycott metaphors could be developed from an examination of how boycotts foster human development and democratic self-advancement through group action. The historical origins of the word boycott, for example, illustrate how the collective action of boycott advances the political identity of disempowered groups in society. We should think more about the role of boycott in Irish history and in American labor history. The history of boycott in Ireland and in America illustrates how boycott helped foster and shape a mass movement in labor and civil rights that was essential in bringing justice and social equality in the law and society. As an act of expression, or as an example of collective identity politics, boycott has been an important practice in the social and economic development of societies. This does not mean that boycotts are always necessary for achieving democratic values—that would be fantasy thinking—but rather it only means that law's regulation of boycott should be more sensitive to the role boycott performs in creating group identity in our culture and our society.

New metaphors of boycott "boycott is communicative action," "boycott is norm regulation," "boycott is contestability," "boycott is democratic practice" would enable judges to better acknowledge the democratic and free speech values of boycott practice. The metaphor "boycott is communicative action" might also enable legal decision makers to see the link between boycott and the political rally and the mass demonstration. At the very least, such an understanding of boycott could be used to recast the meaning of the default metaphors used in the boycott case law. New meaning of boycott might encourage judges and other lawmakers to adopt an understanding of labor and consumer boycotts and cyberboycotts more in keeping with the actual practices of these boycotts in America today.

To adopt new metaphors, judges do not have to turn their backs on stare decisis; judges can find new metaphors in cases like *Claiborne Hardware*. The metaphor of boycott as "soap box oratory" that enabled the Supreme Court in *Claiborne Hardware* to extend First Amendment protection to a civil rights boycott must be given more sway in other fields of law, especially labor and consumer boycotts. Instead of analyzing boycott activity in terms of the standard judicial metaphors, the legal meaning of boycotts could be re-examined by re-examining the history of the word. The history of the word provides a powerful illustration of how Irish tenants understood the meaning of their boycott against Captain Boycott as a deliberative democratic practice aimed at the unrestrained effects of illegitimate power and authority.

Of course, once it is widely recognized that legal descriptions of boycott phenomena are largely the product of metaphoric manipulation, that awareness itself should bring about renewed interest in the psychology of judging. Once legal thinkers understand the significance of metaphoric reasoning in the boycott case law, they may assume a new critical stance toward not only boycotts, but the legal mind itself. To do this, legal thinkers must recognize what Jerome Frank in the epigraph clearly realized, that judges are fallible human beings who possess a fallible imagination. We need to develop therefore a more explicit understanding of how the legal mind works. In this book, I have attempted to show how the link between cognitive theory and ideology might provide such an understanding.

Metaphor can become a way of exploiting the ambiguities in the law, and in the process of exploitation, metaphor can bring about real substantive changes in the law. A good analogy or a good metaphor may possess a sense of rightness, but it would be implausible to claim that there is only one right metaphor for every legal question. Because metaphor is part of the law and its process, judges and their institutions create and enforce the imaginative possibilities of law's metaphors. However, "we tend to forget that the judiciary is an institution when considering the rule of law."[1] We ignore how the institution of the judiciary influences the legal mind. The experience of adjudication as constraint is, as Duncan Kennedy has suggested, a social construct of an institutional culture that is obsessively committed to the denial of the political in bureaucratic workplaces.

In the institutions in which we work, we experience the same sort of denial. We are encouraged to be good colleagues and good team players and to maintain viewpoint neutrality. We are encouraged to suppress ideological concerns in our institutional environments. Like judges, we too, have reason to be anxious about our role as lawyers, judges, law professors, administrators, managers, students, workers, and so forth. We should be concerned about how our imagination and ideology is shaped by our institutional and bureaucratic workplaces. Does this mean we, too, are powerless to question this? Kennedy's answer is "that judges are like the rest of us. In our various positions within the bureaucratic institutions of our system, we do the same. Like them, we have to confront the question of bad faith, and, like them, we might gain from critique a margin for boldness."[2]

Because judges both select and are seized by metaphors, metaphor carries considerable power and authority in the law. This power can be critiqued. The denial and suppression of the ideological in the law can be challenged, scrutinized, and critiqued by examining how imagination and ideology enable lawmakers to deny the ideology of their work. The violence of the law can be exposed. New metaphors establishing new default rules in the law can be discovered for evaluating the ethos of law's authority. Understanding law's character can permit us to explore and analyze the legitimacy of legal authority in a new way. Legal metaphors that are deeply entrenched in the judicial imagination can be revealed to be "dead metaphors" that no longer accurately capture the meaning of phenomena.[3] New legal doctrine and new legal rights can be created through the effort to bring out different imaginative ideas for enhancing legal thought. All of this can bring about a margin for boldness. "The reptile hidden in the weeds" can be exposed if only we look to the source responsible for its concealment.

I hope I have shown why the word boycott has had an interesting and controversial history. The word and its practice has influenced the development of law and culture in Ireland and in America. And, yet, what is perhaps the most interesting aspect of this word is that after more than a century of usage, we are still attempting to discover its meaning. We owe a great debt to Captain Boycott and the Irish tenants of County Mayo since they have provided us with an extremely interesting and important word. The search for the meaning of this word will continue to provoke controversy and require a margin of boldness as each new generation struggles to understand the nature and significance of boycott for their time and their era.

Notes & Index

NOTES & INDEX

NOTES

NOTES

PROLOGUE: BOYCOTT AND THE REPTILE HIDDEN IN THE WEEDS

1. See *NAACP v. Claiborne Hardware Co.*, 458 U.S. 886, 888 (1982).

2. The foreground/background shift is a technique used by both critical legal studies and cognitive legal scholars. See Duncan Kennedy, *A Critique of Adjudication {fin de siècle}* 248 (1997); Steven L. Winter, *An Upside/Down View of the Countermajoritarian Difficulty*, 69 Tex. L. Rev. 1881, 1881–1890 (1997).

3. 458 U.S. 886 (1982).

4. 456 U.S. 212 (1982).

5. 493 U.S. 411 (1990).

6. See Eleanor Rosch, *Cognitive Representations of Semantic Categories*, 104 J. of Experimental Psychology 192 (1975).

7. See Eleanor Rosch, *Principles of Categorization*, in *Cognition and Categorization* 27, 35–37 (Eleanor Rosch and Barbara B. Lloyd eds. 1978); Steven L. Winter, *Radial Categories*, in *A Clearing in the Forest: How the Study of the Mind Changes Our Understanding of Life and Law* (Univ. of Chicago Press, forthcoming).

8. George Lakoff, *Women, Fire, and Dangerous Things: What Categories Reveal about the Mind* 79–114 (1987).

9. Ludwig Wittgenstein, *Philosophical Investigations* 31e (G. E. M. Ancombe trans. 1953).

10. See Steven L. Winter, *Radial Categories*, in *Clearing in the Forest* supra.

11. Id. at 20. See also George Lakoff, *Women, Fire, and Dangerous Things* 80–81 (1987).

12. This example is taken from Benjamin Lee Whorf, *Language, Thought, and Reality: Selected Writings of Benjamin Lee Whorf* 260 (John Caroll ed. 1956). Steven L. Winter has illustrated how this example establishes how the linguistic category *hand* is a radial category. Steven L. Winter, *Compositional Structure*, in *Clearing in the Forest* supra.

13. George Lakoff, *Women, Fire, and Dangerous Things* supra at 84. The idealized cognitive model of mother thus has certain prototypical effects that permit us to understand extensions from the radial category to subcases of the

category *mother*. Another popular example is the category *bachelor*. Id. at 85–86. That category is normally defined as *unmarried men*. The pope is unmarried, and yet it would be odd to refer to him as a bachelor. What permits us to rule the pope out of the category *bachelor* are the background assumptions from our culture used to identify unmarried men of typical marriageable age who are available for heterosexual marriage. A set of normative background assumptions enable us to classify various males as being *in* or *out* of the bachelor category.

14. Chapter 1 will examine the source of the Zulu metaphor. Suffice it to say that there is a long history to the use of African metaphors in Irish literature and culture. See Declan Kiberd, *Inventing Ireland: The Literature of the Modern Nation* 407–8, 611 (1996). Roddy Doyle's story, "The Commitments," subsequently made into a highly successful movie, for example, depicted poor teenagers in contemporary Dublin as "soul" musicians who saw themselves as the "Blacks" of Europe and Ireland. Roddy Doyle, *The Barrytown Trilogy* 13 (1992) ("the Irish are the niggers of Europe, and Dubliners are the niggers of Ireland, and the Northside Dubliners are the niggers of Dublin.").

15. Chapter 2 will examine the source of the tiger and murder metaphors of labor boycott adjudications at early common law.

16. Gary Peller, *The Metaphysics of American Law*, 73 Calif. L. Rev. 1151, 1182 (1985).

17. In the last decade or so, there has been new insight developed from the study of how legal interpretation of rules is invariably unpredictable. Critical legal studies scholars, as well as legal feminists, law and literature, and critical race theorists, have insisted that legal decision makers have a choice between two (or more) interpretations or definitions of a particular legal rule or doctrine, and that the choice made can have a profound ideological consequence for the adjudication of some cases. See Gary Minda, *Postmodern Legal Movements: Law and Jurisprudence at Century's End* 106–88 (1995). Much of the effort of the critics has focused on how judicial interpretations of the formal rules have distinct ideological effects for determining the interests of groups. Duncan Kennedy, *A Critique of Adjudication* supra at 59–66. In building on this work, this book attempts to show how the cognitive process of factual phenomena is fundamental for understanding the ideology of adjudication of group boycotts. Cognitive theory and the study of metaphor can offer useful insight for understanding why predictable and clear rules (rule determinacy) can be as problematic, and perhaps even more troubling, as rule indeterminacy, which has been the focus of much of the criticism of critical legal studies. The formal legal rules may seem predictable, clear, and even fair on the surface of the legal text, but, as this book will argue, there is a background to the text, shaped by an imaginative and metaphoric form of reason that give the rules a distinct normative and ideological orientation. We should be interested in investigating how the background world of meaning influences and shapes the legal mind.

18. John R. Searle, *Metaphor*, in *Metaphor and Thought* 83, 96 (Andrew Ortony ed., 2d ed 1993).

19. Michael Frost, *Greco-Roman Analysis of Metaphoric Reasoning*, 2 J. of Legal Writing 113, 118 (1996), quoting Aristotle's observation that metaphors are devices that "give names to nameless things," in Aristotle's *The Rhetoric of Aristotle* 188 (Leon Golden trans. 1968).

20. Duncan Kennedy, *A Critique of Adjudication* supra at 211.

21. See Michael Frost, *Greco-Roman Analysis of Metaphoric Reasoning* supra at 115–28.

22. Thomas Ross, *Metaphor and Paradox*, 23 Ga. L. Rev. 1053, 1053 (1989).

1. CAPTAIN BOYCOTT, THE IRISH REVOLUTION, AND METAPHOR

1. The historical sources relevant to the boycott of Captain Boycott, from which the discussion in the text principally draws, include: T. W. Moody, *Davitt and Irish Revolution, 1846–82* (1981); Janet Marlow, *Captain Boycott and the Irish* (1973); T. H. Corfe, *The Troubles of Captain Boycott, Part I and II*, in 14 *History Today* 758–64, 854–62 (1964); A. Matris, *A Bad Word Made in Connacht*, 14 The Catholic Bulletin 798 (1924). For a history of the Irish land question in nineteenth-century Irish history, see Philip Bull, *Land, Politics, and Nationalism: A Study of the Irish Land Question* (1996); W. E. Vaughan, *Landlords and Tenants in Mid-Victorian Ireland* (1994); W. E. Vaughan, *Landlords and Tenants in Ireland, 1848–1904* (1984); Barbara L. Solow, *The Land Question and the Irish Economy, 1870–1903* (1971). For materials relevant to Irish nationalism and the sociopolitical history of nineteenth-century Ireland see Peter Grey, *The Irish Famine* (1995); Cecil Woodham-Smith, *The Great Hunger* (1962); J. E. Pomfret, *The Struggle for Land in Ireland, 1800–1923* (1930).

2. T. H. Corfe, *The Troubles of Captain Boycott, Part I*, in 14 supra at 758–64 (1964).

3. It was impractical for Irish landlords to reside on their estates for a number of reasons. First, because their estates were so vast, they could not live simultaneously on all their estates. Second, their role as the social and political leaders necessitated residences in other places. The earl of Erne, for example, was chief secretary of Ireland on three occasions and viceroy of India from 1869–1872. W. E. Vaughan, *Landlords and Tenants in Mid-Victorian Ireland* supra at 4.

4. Id. at 132.

5. Id. at 1.

6. See T. W. Moody, *Davitt and Irish Revolution* 418–19 (1981).

7. See W. E. Vaughan, *Landlords and Tenants in Mid-Victorian Ireland* supra at 44–67. Professor Vaughan's analysis of estate management shows that the great landlords of nineteenth-century Ireland relied upon trained professional agents to manage their vast estates. "The training of agents was as varied as their functions. Some were solicitors. . . . some added a knowledge of agriculture to

a liberal education. . . . some were ex-soldiers, such as Captain Boycott." Id. at 110. Vaughan notes that it was "widely believed that agents were often the cause of trouble between landlords and tenants." Id. at 111. One agent is said to have ordered a tenant to "decapitate a dog and present its severed head at the office, because he disapproved of tenants keeping hunting dogs." Id. at 111–12.

8. Id. at 159–60.

9. James Redpath, *Talks of Ireland* 215 (1881). See also H. W. Laidler, *Boycotts and the Labor Struggle: Economic and Legal Aspects* 23 (1913).

10. W. E. Vaughan, *Landlords and Tenants in Mid-Victorian Ireland* supra at 48; W. E. Vaughan, *Landlords and Tenants in Ireland, 1848–1904* 14 (1984).

11. While there was disagreement on the question of whether rent levels at Lord Erne's Mayo estates were above market evaluations, no evidence could be found to indicate that he or his agent were "rackrenting." See also Janet Marlow, *Captain Boycott and the Irish* 136 (1973).

12. W. E. Vaughan, *Landlords and Tenants in Mid-Victorian Ireland* supra at 124–25.

13. Id. at 111–12.

14. Forty-odd years earlier, following the Great Irish Famine of 1846–47, a secret society known by an Irish woman's name, "Molly Maguire," operated in north central Ireland to pressure English landlords and their agents to give food and assistance to the starving poor. The "Mollies" perpetuated a regime of resistance based on acts of violence and murder. In America, the Molly Maguires immigrated to the coal fields of western Pennsylvania and became a formidable secret society that was also known to practice acts of violence against the coal companies and their agents. See Harold W. Aurand, *From the Molly Maguires to the United Mine Workers, 1896–97* (1980); Wayne G. Broehl Jr., *The Molly Maguires* (1964). The Irish peasant farmers involved in the boycotts during the Land War period, however, were less organized as a group and were generally committed to nonviolent means of civil disobedience. While acts of violence against landlords and their agents did occur during the Land War period, they were not numerous. See W. E. Vaughan, *Landlords and Tenants in Mid-Victorian Ireland* 1661 (1994). It is quite likely, however, that the violence associated with the Irish "Mollies" in north central Ireland colored the way the Irish establishment saw the tenant boycotts of the later Land War period.

15. H. W. Laidler, *Boycotts and the Labor Struggle* supra at 23–27 quoting 5 Mag. of W. History 212–14 (1886).

16. See T. W. Moody, *Davitt and Irish Revolution* 846–82 (1981). See also W. E. Vaughan, *Landlords and Tenants in Mid-Victorian Ireland* supra at 109–10, 178.

17. Philip Bull, *Land, Politics, and Nationalism* (1996). Professor Bull argues that the nexus between the issues of land and Irish nationalism was so strong in the nineteenth century that "one issue became effectively a metaphor

for the other." Id. at 4. The metaphor developed as "a consequence of the growing confidence of the tenant farmers, for whom advances in their tenure conditions, culminating in the 1881 Land Act, had engendered expectations of eventual control of their land and with it a new status for themselves socially which could only be fully realized through an acknowledgment of their distinctive nationality—a symbolic reversal of the past demeaning subjection of their Irish and Catholic identity." Id. at 95.

18. For background concerning the Irish Land League, see Declan Kiberd, *Inventing Ireland: The Literature of the Modern Nation* 87–88 (1996); Joseph Lee, *The Land War*, in *Milestones in Irish History* 106 (Liam De Paor ed. 1986); T. W. Moody, *Davitt and Irish Revolution* (1981).

19. F. S. L. Lyons, *Ireland since the Famine* 167 (1963).

20. See T. W. Moody, *Davitt and Irish Revolution* supra at 418–19; T. H. Corfe, *The Troubles of Captain Boycott, Part I*, in 14 *History Today* at 762 (1964).

21. Captain Boycott's escapades on Achill Island are described in Theresa McDonald's *Achill Island: Archaeology, History, Folklore* 171, 174, 179, 183, 189, 191, 198, 230–33, 274, 298, 315 (1997).

22. Id. at 232–33.

23. Id.

24. Id.

25. T. H. Corfe, *The Troubles of Captain Boycott, Part I*, in 14 *History Today* 758, 759 (1964).

26. W. E. Vaughan, *Landlords and Tenants in Mid-Victorian Ireland* supra at 112.

27. In the spring of 1997, I visited Lord Erne's Lough Mask House, which is situated on the outskirts of Ballinrobe, Ireland. The house is privately owned. The current owner, a Mr. John Daly, purchased the house from Boycott's estate. The house is located on plantation-like grounds, with an iron gate, gate house, and a beautiful winding road. The house itself is boxlike. The ruins of a castle are located behind the house. While the house is not as big as one might expect, it was a considerable structure when compared to the other small farmhouses located in the area.

On the day I visited the Lough Mask House, I was greeted by Mr. Daly's wife, who informed me that the Daly family had a rather good impression of Captain Boycott. Ms. Daly's view of the boycott affair was that the Captain was "in the wrong place, at the wrong time;" that he "was just doing his job, collecting what amounted to 'taxes;'" and "Captain Boycott was the real victim." I had the distinct impression that Ms. Daly was somehow emotionally affected by what happened to the "poor" Captain and that she wanted to set the record straight once and for all. As I left the Lough Mask House that day, I wondered if the "poor" Captain Boycott would have thought kindly of Ms. Daly's gallant effort to defend his reputation.

28. The only authoritative history of Michael Davitt and the Land League is T. W. Moody, *Davitt and Irish Revolution* (1981). Moody had sole possession of Davitt's personal papers for many years after Davitt's death. The Davitt papers are now held at the Library at Trinity College, Dublin, Ireland. Moody's book is now out of print. As Janet Marlow has noted in her book on Captain Boycott, which is also out of print, Michael Davitt has never been accorded "proper stature" in Ireland even though he, along with Charles Parnell, was a key player in the Irish revolution during the nineteenth and twentieth centuries. Janet Marlow, *Captain Boycott and the Irish* supra at 276.

29. T. W. Moody, *Davitt and Irish Revolution* supra at xv–xvi.

30. Id. at xvi. The new departure represented by the Land League was a strategic response to the economic crises of 1879 that had raised new questions about the legitimacy of the landlord-tenant relation.

31. Quoted in T. W. Moody, *Davitt and Irish Revolution* supra at 438.

32. There was some dispute about the actual rent reduction granted by Lord Erne. See Janet Marlow, *Captain Boycott and the Irish* supra at 136, 158. In a subsequent hearing before the Bessborough commission, Boycott stated that Lord Erne had granted a 20 percent abatement, but on other occasions, he stated that it was only 10 percent. Id. at 158 (footnote). T. H. Corfe reported that the rent reduction amounted to 2s. in the pound. T. H. Corfe, *The Troubles of Captain Boycott, Part I* supra at 761.

33. Janet Marlow, *Captain Boycott and the Irish* supra at 138.

34. Id.

35. Conditions in the west of Ireland were, even at this time, still affected by the Great Potato Blight of 1845–50. See Peter Grey, *The Irish Famine* (1995); Cecil Woodham-Smith, *The Great Hunger* (1962). The *Freeman's Journal*, an Ulster newspaper covering the west of Ireland, reported that in Mayo there was "[a]ir sick with the smell of the potato blight" and "[d]ay after day nothing but lightning and rain to spread the havoc." T. H. Corfe, *The Troubles of Captain Boycott, Part I* supra at 760.

36. Janet Marlow, *Captain Boycott and the Irish* supra at 136. It was far from clear whether the dispute was the result of the arbitrary manner in which rent was collected by Captain Boycott or the inflexible position maintained by Lord Erne on the question of the rent abatement. Indeed, the record fails to refute the distinct possibility that Captain Boycott was merely doing his job as a rent collector and that Lord Erne was charging a fair rent under the conditions. His offer of a 10 percent rent reduction may have been fair given prevailing agricultural incomes. For economic evidence suggesting that landlords were at this time charging fair market rent see W. E. Vaughan, *Landlords and Tenants in Mid-Victorian Ireland* supra at 44–66. See also W. E. Vaughan, *Landlords and Tenants in Ireland, 1848–1904* (1984).

37. T. H. Corfe, *The Troubles of Captain Boycott, Part I* supra at 760.

38. Id.

39. Captain Boycott's residence at Achill Island, both before and after the boycott, is noted in Theresa McDonald's *Achill Island: Archaeology, History, Folklore* 230–33, 274, 298, 336 (1997).

40. See T. H. Corfe, *The Troubles of Captain Boycott, Part I* supra at 762–63.

41. Janet Marlow, *Captain Boycott and the Irish* supra at 138.

42. Id. at 138–39.

43. T. H. Corfe, *The Troubles of Captain Boycott, Part II* supra at 855.

44. Janet Marlow, *Captain Boycott and the Irish* supra at 151–52, 157–58.

45. Id. at 157.

46. Id.

47. T. W. Moody, *Davitt and Irish Revolution* supra at 438.

48. Id. at 450–51.

49. Id. at 453.

50. Id. at 454.

51. Janet Marlow, *Captain Boycott and the Irish* supra at 263. This money failed to cover his total expenses incurred during the military takeover of his estate. Id.

52. This account is provided in Janet Marlow's book, *Captain Boycott and the Irish* supra at 145. T. H. Corfe suggests that the term *boycott* may have first been used in Ulster, where the *Belfast Newsletter* had proposed a boycott relief fund for Captain Boycott, contributing to the identification of the captain's name with the boycotting activities directed against him. T. H. Corfe, *The Troubles of Captain Boycott, Part II* supra at 857. But Corfe also notes that Father O'Malley suggested the use of the name and that it was James Redpath, the American journalist, who popularized it in letters to American newspapers. Id. at 858. Corfe notes that "[b]y November 9th an Irish reporter [near] Ballinrobe [where Lord Erne's Lough Mask House was located] was writing about the policy which has added the ugly word 'boycotting' to the English language." Id. Two days later, the same reporter announced that Captain Boycott's "fame has immortalized his name in the English dictionary." Id.

53. Janet Marlow, *Captain Boycott and the Irish* supra at 145.

54. See W. E. Vaughan, *Landlords and Tenants in Mid-Victorian Ireland* supra at 178–79.

55. The novel was published by Michael Rooney, *Captain Boycott* (1946). The movie *Captain Boycott* was not successful. A movie reviewer stated that "[w]hat might have been a profound and moving picture becomes the light prank of a series of puppets dangled against a diffused naive background." The acting was described as "weak," and the historical importance of the event was lost in the script. Liam O'Laughire, *Captain Boycott*, 16 The Bell 64–68 (1947–48).

56. While the word *boycott* has a relatively recent origin, what we now know to be a boycott—a collective effort to withdraw and to induce others to

withdraw social and economic relations with another—has had a long and ancient history (*Webster's New International Dictionary*, 3d ed., s.v. "boycott"). Groups of people were boycotting since the very dawn of recorded history.

57. The Great Mutiny took place in the year 1797 when sailors in the British Navy refused to take orders from their superiors and threatened a revolution at large during England's war with France. These events helped to frame Herman Melville's epic story *Billy Budd and the Encantadas* (1891).

58. See W. E. Vaughan, *Landlords and Tenants in Mid-Victorian Ireland* supra at 161.

59. The orthodox interpretation of this period found in J. E. Pomfret's classic work *The Struggle for Land in Ireland, 1800–1923* (1930) was that predatory landlordism was a central cause of agrarian agitation and land reform in Ireland. It was Pomfret who helped to give predatory landlordism a central place in nineteenth-century Ireland. The accuracy of Pomfret's predatory landlord thesis has been recently questioned by a number of contemporary Irish historians. See W. E. Vaughan, *Landlords and Tenants in Mid-Victorian Ireland* (1994); Barbara L. Solow, *The Land Question and the Irish Economy, 1870–1903* (1971).

W. E. Vaughan and Barbara Solow suggest that the orthodox view, which placed emphasis on the predatory landlordism thesis, was based on an inaccurate description of what the landlord-tenant relation was like for the average tenant. W. E. Vaughan describes how most landlords were not like Captain Boycott. They did not exploit their tenants by extracting large rent increases; rent increases were in fact only about 20 percent higher during the Land War years. Evictions were not common, and except for a few cases like Captain Boycott, landlords as a group were neither "bad" nor predatory as they have been made out to be. Barbara Solow's study of the period suggests that most Irish tenants during the Land War period paid well below a fair market rent. See also Philip Bull, *Land, Politics, and Nationalism* (1996).

60. As Professor Vaughan has noted:

> It is difficult now, looking back to the 1960s and early 1970s, to recapture the power of this interpretation, which gave the predatory landlord a central place in nineteenth-century Irish history. It was what most people believed; it was a belief shared by many who shared few other beliefs; it had a powerful teleological attraction in that it explained the land war and the abolition of landlordism. (W. E. Vaughan, *Landlords and Tenants in Mid-Victorian Ireland* at vi. [1994]).

61. Id. at 20–102.

62. See Barbara L. Solow, *The Land Question and the Irish Economy, 1870–1903* (1971).

63. W. E. Vaughan, *Landlords and Tenants in Mid-Victorian Ireland* supra at viii.

64. Id.

65. Id.

66. Id. at vi.

67. W. E. Vaughan, *Landlords and Tenants in Ireland, 1848–1904* supra at 31–32, citing, James Donnelly Jr., *Landlord and Tenant in Nineteenth-Century Ireland* (1973); Samuel Clark, *The Social Composition of the Land League*, 17 Ir. Hist. Stud. 68 (Sept. 1971).

68. W. E. Vaughan, *Landlords and Tenants in Ireland, 1848–1904* supra at 35.

69. Id. (emphasis added).

2. ORIGINS OF BOYCOTT IN AMERICA

1. See, e.g., Christopher L. Tomlins, *The State and the Unions, Labor Relations Law, and the Organized Labor Movement in America, 1880–1960* (1985); Almont Lindsey, *The Pullman Strike* 16 (1942).

2. Stereotypes of landlord and tenant in Ireland during Captain Boycott's day are described in Philip Bull, *Land, Politics, and Nationalism* 10 (1996).

3. See Pauline Maier, *From Resistance to Revolution: Colonial Radicals and the Development of American Opposition to Britain, 1765–1776* 114–22 (1972).

4. Id. "The enduring arguments for nonimportation were, then, above all political. It offered the 'wisest and only peaceful method' for Americans to recover their liberty. Moreover, that was legal and seemed to promise success." Id. at 119.

5. C. Edwin Baker, *Human Liberty and Freedom of Speech* 189 (1989). Professor Baker explains how the "economic or social boycott" parallels the mass demonstration of our revolution:

> In both the demonstration and the boycott, people combine into a group, an assembly or association, and they embody their expression of values in their practice. In both, people hope and expect that this form of expression will be disruptive and exert pressure to change. In both cases, disruption results when each member of the group individually acts in a way that she clearly has a right to act, but in a way contrary to the normal routine that others expect and on which, to some extent, others depend. Although in both the boycott and the mass demonstration, the possibility of placing pressure on others can be crucial to the motivation of the participants, their protest behavior is also in itself expressive, value-based conduct, independent of the pressure they impose. The boycotter affirms that under present conditions she considers purchases from or interactions with the boycotted party to be objectionable. The rally participant considers her participation, the protest symbolized by her presence, to be ethically and personally the right thing to do at this time.

6. See Hagai Hurvitz, *American Labor Law and the Doctrine of Entrepreneurial Property Rights: Boycotts, Courts, and the Judicial Reorientation of 1886–1895*, 8 Ind. Rel. L. J. 307 (1986); Ellen Kelman, *American Labor Law and Legal Formalism: How 'Legal Logic' Shaped and Vitiated the Rights of American Workers*, 58 St. John's L. Rev. 1 (1983).

7. See *State v. Glidden*, 8 A. 890 (Conn. 1887); *Grump v. Commonwealth*, 84 Va. 927 (1888).

8. See James B. Atleson, *Confronting Judicial Values: Revisiting the Law of Work in a Common Law System*, 45 Buff. L. Rev. 435, 440 (1997).

9. Id. See generally William Forbath, *Law and the Shaping of the American Labor Movement* (1991).

10. See Duncan Kennedy, *A Critique of Adjudication* 249 (1997). "Labor and capital [were] each organized, with individual workers and unions on one side and capitalist enterprises of different sizes and structures on the other." Id.

11. See M. Turner, *The Early American Labor Conspiracy Cases: Their Place in Labor Law* 39–58 (1967). "No American workers were sentenced to jail before the Civil War, and most fines ranged $1.00 to $10.00." V. Hattam, *Unions and Politics: The Court and American Labor* 57–58 (Ph.D. dissertation, 1987), cited in W. Forbath, *The Shaping of the American Labor Movement*, 102 Harv. L. Rev. 1111, 1150, n. 170 (1989). See also Gary Minda, *The Common Law, Labor, and Antitrust*, 11 Indus. Rel. L. J. 461, 487 (1989); Wyth Holt, *Labor Conspiracy Cases in the United States 1805–1842: Bias and Legitimation in Common Law Adjudication*, 22 Osgoode Hall L. J. 591 (1984).

12. See Christopher Tomlins, *Law, Labor, and Ideology in Early American Republic* pt. 2 (1993).

13. See William Forbath, *Law and the Shaping of the American Labor Movement* supra; Robert J. Stanfeld, *The Invention of Free Labor: The Employment Relation in English and American Law and Culture* 1350–1870 (1991).

14. 8 A. 890 (Conn. 1887).

15. Id. at 898.

16. Id. at 894.

17. Id.

18. Id. at 896–97 (quoting the story as narrated by Mr. Justin McCarthy, "an Irish gentleman of learning and ability," who, according to Judge Carpenter, was recognized as "good authority" [896–97]) (emphasis added).

19. Id. at 896.

20. Id.

21. Id.

22. Id.

23. See George Lakoff and Mark Turner, *More Than Cool Reason: A Field Guide to Poetic Metaphor* 166–69 (1989).

24. Id. at 166.

25. Id.

26. Id. at 170–72.

27. Id. at 172.

28. The metaphoric meaning of the tiger metaphor can be helpful for explaining why *wildcat* strikes (strikes by employees without union authorization) have been found to be illegal even when they would be lawful when authorized by the union. Unauthorized strikes are imaginatively structured by the knowledge of a wild animal, known to have bestial instincts and a drive toward violence.

29. Consider, for example, the less threatening image of tigers in William Blake's wonderful poem, "The Tyger":

Tyger! Tyger! burning bright
In the forests of the night,
What immortal hand or eye
Could frame thy fearful symmetry?

In what distant deeps or skies
Burnt the fire of thine eyes?
On what wings dare he aspire?
What the hand dare seize the fire?

And what shoulder, and what art,
Could twist the sinews of thy heart?
And when thy heart began to beat,
What dread hand forged thy dread feet?

What the hammer? what the chain?
In what furnace was thy brain?
What the anvil? what dread grasp
Dare its deadly terrors clasp?

When the stars threw down their spears,
And watered heaven with their tears,
Did he smile his work to see?
Did he who made the Lamb make thee?

Tyger! Tyger! burning bright
In the forests of the night,
What immortal hand or eye,
Dare frame thy fearful symmetry?

30. *State v. Glidden,* 8 A. 890, 897 (Conn. 1887).

31. Id. at 897.

32. The Zulu analogy was a popular reference made in nearly all newspaper accounts of the Captain Boycott story. See Janet Marlow, *Captain Boycott and the Irish* 157–58 (1973). In January 1879, one year before the Captain Boycott incident, Zulus had inflicted a disastrous defeat on a British force in Isandula, Africa.

33. Id. at 894.

34. Id. at 897.

35. 84 Va. 927, 6 S.E. 620 (1888).

36. *Grump,* 84 Va. at 939.

37. 221 U.S. 418 (1911). For the historical background of the decision, see Laidler, *Boycotts and the Labor Struggle* 134–50 (1913); Harold C. Livesay, *Samuel Gompers and Organized Labor in America* 144–47, 162 (1978).

38. 221 U.S. at 439 (emphasis added).

39. Id. at 439.

40. The *American Federationist* was established in 1893 by the American Federation of Labor (AFL). Gompers served as the newspaper's editor, reporter, columnist, and proofreader. The AFL's "We Don't Patronize" list was in fact compiled in response to the blacklist, one of the most insidious but effective forms of boycott practiced by employee groups.

41. *Gompers v. Bucks Stove & Range Co.,* 221 U.S. at 420–21 n. 1 (1911). Gompers and two other union officers denied the court's injunction and were subsequently cited for contempt of court. The conviction was upheld by the Supreme Court of the District of Columbia, and Gompers received a one-year sentence. During the appeal process, however, the president of the Bucks Stove & Range Company died, and his successor dropped the case against Gompers, allowing Gompers to avoid a term in jail.

42. *Gompers,* 221 U.S. at 451–52. Because the union and the company settled the civil action from which the civil contempt proceedings arose, the Court concluded that the contempt convictions against Gompers and other union leaders could not stand. Id.

43. The *Gompers* decision, along with the Court's decision in *Lowe v. Lawlor,* 208 U.S. 274 (1908) [the *Danbury Hatters* case], ushered in the infamous era of the labor injunction. See Felix Frankfurter and Nathan Greene, *The Labor Injunction* (1930).

44. *Gompers,* 221 U.S. at 439.

45. Id.

46. Id.

47. Id.

48. Id. at 437. The Court cited in support of its conclusion a number of state and federal decisions finding that publication of a boycott could be a means of continuing an unlawful object.

49. Id.

50. The publicity could be seen as analogous to so-called signal picketing, which courts have since treated as conduct involving "an automatic response to a signal rather than a reasoned response to an idea." See *NLRB v. Retail Store Employees Union, Local 1001 (Safeco)*, 447 U.S. 607, 619 (1980) (Stevens, J., concurring). Other justices have made similar distinctions. See, e.g., *Bakery & Pastry Drivers Local 802 v. Wohl*, 315 U.S. 769, 776–77 (1942) (Douglas, J., concurring) (distinguishing between speech and speech-plus activity); see also *Amalgamated Food Employees Union Local 590 v. Logan Valley Plaza, Inc.*, 391 U.S. 308, 336 (1968) (Harlan, J., dissenting); *NAACP v. Buton*, 371 U.S. 415, 453 (1963) (Harlan, J., dissenting).

51. A number of subsequent decisions of the Court seem to cast a dark shadow of doubt over the *Gompers* decision. In *Police Dep't of the City of Chicago v. Moseley*, for example, the Supreme Court invalidated an ordinance that prohibited picketing near public schools unless the picketing was related to a labor dispute (408 U.S. 92 [1972]). As Justice Marshall argued for the majority, "[The infirmity of the ordinance is] that it describes permissible picketing in terms of its subject matter. . . . [A]bove all else, the First Amendment means that government has no power to restrict expression because of its message, its idea, its subject matter, or its content." Id. at 95–96; see also *Carey v. Brown*, 447 U.S. 455 (1980) (holding that peaceful residential picketing deserves as much protection as communications concerning an employer's stand on civil rights or other political matters).

52. Steven L. Winter, *Clearing in the Forest* supra at 15.

53. *State v. Glidden*, 8 A. 890, 894 (Conn. 1887).

54. 310 U.S. 88, 104–5 (1940).

55. See, e.g., *Giboney v. Empire Storage & Ice Co.*, 336 U.S. 490, 501 (1949); *NLRB v. Retail Store Employees Union, Local 1001 (Safeco)*, 447 U.S. 607, 612–13 (1980).

56. *NLRB v. Retail Store Employees Union, Local 1001 (Safeco)*, 447 U.S. 607 (1980).

57. The idea that legal decision making is dependent on the embeddedness of *sedimentation* of background assumptions can be attributed to Merleau-Ponty. See Steven L. Winter, *An Upside/Down View of the Countermajoritarian Difficulty*, 69 Tex. L. Rev. 1881, 1883 n. 7 (1997), citing, M. Langer, *Merleau-Ponty's Phenomenology of Perception: A Guide and Commentary* 34 (1989).

58. See Samuel Yellen, *American Labor Struggles* 3 (1980).

59. Id. at 21–40.

60. Id. at 42.

61. Christopher L. Tomlins, *The State and the Unions* 11 (1985).

62. See Harold C. Livesay, *Samuel Gompers and Organized Labor in America* 21–40 (1978).

63. Id. at 40.

64. For a general historical account of the "Riot," see Paul Avrich, *The Haymarket Tragedy* 197–214 (1984).

65. Samuel Yellen, *American Labor Struggles* supra at 828.

66. See Paul Avrich, *The Haymarket Tragedy* 208 (1984).

67. See Christopher L. Tomlins, *The State and the Unions* supra at 59.

68. See Laidler, *Boycotts and the Labor Struggle* supra at 72.

69. Id.

70. See Christopher L. Tomlins, *The State and the Unions* 60–67 (1985).

71. See Wayne G. Broehl Jr., *The Molly Maguires* 1–70 (1964).

72. See T. W. Moody, *Davitt and Irish Revolution* 418–20, 438 (1981).

73. The Haymarket incident was more a police riot than a labor riot. See Paul Avrich, *The Haymarket Tragedy* (1984).

74. For an analysis of subsequent images of violence in Labor jurisprudence see Dianne Avery, *Images of Violence in Labor Jurisprudence: The Regulation of Picketing and Boycotts, 1894–1921*, Buff. L. Rev. 1, 37 (1989). See also *Casey v. Cincinnati Typographical Union No. 3*, 45 F. 135, 143 (6th Cir. 1891). See also *Toledo A.A. & N.M. Ry. Co. v. Pennsylvania Co.*, 54 F. 730, 738 (6th Cir. 1893) ("As usually understood, a boycott is a combination of many to cause a loss . . . by coercing others." [738]).

75. *Consolidated Steel & Wire Co. v. Murray*, 80 G. 811, 819–20 (N.D. Ohio 1897).

76. Id. at 828.

77. Hagai Hurvitz, *American Labor Law and the Doctrine of Entrepreneurial Property Rights: Boycotts, Courts, and the Judicial Reorientation of 1886–1895*, 8 Ind. Rel. L. J. 307, 311 (1986), citing and quoting, *People v. Wilzig*, 4 N.Y. Crim. 403, 426–28 (N.Y. Cty. of Oyer and Terminer 1886).

78. *Gray v. Building Trades Council*, 97 N.W. 663, 666 (Minn. 1903).

79. *Casey v. Cincinnati Typographical Union No. 3*, 45 F. 135, 143 (6th Cir. 1891). See also *Toledo A.A. & N.M. Ry. Co. v. Pennsylvania Co.*, 54 F. 730, 738 (6th Cir. 1893) ("As usually understood, a boycott is a combination of many to cause a loss . . . by coercing others" [738]).

80. *Oxley Stove Co. v. Coopers' Int'l Union of N. Am.*, 72 F. 695, 698–99 (D. Kansas 1896).

3. BOYCOTTS AND COGNITIVE THEORY

1. Eve V. Clark and Herbert H. Clark, *When Nouns Surface as Verbs*, 55 Language: J. of Linguistic Soct'y of America 767, 781 (1979).

2. See chapter 7 infra.

3. See Mark Johnson, *The Body in the Mind: The Bodily Basis of Meaning, Imagination, and Reason* xv (1987). The discussion in this chapter and in chapter 4 will focus primarily on how cognitive theory helps to explain the judicial

adjudication of boycott problems in the case law. Cognitive theory also helps to explain the way legislators understand boycott phenomena. The metaphor "boycott as disease," for example, has influenced the way legislators have understood secondary labor boycotts. See chapter 5 supra. Judges and legislators have both used patterns of prereflective thought based on physical and cultural experiences in organizing their abstract conceptualizations about phenomena.

4. George Lakoff and Mark Turner, *More Than Cool Reason: A Field Guide to Poetic Metaphor* 114, 116 (1989). See also Johnson, *Body in the Mind*; George Lakoff, *Women, Fire, and Dangerous Things* (1987); Michael J. Reddy, *The Conduit Metaphor: A Case of Frame Conflict in Our Language about Language*, in *Metaphor and Thought* 164, 284 (Andrew Ortony ed., 2d ed. 1993).

5. Lakoff and Turner, *More Than Cool Reason* supra at 116.

6. George Lakoff and Mark Johnson, *Metaphors We Live By* 4 (Chicago 1980).

7. Id. at 29.

8. See Michael J. Reddy, *The Conduit Metaphor* supra at 165.

9. Id.

10. Id.

11. See Edward Rubin and Malcolm Feeley, *Creating Legal Doctrine*, 69 So. Calf. L. Rev. 1989, 2021 (1996).

12. Id.

13. Id.

14. Id., citing *Dombrowski v. Pfister*, 380 U.S. 479, 487 (1965) ("The chilling effect upon the exercise of First Amendment rights may derive from the fact of the prosecution, unaffected by the prospects of its success or failure."). Id.

15. George Lakoff and Mark Johnson, *Metaphors We Live By* supra at 71.

16. George Lakoff, *Women, Fire, and Dangerous Things* supra at 45.

17. Prototype theory developed in the field of cognitive psychology is used to explain how conceptual thinking depends on prototypes or categories. See, e.g., Eleanor Rosch, *Cognitive Representations of Semantic Categories*, 104 J. of Experimental Psychology 192 (1975). Professor Lawrence Solan has recently applied prototype theory to the interesting task of interpreting criminal statutes. See Lawrence M. Solan, *Law, Language and Lenity* 40 (William & Mary L. Rev., forthcoming). George Lakoff developed the idea of radial category to explain the cognitive significance of the prototype effects of ideological cognitive models. See George Lakoff, *Women, Fire, and Dangerous Things* supra at 79–114.

18. See Steven L. Winter, *Radial Categories*, in *Clearing in the Forest* supra at 18–19. The idea of radial category was coined by George Lakoff. See George Lakoff, *Women, Fire, and Dangerous Things* supra at 79–114.

19. Winter, *Radial Categories*, in *Clearing in the Forest* supra at 3.

20. The concept of an *image schemata* has been developed by cognitive

theorists to describe the imaginative devices we use to organize our thoughts into patterns in order to comprehend complex data. See Johnson, *Body in the Mind* supra at 28. Because image schemata are linked to our experience, they give rise to what cognitive theorists call *prototypical* effects—recurring or corresponding relations between the culturally shared experiences of individuals in a given society and the cognitive process. Steven L. Winter has shown how the image-schematic model of cognitive theory structures the legal conception of a cause of action and thus distorts the law of standing. See Steven L. Winter, *The Metaphor of Standing and the Problem of Self- Governance*, 40 Stan. L. Rev. 1371 (1988).

21. *Idealized cognitive model* (ICM) is a technical term used in cognitive theory to describe detailed imaginative narratives drawn from human experiences to organize complex knowledge about the world. See, e.g., George Lakoff, *Women, Fire, and Dangerous Things* 45, 56–57 (1987). See also Steven L. Winter, *Radial Categories*, in *Clearing in the Forest* supra. Gerald Lopez has used the concept of "stock structory" or "stock story" to capture the meaning of what cognitive theorists call an idealized cognitive model. See Gerald P. Lopez, *Lay Lawyering*, 32 UCLA Rev. 1 (1984). ICMs are thus like stock stories, folk theories, or image-schemata upon which we intuitively rely to organize our knowledge about the diverse inputs of daily life. ICMs share certain core features. All ICMs are (1) grounded in direct physical or cultural experience; (2) highly generalized to capture some, but not all, of a covered fact situation; (3) unconscious or intuitive structures of thought that operate automatically in the thought process; and (4) neither determinant nor objective characterizations of reality. These features are what produce prototype effects. See George Lakoff, *Women, Fire, and Dangerous Things* supra at 68–76.

22. An image schema is an "abstract pattern in our experience and understanding that [is] not propositional in any of the standard senses of that term, and yet [it is] central to meaning and to the inferences we make." Mark Johnson, *Body in the Mind* supra at 2, 75.

23. Winter, *Transcendental Nonsense, Metaphoric Reasoning, and the Cognitive Stakes for Law*, 137 U. Pa. L. Rev. 1105, 1132 (1989).

24. Id.

25. Johnson, *Body in the Mind* supra at 79.

26. Id. at 1383.

27. Id. at 90.

28. Id.

29. Mark Johnson has noted that there are at least seven common force image schemata that operate constantly in structuring our experience of force. See Johnson, *Body in the Mind* supra at 45. They are compulsion, blockage, counterforce, diversion, removal of restraint, enablement, and attraction. Id. at 45–48.

30. Id. at 13. Johnson notes, "[T]hough we forget it so easily, the meaning of 'physical force' depends on publicly shared meaning structures that emerge from our bodily *experience* of force." Id.

31. Id. at 45.

32. "Sometimes the force is irresistible, such as when the crowd gets completely out of control, other times the force can be counteracted, or modified. In such cases of compulsion, the force comes from somewhere, has a given magnitude, moves along a path, and has a direction." Id.

33. "A magnet draws a piece of steel toward itself, a vacuum cleaner pulls dirt into itself, and the earth pulls us back down when we jump. There is a common schematic structure of attraction shared by these experiences." Id. at 37.

34. "When a baby learns to crawl, for instance, it encounters a wall that blocks its further progress in some direction. The baby must either stop, ceasing its exertion of force in the initial direction, or it must redirect its force. It can try to go over the obstacle, around it, or even through it, where there is sufficient power to do so. In such a case the child is learning part of the meaning of force and of forceful resistance in the most immediate way." Id. at 45.

35. Johnson, *Body in the Mind* supra at 13–14.

36. 261 U.S. 86 (1923).

37. Id. at 91 (emphasis added).

38. Id.

39. James B. Atleson, *Values and Assumptions in American Labor Law* (1983).

40. Id. at 97–107.

41. For a summary of the intellectual and political movement in law known as the "critical legal studies movement," see Gary Minda, *Postmodern Legal Movements: Law and Jurisprudence at Century's End* 106–27 (1995).

42. See Duncan Kennedy, *A Critique of Adjudication* (1997).

43. Id. at 69.

44. Id. at 97–104.

45. Id. at 118.

46. See James B. Atleson, *Values and Assumptions in American Labor Law* 1–16 (1983). See also Katherine Stone, *The Post-War Paradigm in American Labor Law*, 90 Yale L. J. 1509 (1981); Karl Klare, *Judicial Deradicalization of the Wagner Act and the Origins of Modern Legal Consciousness, 1937–1941*, 62 Minn. L. Rev. 265 (1978).

47. Duncan Kennedy, *A Critique of Adjudication* supra 109–111.

48. Id.

49. Richard A. Posner, *Bad Faith* [Review of Duncan Kennedy, *A Critique of Adjudication {fin de siècle}* (1997)], The New Republic 34 (June 9, 1997).

50. Morton Horwitz has shown how the conception of "corporate personality" came to dominate legal thinking at the turn of the century. See Morton

Horwitz, *The Transformation of American Law, 1870–1960: The Crisis of Legal Orthodoxy* 111–14 (1992); Morton Horwitz, *Santa Clara Revisited: The Development of Corporate Theory*, 88 W. Va. L. Rev. 173 (1985).

51. By the turn of the century, corporations, like real persons, could sue and be sued. For federal court diversity purposes, a corporation counted as one person. Corporations were regarded as being capable of exercising freedom of action. The result was the rise, by the end of the nineteenth century, of "the modern business corporation, organized to pursue private ends for individual gains." Morton Horwitz, *The Transformation of American Law: 1780–1860* at 111 (1977).

52. I do not wish to be read as believing that some correct or true metaphor can be discovered to ground legal analysis in some objective framework.

53. Harold C. Livesay, *Samuel Gompers and Organized Labor in America* 145–47 (1978).

54. Haig Bosmajian, *Metaphor and Reason in Judicial Opinions* 37 (1992).

55. George Lakoff and Mark Johnson, *Metaphors We Live By* 236 (Chicago 1980).

56. Haig Bosmajian, *Metaphor and Reason in Judicial Opinions* at 19–29.

57. Susan Sontag, *Illness as Metaphor* 84 (1977).

58. Edward Rubin and Malcolm Feeley have explained: "A notable feature of both analogy and metaphor, as opposed to deductive reasoning, is that they produce fully realized ideas." Edward Rubin and Malcolm Feeley, *Creating Legal Doctrine*, 69 So. Calif. L. Rev. 1989, 2021 (1996).

59. Michael J. Reddy, *The Conduit Metaphor* supra at 164.

60. Id. at 185–88. See also C. Edwin Baker, *Human Liberty and Freedom of Speech* 94–96 (1989).

61. The term *private sovereignty* is borrowed from Avian Soifer's *Law and the Company We Keep* 82 (1995).

62. Duncan Kennedy, *A Critique of Adjudication* supra at 156.

4. METAPHOR AND ADJUDICATION

1. Richard A. Posner, *Law and Literature: A Misunderstood Relation* 2 (1988).

2. Id. See also Richard A. Posner, *Overcoming Law* 523–24 (1995).

3. Posner, *Law and Literature* supra at 2, n. 1, citing Donald Davison, *What Metaphors Mean* in *On Metaphor* 29 (Sheldon Sacks ed. 1979).

4. See Posner, *Overcoming Law* supra. See also Richard A. Posner, *The Problems of Jurisprudence* 454–69 (1990).

5. Posner, *The Problems of Jurisprudence* supra at 460.

6. Id. at 362. See also Neil Duxbury, *Pragmatism Without Politics*, 55 Mod. L. Rev. 594 (1992).

7. Posner, *Overcoming Law* supra at 524.

8. Id. at 523.

9. 231 N.Y. 229, 131 N.E. 898 (1921); Richard A. Weisberg, *When Lawyers Write* 10 (1987). See also Richard A. Weisberg, *Judicial Discretion, or the Self on the Shelf*, 10 Cardozo L. Rev. 105 (1988).

10. See Richard A. Posner, *Cardozo: A Study in Reputation* 48–57 (1990).

11. See Richard A. Posner, *Bad Faith* [Review of Duncan Kennedy, *A Critique of Adjudication {fin de siècle}* (1997)], The New Republic 34 (June 9, 1997).

12. See Richard A. Weisberg, *When Lawyers Write* supra at 10.

13. See Posner, *Bad Faith* supra.

14. See Gary Minda, *Postmodern Legal Movements: Law and Jurisprudence at Century's End* 13–23 (1995). Christopher Columbus Langdell, the author of the first modern law school case book, ushered in the era of jurisprudence known as formalism. According to Langdell, law was science that consisted of a finite set of enduring legal principles that could be discovered in appellate court decisions. The refinement of Langdellian thought gave way to the idea that law could be studied as a formal system of logically derived norms based on an underlying defensible philosophy. Id. at 24–43. Much later, legal philosophers such as Ronald Dworkin challenged this notion of law by bringing a much more normative perspective to describe judicial activity. Id. at 44–62.

15. Legal realism, dominant in the 1920s and 1930s, was a jurisprudential movement that transformed the nineteenth-century view of the judge as "living oracle" and set the stage for the emergence of modern jurisprudence. See Minda, *Postmodern Legal Movements* supra at 25–33.

16. Posner, *Bad Faith* supra at 34.

17. For my analysis of these ideas, see Gary Minda, *Postmodern Legal Movements* at 37. The post–World War II generation of legal scholars thus believed that "judicially conceived notions of self-restraint and the duty to render a 'reasoned decision' would establish constraints on the freedom of a judge to decide difficult legal problems based on the judge's particular policy predilections." Id.

18. See Edward L. Rubin, *The New Legal Process, the Synthesis of Discourse, and the Microanalysis of Institutions*, 109 Harv. L. Rev. 1392 (1996).

19. See, e.g., Ronald Dworkin, *Law's Empire* (1986).

20. See, e.g., Posner, *Overcoming Law* supra.

21. See Ronald Dworkin, *Law's Empire* supra at 255, 405–6. See also Paul F. Campos, *Jurismania: The Madness of American Law* 115–16 (1998).

22. See Richard A. Posner, *Bad Faith* supra at 34. Judge Posner, however, does better than most judges. He recognizes the relevance of prototype theory in analyzing federal criminal statutes. See *Fitzgerald v. Chrysler Corp.*, 116 F.3d 225 (7th Cir. 1997).

23. See *O'Shea v. Riverway Towing*, 677 F.2d 1194 (7th Cir. 1982).

24. See Edward L. Rubin, *The New Legal Process, the Synthesis of Discourse, and the Microanalysis of Institutions,* 109 Harv. L. Rev. 1393 (1996).

25. See Edward L. Rubin, *Legal Reasoning, Legal Process, and the Judiciary as an Institution,* 85 Calif. L. Rev. 265, 280–81 (1997).

26. See Edward Rubin and Malcolm Feeley, *Creating Legal Doctrine,* 69 So. Calif. L. Rev. 1989 (1996).

27. See Richard A. Posner, *Bad Faith* supra at 34.

28. See, e.g., C. Edwin Baker, *Human Liberty and Freedom of Speech* 194–95, 222 (1989).

29. See Steven L. Winter, *How Do Rules Work?,* in *A Clearing in the Forest: How the Study of the Mind Changes Our Understanding of Life and Law* (Univ. of Chicago Press, forthcoming). See also Paul F. Campos, *Jurismania* supra at 81–121.

30. See Minda, *Postmodern Legal Movements* supra at 25–33. See also Neil Duxbury, *Jerome Frank and the Legacy of Legal Realism,* 18 J. of Law & Soc'y 175 (1991).

31. Jerome Frank, *Law and the Modern Mind* 33 (1930).

32. Id. at 35.

33. See Jerome Frank, *Law and the Modern Mind* supra at 19. See also Robert Jerome Glennon, *The Iconoclast as Reformer: Jerome Frank's Impact on American Law* 47–50 (1985).

34. See Jerome Frank, *Law and the Modern Mind* supra at 19.

35. Id.

36. Id. at 37.

37. See, e.g., Sigmund Freud, *Civilization and Its Discontents* 82 (J. Strachey trans. 1961).

38. Duncan Kennedy, *A Critique of Adjudication* supra at 190.

39. Id. at 192.

40. Id. at 199–200, quoting Jean-Paul Sartre, *Being and Nothingness: An Essay on Phenomenological Ontology* 89–90 (H. Barnes trans. 1965).

41. Id.

42. Kennedy, *A Critique of Adjudication* supra at 182–192.

43. Id. at 203.

44. Id.

45. Id. at 156.

46. See Steven Pinkin, *How the Mind Works* 332 (1997). Psychological studies of metaphor involve *mediational approaches* that attempt to explain how metaphor mediates information based on similarity, relational, and integrative reactions. See Allan Paivo, *Psychological Process in the Comprehension of Metaphor* in *Metaphor and Thought* 150, 154–55 (A. Ortony ed. 1979).

47. Pinkin, *How the Mind Works* supra at 65–66.

48. Id. at 355. Pinkin believes that aspects of the "language of thought" is "hard wired" in the brain. Pinkin acknowledges, however, that there is an inter-

action between the hard wire of the brain and learning from social context and that metaphor is an important cognitive engine of the mind, as distinguished from the brain. Id. at 352–58.

49. Kennedy, *A Critique of Adjudication* supra at 202.

50. Id. at 191–92.

51. See Jerome Frank, *Law and the Modern Mind* supra at 37. For the modern psychoanalytic understanding of psychological denial see Jerrold S. Maxmen, *Essential Psychopathology* 68 (1986). See also *American Psychiatric Glossary* (1994).

52. Maxmen supra at 68.

53. See id.

54. Kennedy, *A Critique of Adjudication* supra at 202.

55. Robert Cover, *The Supreme Court 1982 Term: Foreword, Nomos, and Narrative*, 97 Harv. L. Rev. 4, 53 (1983).

56. See, e.g., Kennedy, *A Critique of Adjudication* supra at 248; Steven L. Winter, *An Upside/Down View of the Countermajoritarian Difficulty*, 69 Tex. L. Rev. 1881, 1881–90 (1997).

57. A classic example would be the landmark opinion in *MacPherson v. Buick Motor Co.*, 217 N.Y. 382 N.Y. 382, 111 N.E. 1050 (1916), where Judge Cardozo invoked the metaphor of "foreseeable danger" to bring about a shift from the old privity rule that limited manufacturer liability for defective products to immediate purchasers to a new rule that extended liability to all foreseeable risks of all users. The metaphor of "foreseeable danger" thus became a new default metaphor in product liability cases that effectively did away with the citadel of the privity rule in negligence cases. See William L. Prosser, *The Assault upon the Citadel: Strict Liability to the Consumer*, 69 Yale L. J. 1099 (1960).

5. Radial Category of Secondary Labor Boycotts

1. See *Labor-Management Reporting and Disclosure Act of 1959*, Pub. L. No. 86–257, 704, 73 Stat. 519 (codified as amended at 29 U.S.C. 158[b][4] [1988]). The statute distinguishes between primary and secondary labor activity. Without the distinction, the statutory prohibition created to forbid secondary labor boycotts, read literally, would "ban most strikes historically considered to be lawful, so-called primary activity." *Local 761, Int'l Union of Electrical, Radio & Machine Workers v. NLRB*, 366 U.S. 667, 672 (1961). However, as Justice Frankfurter once observed, the primary/secondary distinction of federal labor law "does not present a glaringly bright line." Id. at 673.

2. 341 U.S. 665 (1951).

3. Id. at 670–71. Statutory regulation of secondary boycotts has mainly involved construction site cases where both the primary or the secondary employers are working on a common situs. See, e.g., *Denver Building & Const. Trades*, 341 U.S. 675 (1951). The Labor Board and courts have been more will-

ing to find picketing at a common construction situs to violate the secondary boycott provision of federal labor law. This has led to what Julius Getman and Bertrand Pogrebin have called an "economically deceptive and ideologically confusing" law of secondary labor boycotts. Julius G. Getman and Bertrand B. Pogrebin, *Labor Relations: The Basic Processes, Law and Practice* 259 (1988).

4. See Simon Head, *The New, Ruthless Economy*, New York Review of Books, February 29, 1996, p. 47; Keith Bradsher, *Need to Cut Costs? Order Out: Outsourcing Saves Money, but Labor is Frustrated*, New York Times, April 11, 1996, D1.

5. See Howard Lesnick, *The Gravamen of the Secondary Boycott*, 62 Colum. L. Rev. 1363, 1415 (1962) ("A major asserted basis for restricting secondary activity was the legislative desire to discourage what may be called the metastasis of labor disputes: the fanning out of unrest from the struck plant to those doing business with it.") (citing 93 Cong. Rec. 4323 [daily ed. April 29, 1947], reprinted in 2 *Legislative History of Labor Management Relations Act*, 1947, at 1107 [1985]) (remarks of Senator Taft).

6. Lesnick, *Gravamen of Secondary Boycott* supra at 1415.

7. Id. Section 8(b)(4)(ii)(B) of the National Labor Relations Act thus prohibits labor unions from coercing one business to cease dealing with another business, where *coercion* is defined to include the use of means other than non-picketing publicity. See 29 U.S. 158 (b)(4)(ii)(B) (1988).

8. Susan Sontag, *Illness as Metaphor* 6 (1977).

9. Clyde W. Summers and Harry H. Wellington, *Labor Law: Cases and Materials* 280–81 (1968).

10. 29 U.S.C. 157, 158 (a)(i); see *NLRB v. Local 307, Plumbers, United Ass'n of Journeymen and Apprentices of Plumbing and Pipefitting Indus. of United States and Canada*, 469 F.2d 403, 406 (7th Cir. 1972).

11. Prototype theory was initially developed by the work of cognitive psychologists. See, e.g., Eleanor Rosch, *Cognitive Representations of Semantic Categories*, 104 J. of Experimental Psychology 192 (1975).

12. Mark Johnson, for example, has shown how the metaphor "body as machine" was the underlying imaginative device structuring early medical theories of disease. See Mark Johnson, *The Body in the Mind: The Bodily Basis of Meaning, Imagination, and Reason* 130 (1987). Thus, medical metaphors "such as those of isolated parts, functional assemblies, and repair and replacement of malfunctioning units" structured medical evidence in the nineteenth century. Id. As Johnson claims, "[T]he body as machine metaphor was not merely an isolated belief; rather, it was a massive experiential structuring that involved values, interests, goals, practices, and theorizing." Id.

13. *Railway Labor Act*, 45 U.S.C. 151–88 (1988). The United States Supreme Court rejected the view that the Railway Labor Act should be judicially interpreted to prohibit secondary boycott. See *Burlington Northern R.R. Co. v. Broth-*

erhood Maintenance of Way Employees, 481 U.S. 429 (1987).

14. See Peter Meijes Tiersma, *Nonverbal Communication and the Freedom of Speech*, 1993 Wis. L. Rev. 1525 (1994); Lawrence B. Solan, *Freedom of Communicative Action: A Theory of the First Amendment Freedom of Speech*, 83 NW. U. L. Rev. 54 (1989).

15. Tiersma, *Nonverbal Communication* supra at 1531.

16. 310 U.S. 88 (1940).

17. 312 U.S. 287, 293 (1941).

18. See *United States v. Grace*, 461 U.S. 171, 176 (1983); Tiersma, *Nonverbal Communication* supra at 1536.

19. See, e.g., *Teamsters Local 695 v. Vogt*, 354 U.S. 284 (1957); *Teamsters Local 802 v. Wohl*, 315 U.S. 769 (1942); *Cox v. Louisiana*, 379 U.S. 559 (1965).

20. In First Amendment jurisprudence, there is an important distinction between *coverage* and *protection*. Activity may be *covered* by the First Amendment and yet remain *unprotected* if the activity is found to warrant a lower level of First Amendment protection. See Frederick Schauer, *Free Speech: A Philosophical Enquiry* 89–91 (1982).

21. See 49 Stat. 449 (1935), as amended; 29 U.S.C. 158(b)(4) (1988).

22. Id. at 807(g).

23. 377 U.S. 58 (1964).

24. See, e.g., C. Edwin Baker, *Human Liberty and Freedom of Speech* 70–73 (1989); Lawrence B. Solum, *Freedom of Communicative Action: A Theory of the First Amendment Freedom of Speech*, 83 NW. U. L. Rev. 54, 109–10 (1989).

25. See, e.g., John R. Searle, *Speech Acts: An Essay in the Philosophy of Language* 16 (1970).

26. John Hart Ely, *Flag Desecration: A Case Study on the Roles of Categorization and Balancing in the First Amendment Analysis*, 88 Harv. L. Rev. 1482, 1495–96 (1975).

27. *NAACP v. Claiborne Hardware Co.*, 458 U.S. 886, 910 (1982) (J. Stevens, for the Court).

28. *Gompers v. Bucks Stove & Range Co.*, 221 U.S. 418, 439 (1911). Justice Stevens recognized nonetheless that governmental regulation of otherwise protected expression may be justified in "certain narrowly defined instances." Id. at 912 (citing *United States v. O'Brien*, 391 U.S. 367 [1968]). He specifically noted that this might be the case when "[a] nonviolent and totally voluntary boycott may have a disruptive effect on local economic conditions." Id.; see also *NLRB v. Retail Store Employees Union, Local 1001 (Safeco)*, 447 U.S. 607, 616 (1980).

29. See C. Edwin Baker, *Human Liberty and Freedom of Speech* supra at 70–73.

30. Thomas Emerson's influential First Amendment scholarship is responsible for the signal theory of labor picketing. See Thomas Emerson, *The System of Freedom of Expression* 445 (1971). Emerson argued that there was a

fundamental difference between labor picketing and nonlabor picketing. He claimed that labor picketing was different because of its "signal effect." As he explained: "[the] labor picket line is ... not so much a rational appeal to persuasion as a signal for the application of immediate and enormous economic leverage, based upon an already prepared position." Nonlabor picketing is "directed much more to the general public than to their own members.... [It] is a call to reason, not the application of economic coercion, and as such must be classified as expression." Id. C. Edwin Baker, however, notes how Emerson has uncritically equated "pressure" with "coercion." Because pressure is not the equivalent of coercion, the distinction between labor and nonlabor picketing based on signal, fails to explain why liberty theory would protect nonlabor picketing but not labor picketing. C. Edwin Baker, *Human Liberty and Freedom of Speech* supra at 72.

31. 377 U.S. 58 (1964).

32. A labor picket that follows the product, pickets the store or business that carries the product produced by the picket's employer.

33. 477 U.S. 607 (1980).

34. See J. Getman and J. Blackburn, *Labor Relations: Law, Practice, and Policy* 257 (1983).

35. 485 U.S. 568 (1988).

36. See Rick Fantasia, *Cultures of Solidarity* 82–85 (1988) (examining how signals are important features of wild-cat strikes); Dennis Chong, *Collective Action and the Civil Rights Movement* 103–40 (1991) (examining how signaling effects of groups solve collective action problems). See generally Avery Katz, *Taking Private Ordering Seriously*, 144 U. Pa. L. Rev. 1745 (1997); Richard H. McAdams, *Group Norms, Gossip, and Blackmail*, 144 U. Pa. L. Rev. 2237 (1997); Cass R. Sunstein, *On Expressive Function of Law*, 144 U. Pa. L. Rev. 2021 (1997); Peter J. Spiro, *New Global Potentates: Non-Governmental Organizations and the "Unregulated" Marketplace*, 18 Cardozo L. Rev. 957 (1997).

37. *Oxford English Dictionary* vol. 6 at 1070 (2d ed. 1989).

38. Id. at 680.

39. As Justice Stevens has expressed the idea: "Indeed, no doubt the principal reason why handbills containing the same message are so much less effective than labor picketing is that the former depend entirely on the persuasive force of the idea." *NLRB v. Retail Store Employees Union, Local 1001 (Safeco)*, 447 U.S. 607, 619 (1980) (Stevens, J., concurring).

40. *Edward J. DeBartolo Corp. v. Florida Gulf Coast Bldg. & Const. Trade Council (DeBartolo II)* 485 U.S. 568, 580 (1988).

41. See Karl Klare, *Judicial Deradicalization of the Wagner Act and the Origins of Modern Legal Consciousness, 1937–1941*, 62 Minn. L. Rev. 265 (1978); and Katherine Stone, *The Post-War Paradigm*, 90 Yale L. J. 1509 (1981).

42. See Katherine Stone, *The Post-War Paradigm* supra.

6. RADIAL CATEGORY OF CIVIL RIGHTS BOYCOTTS

   1. 339 U.S. 460 (1950).

   2. In *Hughes v. Superior Court of California*, 339 U.S. 460 (1950), the Supreme Court, speaking through Justice Frankfurter, concluded that sound public policy, and not any formal legislative prohibition, forbid the use of racial quotas in hiring. Hence, peaceful picketing carried on with the objective of forcing a supermarket to hire blacks violated the state's public policy forbidding racial discrimination. The case is important for creating a new conservative theory of picketing that downplayed the First Amendment aspect of picketing expression. Hence, picketing to achieve illegal objects was found to be outside the protection normally accorded to picketing by the First Amendment in *Thornhill v. Alabama*, 310 U.S. 88 (1940).

   3. 310 U.S. 88 (1940). In *Thornhill*, the Supreme Court held that picketing involved forms of expression that were protected by the First Amendment. The Court, however, has found that the constitutional protection extended to picketing is not absolute. This has led to a number of Supreme Court cases that are difficult to justify in light of the *Thornhill* decision. For example, the vague justification offered by Justice Frankfurter in *Hughes v. Superior Court*, allowing the State to enjoin picketing by a civil rights group, raised (or should have raised) constitutional problems.

   One might attempt to justify state regulation of nonlabor boycotts on three different legal grounds: (1) they lead to violence, (2) they have harmful secondary effects, and (3) they attempt to achieve objectives that violate public policy. See Randall L. Kennedy, *Martin Luther King's Constitution: A Legal History of the Montgomery Bus Boycott*, 98 Yale L. J. 999, 1041 (1989). The first ground, violence, is a justifiable ground when evidence of violence or potential violence is shown, but this ground is inapplicable when there is no evidentiary support to link the boycott to violence, which is the case in many peaceful civil rights boycotts. The notion that a civil rights boycott can be enjoined if it constitutes a secondary boycott is equally problematic since secondary parties pressured by the boycott are not innocent parties in the sense that they have no connection to the underlying dispute provoking the boycott. Id. After all, the targets of a civil rights boycott will be the entire community responsible for the illicit discrimination. In any event, the fact that some disinterested parties might be pressured is hardly a good reason to curtail constitutional protection since "[a]ll societies permit some means of exercising power over other people." C. Edwin Baker, Human Liberty and Freedom of Speech 189 (1989). The third ground, public policy, is also troubling since the term public policy is difficult to define and often becomes just an excuse for hiding judicial policy predilections.

   4. 339 U.S. at 465–66.

   5. See Robert Jerome Glennon, *The Role of Law in the Civil Rights Move-*

ment: *The Montgomery Bus Boycott, 1955–1957,* 9 Law & History Rev. 59, 72 (1991). Note, *The Common-Law and Constitutional Status of Anti-Discrimination Boycotts,* 66 Yale L. J. 397, 397–98 (1957).

6. 458 U.S. 886 (1982).

7. Id. at 911. Justice Stevens relied upon a number of First Amendment cases dealing with other forms of expressive conduct without considering their applicability to labor boycotts. Id. at 910–13 (citing *Organization for a Better Austin v. Keefe,* 402 U.S. 415 [1971] [distribution of leaflets]; and *United States v. O'Brien,* 391 U.S. 367 [1968] [burning draft card]).

8. 458 U.S. at 906–13.

9. Id. at 903–4. Justice Stevens's response to this was that "there is no evidence—apart from the speeches themselves—that . . . threatened acts of violence." Id. at 929. Applying the Court's decision in *Milk Wagon Drivers Union, Local 753 v. Meadowmoor Dairies, Inc.,* 312 U.S. 287, 293 (1941), which held that "insubstantial findings" of "trivial rough incident[s]" and "moment[s] of animal exuberance" fail to invalidate otherwise peaceful picketing, Justice Stevens concluded that the findings in the record were "constitutionally inadequate to support the damages judgment against [the leader of the boycott]." *Claiborne Hardware,* 458 U.S. at 929.

10. Id. at 934 (emphasis added).

11. Id. at 907.

12. Id.

13. 680 P.2d 1086 (Cal. 1984).

14. Id. at 1092 (quoting *Claiborne Hardware,* 458 U.S. at 914).

15. See Gary Peller, *Reason and the Mob: The Politics of Representation,* 2 Tikhun 28, 31 (1987).

16. C. Edwin Baker, *Human Liberty and Freedom of Speech* supra at 184.

17. G. Le Bon, *The Crowd* (2d ed 1969) (originally published in 1895).

18. Id., cited in C. Edwin Baker, *Human Liberty and Freedom of Speech* supra at 184.

19. See Jane Mayer and Jill Abramson, *Strange Justice: The Selling of Clarence Thomas* 95 (1994); *The Thomas Nomination: Excerpts from Senate Hearings on the Thomas Nomination,* New York Times, Oct. 13, 1991, A30.

20. See Kimberle Crenshaw, *Whose Story Is It? Feminist and Antitrust Appropriations of Anita Hill,* in *Race-ing Justice, En-Gendering Power* 402 (T. Morrison ed. 1992).

21. 365 U.S. 127 (1961).

22. Id. at 138.

23. Id.

24. See, e.g., Robert A. Dahl, *Pluralist Democracy in the United States: Conflict and Consent* (1967); see also Gary Minda, *Interest Groups, Political*

Freedom, and Antitrust, 41 Hastings L. J. 905, 937–42 (1990) (describing how pluralist ideology provided the Warren Court with a conception of politics that optimistically accepted the legitimacy of interest group influence in the political process). The underlying pluralistic perspective that explains Justice Black's view of the role of interest group petitioning can be found in the concluding paragraph of Justice Black's opinion:

> In rejecting each of the grounds relied upon by the courts below to justify application of the Sherman Act to the campaign of the railroads . . . we have restored what appears to be the true nature of the case—a "no-holds-barred fight" between two industries both of which are seeking control of a profitable source of income. Inherent in such fights, which are commonplace in the halls of legislative bodies, is the possibility, and in many instances even the probability, that one group or the other will get hurt by the arguments that are made. In this particular instance, each group appears to have utilized all the political powers it could muster in an attempt to bring about the passage of laws that would help it or injure the other. But the contest itself appears to have been conducted along lines normally accepted in our political system, except to the extent that each group has deliberately deceived the public and public officials. And that deception, reprehensible as it is, can be of no consequence so far as the Sherman Act is concerned. (Noerr, 365 U.S. at 144–45).

25. See Edward M. Purcell Jr., *The Crisis of Democratic Theory* 211 (1973); see also Nancy S. Ehrenreich, *Pluralist Myths and Powerless Men: The Ideology of Reasonableness in Sexual Harassment Law,* 99 Yale L. J. 1177, 1188 (1990).

26. See Cass Sunstein, *Beyond the Republican Revival,* 97 Yale L. J. 1539, 1542 (1988); Robert Dahl, *Dilemmas of a Pluralist Democracy: Autonomy vs. Control* 32 (1992).

27. 250 U.S. 616 (1919).

28. Id. at 630 (Holmes, J., dissenting); see also Steven L. Winter, *Transcendental Nonsense* supra at 1188–89.

29. Steven L. Winter, for example, has shown how the metaphor "marketplace of ideas" supported an important understanding of freedom of speech that came to be associated with several conventional metaphors of the mind and ideas. Winter, *Transcendental Nonsense* supra at 1188–89.

30. See, e.g., C. Edwin Baker, *Human Liberty and Human Freedom of Speech* supra at 14. Baker argues that the confidence legal decision makers have in the power of rationality is misplaced: "People cannot use reason to comprehend a set reality because no set reality exists for people to discover. . . . Our conceptions reflect forms of life rather than reason applied in a metaphorical marketplace of

ideas—although speech within this marketplace may be an important, but not necessarily an especially privileged practice that affects our conceptions." Id.

31. See James G. Pope, *Labor-Community Coalitions and Boycotts: The Old Labor Law, the New Unionism, and the Living Constitution,* 69 Tex. L. Rev. 889 (1991); James G. Pope, *Republican Moments: The Role of Direct Popular Power in the American Constitutional Order,* 139 U. Pa. L. Rev. 287 (1990).

32. See Pope, *Republican Moments* supra at 349–52. According to Professor Pope, the Supreme Court has adopted the principle that boycotts should be constitutionally protected when they advance republican values, i.e., when they "transcend the day-to-day conduct of business as usual." Id. at 349.

33. *International Longshoremen's Ass'n v. Allied Int'l, Inc.,* 456 U.S. 212 (1982); see also Florian Bartosic and Gary Minda, *Labor Law Myth in the Supreme Court, 1981 Term: A Plea for Realistic and Coherent Theory,* 30 UCLA L. Rev. 271, 306–10 (1982).

34. During the *Claiborne Hardware* boycott, third parties were asked not to do business with the targets of the boycott.

35. See Randall L. Kennedy, *Martin Luther King's Constitution: A Legal History of the Montgomery Bus Boycott,* 98 Yale L. J. 1018 (1989); Robert Jerome Glennon, *The Role of Law in the Civil Rights Movement,* 9 Law & Hist. Rev. 59 (1991).

36. Kennedy, *Martin Luther King's Constitution* supra at 1022. But see Glennon, *The Role of Law in the Civil Rights Movement* supra (arguing the importance of subsequent legal decisions upholding the right of boycotters).

37. Glennon, *The Role of Law in the Civil Rights Movement,* 9 Law & Hist. Rev. 59 (1991). See *Browder v. Gayle,* 352 U.S. 903 (1956) (Supreme Court affirming a three-judge court's decision striking down the state and local statutes in Montgomery, Alabama, requiring racial segregation on public buses).

38. Id. at 1066.

39. Id.

40. Randall L. Kennedy, *Martin Luther King's Constitution* supra at 1066.

41. While it is true that constitutional principles of federalism and federal supremacy can also explain the Court's *Claiborne Hardware* decision, those legal principles cannot fully account for why the Court has defined the meaning of boycotts differently in other boycott cases. Constitutional doctrines cannot explain why the legal meaning of boycott changes like the color of a chameleon as legal analysis moves to different social and economic contexts.

42. C. Edwin Baker, *Human Liberty and Freedom of Speech* supra at 189.

43. Id.

7. RADIAL CATEGORY OF COMMERCIAL BOYCOTTS

    1. 33 A. 1 (R.I. 1895).

    2. Id. at 3.

3. Id.

4. 96 Mass. 499 (1867).

5. Id. at 503–4.

6. 106 Mass. 1 (1870).

7. Labor law scholars have struggled hard to answer this question. See Charles D. Gregory and Harold H. Katz, *Labor and the Law* 55–59 (3d ed 1979).

8. See generally Rudolph Peritz, *Competition Policy in America, 1888–1992: History, Rhetoric, Law* (1996).

9. For a recent discussion of the relevance of the human body to legal discourse, see Alan Hyde, *Bodies of Law* (1997). See also Johnson, *The Body in the Mind: The Bodily Basis of Meaning, Imagination, and Reason* 75 (1987).

10. Id. Johnson, *Body in the Mind,* supra at 97.

11. Id.

12. 44 N.E. 1077 (1896).

13. Id. at 1081.

14. Mark Tushnet, *The Logic of Experience: Oliver Wendell Holmes on the Supreme Judicial Court,* 63 Va. L. Rev. 975, 1036 (1977). This was not because Holmes sided with the cause of labor. As Tushnet has explained: "Holmes saw his opinions as erecting a structure of legal thought; that he came out on the labor side in *Vegelahn* was as irrelevant as the fact that he came out on the employer's side in most cases involving industrial accidents." Id. at 1040.

15. *Vegelahn,* 44 N.E. at 1081.

16. Thus, unlike nineteenth-century *homo economicus* that assumed the necessity of "regulated, saving, accounting, discipline—an economy that depends on the rational limitation of desire," twentieth-century homo economicus assumed unregulated markets and unlimited expansion of desire. See Susan Sontag, *Illness as Metaphor* 63 (1977).

17. *Vegelahn,* 44 N.E. at 1081.

18. "Workers and employers, then, were competitors, and the law ought to be neutral in their struggle." Tushnet, *The Logic of Experience* supra at 1038.

19. The homeostasis metaphor in Holmesian thought was not the same as the balancing metaphor that assumed that judges could weigh and balance competing policies. The homeostasis metaphor, unlike the balancing metaphor, assumes a dialectical struggle between incommensurable conflicting policies. See Thomas C. Grey, *Plotting the Path of the Law,* 63 Brooklyn L. Rev. 19, 57–58 (1997).

20. See generally Johnson, *Body in the Mind* supra at 331.

21. *Vegelahn,* 44 N.E. at 1081 (Holmes J., dissenting).

22. See Gary Minda, *Rediscovering Progressive Labor Politics: The Labor Law Implications of FTC v. Superior Court Trial Lawyers Assoc.,* 16 Vt. L. Rev. 71, 103–4 (1991).

23. 493 U.S. 411 (1990).

24. 493 U.S. at 425–27; see Stephen Calkins, *The October 1989 Supreme Court Term and Antitrust: Power, Access, and Legitimacy*, 59 Antitrust L. J. 339, 341–55 (1991).

25. 493 U.S. at 427 (quoting *Allied Tube & Conduit Corp. v. Indian Head, Inc.*, 486 U.S. 492, 508 [1988]).

26. 493 U.S. at 426.

27. Id. at 434.

28. Id. at 433–34.

29. Id. at 426.

30. Duncan Kennedy, *A Critique of Adjudication* supra at 185–86.

31. 365 U.S. 127 (1961).

32. C. Edwin Baker, *Human Liberty and Freedom of Speech* 189 (1989).

33. Id. at 189.

34. 234 U.S. 600 (1914).

35. See Herbert Hovenkamp, *Economics and Federal Antitrust Law* 275 (1985).

36. *Broadcast Music, Inc. v. CBS*, 441 U.S. 1 (1979); *Appalachian Coals, Inc. v. U.S.*, 288 U.S. 344 (1933).

37. See Bork, *Antitrust Paradox: A Policy at War with Itself* 330 (1978).

38. See, e.g., *Northwest Wholesale Stationers, Inc. v. Pacific Stationery & Printing Co.*, 472 U.S. 284, 297 (1985) ("[N]ot all concerted refusals to deal should be accorded *per se* treatment."); James A. Rahl, *Per Se Rules and Boycotts under the Sherman Act: Some Reflections on the Klor's Case*, 45 Va. L. Rev. 1165, 1168–73 (1959).

39. See Bork, *Antitrust Paradox* supra at 334, 337–38. Judge Bork's widely cited opinion in *Rothery Storage & Van Co. v. Atlas Van Lines, Inc.*, 792 F.2d 210 (D.C. Cir. 1986), *cert. denied*, 479 U.S. 1033 (1987), illustrates how in antitrust law the ancillary restraint distinction has generated inconsistent results. In *Rothery Storage*, Judge Bork reviewed the current antitrust case law applicable to group boycotts and concerted refusals to deal and concluded that "it has always been clear that boycotts are not, and cannot ever be, per se illegal." Id. at 215. In finding that "any comprehensible per se rule for [group] boycotts ... is out of the question," Judge Bork stated that the per se rule is too rigid, simplistic, and destructive of many common and entirely beneficial business arrangements. Id. (quoting Rahl supra at 1173 note 158). The Supreme Court adopted Judge Bork's analysis in *Northwest Wholesale Stationers, Inc. v. Pacific Stationery & Printing Co.* in concluding that "not all concerted refusals to deal should be accorded per se treatment" (472 U.S. 284, 297 [1985]). However, the Court has also held that when the boycott is found to be an illegal price-fixing conspiracy, then it will be condemned per se. *FTC v. Superior Court Trial Lawyers Ass'n*, 493 U.S. 411, 423–36 (1990); *Palmer v. BRG of Georgia, Inc.*, 498 U.S. 46, 48 (1990) ("We explained that '[u]nder the Sherman Act a combination formed for the purpose and with the

effect of raising, depressing, fixing, pegging, or stabilizing the price of a commodity in interstate or foreign commerce is illegal per se.'" [48]).

If one analyzes these cases by using the form of legal analysis commonly known as *reasoning by analogy*, then it is difficult to understand why some boycotts are held to be per se unlawful, and others are not. If, however, one analyzes the cases not by analogy but rather by radial category extension, then the cases make perfect sense. Antitrust lawyers instinctively understand the meaning of the relevant radial categories because they have been trained to think imaginatively within a structure shaped by the default metaphors of "nakedness" and "ancillary."

40. Herbert Hovenkamp, *Federal Antitrust Policy: The Law of Competition and Its Practice* 201 (1994).

41. Id.

42. *Palmer v. BRG of Georgia, Inc.*, 498 U.S. 46 (1990) (per curiam decision finding that a market allocation agreement between competitors was per se illegal under the Sherman Act).

43. See *Northwest Wholesale Stationers, Inc.*, 472 U.S. at 297 (concluding that rule of reason analysis, not per se rule, was the appropriate standard for determining whether group's boycott of producers violated antitrust laws). But see *FTC v. Superior Court Trial Lawyers Ass'n*, 493 U.S. at 432–36 (applying per se rule to boycott found to be a price-fixing conspiracy); *Palmer*, 498 U.S. 46 (acknowledging importance of adhering to per se rule for regulating classic restraints of trade).

44. Herbert Hovenkamp, *Federal Antitrust Policy* supra at 216.

45. See, e.g., *United States v. Container Corp.*, 393 U.S. 333, 340–41 (1968) (Marshall, J., dissenting).

46. 500 U.S. 322 (1991).

47. Id. at 326. The hospital offered Pinhas a contract for $36,000 per year (later increased by an oral offer to $60,000) for services he would never be asked to perform.

48. Id.

49. Id. at 327.

50. *Pinhas v. Summit Health, Ltd.*, 894 F.2d 1024, 1031–32 (9th Cir. 1989).

51. 444 U.S. 232 (1980). *McLain* involved an alleged conspiracy to fix real estate brokerage commissions. The Court established that Sherman Act litigants need not make a "particularized showing of an effect on interstate commerce caused by [an] alleged conspiracy to fix commission rates" in order to satisfy the interstate commerce requirement for federal court jurisdiction. Id. at 242–43. As the *McLain* Court explained: "To establish the jurisdictional element of a Sherman Act violation it would be sufficient for petitioners to demonstrate a substantial effect on interstate commerce generated by respondents' brokerage activity." Id. at 242.

52. 444 U.S. at 246 (citing *Hospital Bldg. Co. v. Rex Hospital Trustees*, 425 U.S. 738, 745 [1976]).

53. The phrase "infected activities" in the *McLain* decision has created confusion. Some courts read *McLain* as requiring proof that defendant's alleged illegal conduct substantially affected interstate commerce. See, e.g., *Shahawy v. Harrison*, 778 F.2d 636, 640 (11th Cir. 1985); *Western Waste Serv. Sys. v. Universal Waste Control*, 616 F.2d 1094, 1097 (9th Cir.), *cert. denied*, 449 U.S. 869 (1980). Others, perhaps a majority, read *McLain* as merely requiring proof establishing some nexus between defendant's challenged practices and interstate commerce. See, e.g., *Hayden v. Bracy*, 744 F.2d 1338, 1342–43 (8th Cir. 1984); *Furlong v. Long Island College Hosp.*, 710 F.2d 922, 925–26 (2d Cir. 1983). *Pinhas* represents a brewing controversy over the appropriateness of the antitrust jurisdictional test established by *McLain*.

54. *Pinhas*, 500 U.S. at 332.

55. Id.

56. 359 U.S. 207 (1959). The holding in *Klor's* that group boycotts are per se antitrust offenses is seen by antitrust experts as controversial and of doubtful authority. See Herbert Hovenkamp, *Economics and Federal Antitrust Law* 277 (1985) ("The facts of *Klor's* are perplexing, and there is some reason to think the Court would reconsider its decision today" [277]).

57. *Pinhas*, 500 U.S. at 332 (quoting *Klor's*, 359 U.S. at 213).

58. Id. at 338. (Justice Scalia, dissenting). Justice Scalia's dissent was joined by three other justices: Justice O'Connor, Justice Kennedy, and Justice Souter.

59. Id.

60. Id. Justice Scalia noted that the parties acknowledged "that every hospital in Los Angeles has its own peer review process, and that the complaint itself asserts that, well before the offer of the 'sham contract,' 'nearly all' those hospitals had abolished the featherbedding practice that is the object of this conspiracy." Id.

61. *Pinhas*, 500 U.S. at 332 (citing *Klor's, Inc. v. Broadway-Hale Stores, Inc.*, 359 U.S. 207, 213 [1959]).

62. Id.

63. Id.

64. As Justice Stevens explained for the majority, "The competitive significance of the respondent's exclusion from the market must be measured, not just by a particularized evaluation of his own practice, but rather, by a general evaluation of the impact of the restraint on other participants and potential participants in the market from which he has been excluded." Id. at 331. Or, as Justice Scalia put it for the dissent, "As I understand the Court's opinion, the test of Sherman Act jurisdiction is whether the entire line of commerce from which Dr. Pinhas has been excluded affects interstate commerce." Id. at 334.

65. The Court has concluded that proof of market power is not relevant for

determining whether a group boycott constitutes a substantive antitrust violation. See *FTC v. Superior Court Trial Lawyers Ass'n*, 493 U.S. 411 (1990); *Klor's, Inc. v. Broadway-Hale Stores, Inc.*, 359 U.S. 207 (1959). If there is no market power defense for financially interested boycotts, why require proof of market power to establish interstate commerce requirements? One answer is that, under Justice Scalia's view of the commerce requirement, jurisdiction is substantive in nature. The practical significance of this is that there would be a "shift [of] power from juries to judges" in antitrust litigation. In other words, "antitrust plaintiffs [would be required under Scalia's test] to demonstrate anticompetitive effects before courts had power to decide their cases" (Calkins, *The October 1989 Supreme Court Term and Antitrust* supra at 635). In *Trial Lawyers*, the Supreme Court rejected the notion that a market power defense should be recognized to protect a symbolic lawyer boycott from antitrust liability. Justice Scalia, who agreed with the majority in *Trial Lawyers*, was able to reject a market power defense because he, along with the majority, believed that the boycott involved a per se antitrust violation. The per se violation rule in antitrust law applies to cases involving particular types of market restraints, such as price-fixing agreements, that pose an obvious danger to competition and are not balanced by any plausible procompetitive virtue. See *Northern Pac. Ry. v. United States*, 356 U.S. 1, 5 (1958).

66. *Summit Health, Ltd. v. Pinhas*, 500 U.S. 332, 332 (1991).

67. 509 U.S. 764 (1993).

68. 15 U.S.C. 1013(b)(1993).

69. 509 U.S. at 801.

70. Id., citing 2 *Oxford English Dictionary* 468 (2d ed 1989).

71. *Hartford Insurance* 509 U.S. at 802–3.

72. Id. at 804.

73. Id. at 805.

74. Id.

75. Id. at 791–92 (Souter, J., dissenting).

76. Id. at 791.

77. Id. at 802. n. 2 (Scalia, J.).

78. Id. at 794 n. 19 (Souter, J., dissenting).

79. See Antonin Scalia, *The Rule of Law as a Law of Rules*, 56 U. Chi. L. Rev. 1175, 1178–80 (1989).

80. Steven L. Winter, *How Do Rules Work?*, in *Clearing in the Forest* supra at 1.

81. Id. at 7.

8. WHY THE BOYCOTT CHAMELEON HAS BEEN MISUNDERSTOOD

1. The Supreme Court's decision in *Claiborne Hardware* can be explained in light of the Court's historical treatment and commitment to the civil rights

movement—legal treatment of boycott thus depends on the identity of the group boycotting. See generally Harry Kalven Jr., *The Negro and the First Amendment* 123–72 (1965).

2. See Eisner R. Elhauge, *Making Sense of Antitrust Petitioning Immunity*, 80 Calif. L. Rev. 1177 (1992).

3. Michael C. Harper, *The Consumer's Emerging Right to Boycott: NAACP v. Claiborne Hardware and Its Implications for American Labor Law*, 93 Yale L. J. 409 (1984).

4. Harper supra at 410, 420–26. Seth Kupferberg has similarly argued that political strikes by labor unions should be accorded a First Amendment protection analogous to that accorded civil rights boycotts. See Kupferberg, *Political Strikes, Labor Law, and Democratic Rights*, 71 Va. L. Rev. 685 (1985).

5. Harper supra at 422.

6. Id.

7. Id. at 423.

8. Id. at 422.

9. Id. at 425.

10. See Harry Kalven Jr., *The Negro and the First Amendment* (1965).

11. See Richard H. McAdams, *The Origin, Development, and Regulation of Norms*, 96 Mich L. Rev. 338, 386–90 (1997) (discussing the distinction between group and societal norm regulation).

12. See generally Richard H. McAdams, *The Origin, Development, and Regulation of Norms* supra at 362–64 (discussing how private groups enforce group norms).

13. Harper, *The Consumer's Emerging Right to Boycott* supra at 426.

14. Id.

15. The Red Apple boycott has been condemned for being racially motivated. See United States Civil Rights Commission, *Civil Rights Issues Facing Asian Americans in the 1990s* 34–40 (1992).

16. Howard Lesnick, *The Gravamen of the Secondary Boycott*, 62 Colum. L. Rev. 1363 (1962).

17. Id. at 1415 (citing 93 Cong. Rec. 4323 [daily ed. April 29, 1947], reprinted in 2 *Legislative History of the Labor Management Relations Act*, 1947, at 1107 [1985] [remarks of Senator Taft]).

18. Id. at 1414.

19. See Donald S. Engel, *Secondary Consumer Picketing—Following the Struck Product*, 52 Va. L. Rev. 189, 211 (1966).

20. Elhauge, *Making Sense of Antitrust Petitioning Immunity* supra at 1184. Elhauge's *Antitrust Petitioning Immunity* article builds on his earlier article *The Scope of Antitrust Process*, 104 Harv. L. Rev. 667 (1991) dealing with state action immunity. Both articles attempt to advance an *objective* process approach for rationalizing antitrust doctrine.

21. Elhauge, *Making Sense of Antitrust Petitioning Immunity* supra at 1180.

22. Id.

23. Id. at 1197.

24. Id. at 1199 ("[P]etitioners' financial interest in the government's action is irrelevant because our assurance that the restraint furthers the public interest comes not from the petitioners' decision making process but from the government's." [1199]).

25. Id.

26. Id. at 1250. Apparently, train metaphors have become popular among contemporary legal scholars. See, e.g., Bruce Ackerman, *We the People—Foundations* 98–99 (1991) (comparing the American republic to a train moving through constitutional history). Steven L. Winter argues that Ackerman's train metaphor is too quaint and European for mobile America. Winter instead places the judge in the driver's seat of a car driving down a modern freeway. In Winter's view, judges are in the thick of it—always on the freeway and always looking forward, backward, and side-to-side at all other drivers. Steven L. Winter, *Indeterminacy and Incommensurability in Constitutional Law*, 78 Calif. L. Rev. 1441, 1522 (1990).

27. A major obstacle to seeking higher statutory fees was the belief of governmental officials that there was limited public support for higher fees. *Superior Court Trial Lawyers Ass'n v. FTC*, 856 F.2d 226, 229 (D.C. Cir. 1988), *rev'd on other grounds*, 493 U.S. 411 (1990).

28. See *Superior Court Trial Lawyers Ass'n v. FTC*, 856 F.2d at 229–30.

29. Elhauge, *Making Sense of Antitrust Petitioning Immunity* supra at 1211.

30. The preboycott fees were substantially lower than the market price for similar legal services in the district. See *FTC v. Superior Court Trial Lawyers Ass'n*, 493 U.S. at 443 (Brennan, J., concurring in part, dissenting in part).

31. See Gary Peller, *The Politics of Reconstruction*, 98 Harv. L. Rev. 863 (1985) (book review) (discussing a similar tendency within the process-oriented approach of Bruce Ackerman's constitutional law theories).

32. Elhauge, *Making Sense of Antitrust Petitioning Immunity* supra at 1180.

33. See Cass R. Sunstein, *Lochner's Legacy*, 87 Colum. L. Rev. 873, 910–11 (1987).

34. See James G. Pope, *Republican Moments: The Role of Direct Popular Power in the American Constitutional Order*, 139 U. Pa. L. Rev. 287, 294 (1990) (discussing general theoretical and normative arguments for justifying popular protest under a theory of civic republican thought that avoids the large-size problem of modern representative democracies).

35. Id. at 351.

36. The rank-and-file union membership thus had no choice in deciding whether to join the boycott. Id. at 352.

37. Id. at 349.

38. Pope, *Republican Moments* supra at 352 (quoting *International Long-shoremen's Ass'n v. Allied Int'l, Inc.*, 456 U.S. 212, 214 [1982]).

39. Id. at 352.

40. Id. (quoting *Allied Int'l, Inc.*, 456 U.S. at 241).

41. Id. at 349.

42. Id. at 312.

43. *FTC v. Superior Court Trial Lawyers Ass'n*, 493 U.S. 411, 449 (1990) (quoting, *NAACP v. Claiborne Hardware Co.*, 458 U.S. 886, 911 [1982] [Stevens, J.]).

44. Pope, *Labor-Community Coalitions and Boycotts* supra at 924. ("Most [labor-community boycotts] fall between the extremes, where determining the appropriate degree of protection will involve difficult value judgments." [924]).

45. See, e.g., Aviam Soifer, *Law and the Company We Keep* (1995).

46. See Steven L. Winter, *Radial Categories*, in *Clearing in the Forest* supra. Steven L. Winter, *An Upside/Down View of the Countermajoritarian Difficulty*, 69 Tex. L. Rev. 1881, 1925 (1997).

47. See Duncan Kennedy, *A Critique of Adjudication* 3 (1997).

48. Owen M. Fiss, *Objectivity and Interpretation*, 34 Stan. L. Rev. 739 (1982).

9. CHANGING SOCIAL CONCEPTIONS OF BOYCOTT

1. See, e.g., Fredric Jameson, *Postmodernism and Consumer Society*, in *The Anti-Aesthetic: Essays on Postmodern Culture* 111, 112–13 (Hal Foster ed. 1983).

2. See Daniel Yergin and Joseph Stanislaw, *The Commanding Heights: The Battle Between Government and the Marketplace That Is Remaking the Modern World* (1998).

3. See Joshua Karliner, *The Corporate Planet: Ecology and Politics in the Age of Globalization* (1997).

4. See Peter J. Spiro, *New Global Potentates: Non-Governmental Organizations and the "Unregulated" Marketplace*, 18 Cardozo L. Rev. 957 (1997).

5. Douglass Cassel, *Corporate Initiatives: A Second Human Rights Revolution?*, 19 Fordham Int'l L. J. 1963 (1996).

6. See Peter J. Spiro, *New Global Potentates: Non-Governmental Organizations and the "Unregulated" Marketplace*, 18 Cardozo L. Rev. 957 (1997); Kenneth Sheets, *Products under Fire*, U.S. News & World Report, April 16, 1990, at 44.

7. For a comprehensive review of how *ethos* of metaphor was understood 2,000 years ago in Greece and Rome, and how that *classic* understanding compares to the way metaphor is understood in the law, see Michael Frost, *Greco-Roman Analysis of Metaphoric Reasoning*, 2 J. of Legal Writing 113, 115–32 (1996).

8. The boycott bulletin board can be found at http://www.2street.com/boycott/list.phtml.

9. N.Y. Times, Feb. 17, 1996, at sect. 1 p. 3.

10. Id.

11. Id.

12. Id.

13. 65 USLW 4715 (decided June 26, 1997).

14. Id. at 4728 (Justice O'Connor, concurring in part, dissenting in part).

15. Id.

16. See James B. Pope, *Labor-Community Coalitions and Boycotts: The Old Labor Law, the New Unionism, and the Living Constitution*, 69 Tex. L. Rev. 889, 894–97, 901–14 (1991).

17. In 1973, Joseph Coors, patriarch of the Coors family, donated $25,000 to help start up the Heritage Foundation. Steven Greenhouse, *The Coors Boys Stick to Business*, N.Y. Times, Nov. 30, 1986, 3 at 1. Joseph Coors has, at times, provided more than half of the Heritage Foundation's budget. See Paul Richter, *Coors' New Brew: Taking Out the Political Aftertaste*, L.A. Times, Sept. 27, 1987, 4 at 1.

18. See, e.g., Richter, *Coors' New Brew* supra at 1. Feminists boycotted Coors because of the Coors family's strident opposition to the Equal Rights Amendment. African-Americans joined the boycott in response to statements by Bill Coors, Joseph Coors's brother, that "blacks lack 'intellectual capacity'" and that this was one reason Africa has economic problems. Women's, African-American, Hispanic, and homosexual groups also boycotted Coors due to the firm's alleged discriminatory employment practices. Id. at 6.

19. The Coors Beer boycott was initiated by the AFL-CIO in response to the Coors Company's antiunion attitudes and practices. Richter, supra at 1. Opposition to the political views of Joseph Coors led to intensifying and broadening of the boycott. Id.; see also Mark Stencel, *Boycotts: A Touchy Business for Targeted Firms*, L.A. Times, Sept. 11, 1990, D at 2A; *Helms Subject of Beer Boycott by Gays*, United Press International (Jul. 22, 1990) (Lexis, Nexis library, UPI File).

20. See Richter, *Coors' New Brew* supra. Coors's market share decline was attributed to the boycott as well as the aggressive tactics of Coors's competitors. Id. Over the last few years, Coors's market share was substantially diminished. For example, Coors's California market share fell from above 40 percent in 1977 to approximately 14 percent in 1984. Company profits dropped from $67.7 million to $44.7 million. The Coors boycott raises troublesome issues for policy makers concerned with federal competition policy because the boycott restrained the ability of Coors to compete in the market, a consequence that could not be seen as the result of "competition on the merits." If a group of beer competitors had engaged in the same boycott, the boycott would probably have been found to be a per se violation of the antitrust laws. See *Klor's, Inc. v. Broadway-Hale Stores, Inc.*, 359 U.S. 207 (1959) (holding that a group boycott is per se illegal under 1 of Sherman Act); cf., *Catalano, Inc. v. Target Sales, Inc.*, 446 U.S. 643 (1980) (per curiam) (holding that an agreement between beer distributors

to eliminate short term credit formerly granted to retailers is illegal per se).

21. Hardy Green, *On Strike at Hormel: The Struggle for a Democratic Labor Movement* 300 (1990); Charles Heckscher, *The New Unionism: Employee Involvement in the Changing Corporation* (1988). The struggle for a new democratic labor movement is likely to be frustrated by the new legal distinctions established by the Supreme Court's developing boycott doctrine. To be successful in its effort to create a new unionism, labor must be permitted to tie the goal of the consumer campaign to the ultimate goal of winning broad support for collective bargaining. Union organizers must, if they are to succeed in saving the labor movement from extinction, transcend the economics/politics distinction by persuading others that the institutional interests of labor are consistent with the broader social and political interests of other marginalized groups in society. See Gary Minda, *Rediscovering Progressive Labor Politics: The Labor Law Implications of FTC v. Superior Court Trial Lawyers Assoc.*, 16 Vt. L. Rev. 71, 126 (1991).

22. Business Dateline, 38 Florida Trend, no. 6, sec. 1 p. 78 (1994).

23. Phoenix Gazette, Nov. 8, 1995, p. B1.

24. PR News Service, April 15, 1994, Financial News Section.

25. Austin-American Statesmen, Feb. 1, 1995, p. B4.

26. N.Y. Times, Oct. 12, 1994, at A 18.

27. St. Louis Dispatch, May 8, 1994, at 1b.

28. L.A. Times, Oct. 9, 1995, at A 14.

29. The Atlanta Journal and Constitution, September 3, 1995, p. 15A.

30. Recent empirical evidence suggests that labor boycotts involving social issues are more effective at damaging the wealth position of the target company's shareholders. See Pope, *Labor-Community Coalitions and Boycotts* supra at 905–8 note 20; see also Steven W. Pruitt and Monroe Friedman, *Determining the Effectiveness of Consumer Boycotts: A Stock Price Analysis of Their Impact on Corporate Targets*, 9 J. Consumer Pol'y 375, 381, (1986) (discussing long-term study of consumer and union boycotts revealing that stock prices declined by about 3.5 percent). See Steven W. Pruitt et al., *The Impact of Union-Sponsored Boycotts on the Stock Prices of Target Firms*, 9 J. Lab. Res. 285, 289 (1988) (study of union boycotts suggest that the negative effect of boycotts arising immediately after the announcement of the boycott dissipated within one month).

31. Dennis E. Garrett, *Consumer Boycotts: Are Targets Always the Bad Guys?*, Bus. & Soc. Rev., 19 (summer 1986).

32. One justification for consumer-oriented boycotts is that these boycotts seek to provide consumers with more complete information about the product than was offered in the marketplace. The idea of consumer sovereignty suggests that consumers should have full information about the products they consume, including the political practices their purchases might support. This is an argument offered by Professor Harper in advocating a right to boycott as political action. See Harper supra at 421 ("Any secure basis for a

right to boycott must trump a state's efforts to protect its economy from disruption. An individual's decision to join a consumer boycott must be protected precisely because it enables the individual to affect the economy, not in spite of such effects."). Professor Harper acknowledges, however, that the notion of consumer sovereignty found in the "microeconomic welfare doctrine is not a sufficient source for the right to engage in a concerted refusal to patronize, because the doctrine rests on challengeable ethical and empirical assumptions." Id. A more persuasive argument would seek to establish that the right to boycott is "a constitutionally protected political act" and that "[t]he coercion inherent in political boycotts is simply an exercise of the influence that citizens as consumers should be encouraged to exercise." Id. at 425. The same argument can be made in advocating broader legal protection for consumer boycotts incident to labor disputes. See id. at 438–53.

33. In either case, the goal of the boycott was designed to bring pressure on private entities that affirmatively support, through deeds or investments, political practices that some find to be morally reprehensible. See Harper supra at 410.

34. See Richard H. McAdams, *Group Norms, Gossip, and Blackmail,* 144 U. Pa. L. Rev. 2237 (1997); Wendy J. Gordon, *Norms of Communication and Commodification,* 144 U. Pa. L. Rev. 2321 (1996).

35. News Tribune, March 2, 1994, p. f3, quoting Zachary D. Lyons.

36. L.A. Times, May 5, 1995, Part E, p. 2.

37. Peter J. Spiro, *New Global Potentates: Non-Governmental Organizations and the "Unregulated" Marketplace,* 18 Cardozo L. Rev. 957 (1997).

38. Steven L. Winter, *Compositional Structure,* in *Clearing in the Forest* at 1.

39. Id.

10. *Ethos of the Legal Mind*

1. See Michael Frost, *Greco-Roman Analysis of Metaphoric Reasoning,* 2 J. of Legal Writing 113 (1996).

2. Id. at 125–26.

3. Id. at 126.

4. A. Gouldner, *The Dialectic of Ideology and Technology: The Origins, Grammar, and Future of Ideology* 98 (1976), cited and quoted in Robert C. Post, *The Constitutional Concept of Public Discourse,* 103 Harv. L. Rev. 601, 636 (1990).

5. The term *norm entrepreneur* was coined by Cass R. Sunstein to explain how individuals have held up alternative norms of groups to challenge societal norms. See Sunstein, *On the Expressive Function of Law,* 144 U. Pa. L. Rev. 2021, 2030–31 (1996).

6. The term *norm cascade,* also known as *snowball* or *bandwagon effect,* is a metaphoric term used in legal literature about norms to explain how private groups rely on group pressure, including shame, pride, and esteem, to shift behavior and norms in new directions. The metaphor "norm cascade" is based

on the mental image of a water or snow cascade, building slowly at first, then after time gaining support and power in volume and density. See Sunstein supra; Timur Kuran, *Private Truths, Public Lies* (1995).

7. See Cass R. Sunstein, *Legal Reasoning and Political Conflict* 68 (1996).

8. See Steven L. Winter, *Reasoning by Analogy*, in *Clearing in the Forest* supra.

9. Metaphor thus helps to explain how judges use policy analysis as a Trojan horse for the ideological in adjudication. See Duncan Kennedy, *A Critique of Adjudication* supra at 83–92.

10. C. Edwin Baker, *Human Liberty and Freedom of Speech* supra at 190.

11. See generally Robert Post, *Recuperating First Amendment Doctrine*, 47 Stan. L. J. 1249, 1265–1267 (1995).

12. Id.

13. Duncan Kennedy, *A Critique of Adjudication* supra at 3.

14. Jerome Frank, *Law and the Modern Mind* 111 (1930).

15. Stanley Fish, *There's No Such Thing as Free Speech . . . and It's a Good Thing, Too* (1994).

16. Id.

17. There are examples where contestability has led to important changes in the law. See Lawrence Lessig, *Understanding Changed Readings: Fidelity and Theory*, 47 Stan. L. Rev. 395 (1995). There is ample scholarly authority for developing a First Amendment theory of boycott as a contestable democratic social practice. See Robert Post, *Recuperating First Amendment Doctrine*, 47 Stan. L. Rev. 1249 (1995). See also Robert Post, *The Constitutional Concept of Public Discourse: Outrageous Opinion, Democratic Deliberation, and Hustler Magazine v. Farwell*, 103 Harv. L. Rev. 601 (1990).

18. Robert Post, *Recuperating First Amendment Doctrine*, 47 Stan. L. Rev. 1249, 1272 (1995).

19. There is some empirical evidence to support the view that consumer boycotts have had a negative effect on the stock market prices of targeted firms. See Ganett, *Consumer Boycotts: Are Targets Always the Bad Guys?*, 1986 Bus. & Soc'y. Rev., 17, 19; Pruitt and Friedman, *Determining the Effectiveness of Consumer Boycotts: A Stock Price Analysis of Their Impact on Corporate Targets*, 9 J. Consumer Pol'y 381 (1986). It is doubtful, however, that legal intervention to restrain a boycott would encourage citizens to respect the law, or end a boycott. Moreover, what if it is law that is the source of violence? What if violence is itself necessary to preserve law? See Jacques Derrida, *Force of Law: The Mystical Foundation of Authority*, Cardozo L. Rev. 921 (1991).

EPILOGUE: IDEOLOGY AND THE LEGAL MIND

1. Edward Rubin and Malcolm Feeley, *Creating Legal Doctrine*, 69 So. Calif. L. Rev. 1989, 2030 (1996).

2. Duncan Kennedy, *A Critique of Adjudication* supra at 339–40.

3. It is generally thought that *dead metaphors* are no longer real metaphors in that they have been widely accepted in ordinary conversational language. The Dead Metaphor Theory is based on what George Lakoff and Mark Turner see as a basic misconception of Literal Meaning Theory: the notion "that those things in our cognition that are most alive and most active are those that are conscious." Lakoff and Turner supra 129. Metaphors "that are most alive and most deeply entrenched, efficient, and powerful are those that are so automatic as to be unconscious and effortless." Id. at 130. This does not mean that culture and tradition are irrelevant to meaning. Metaphoric understandings of the physical and social world take on new meaning as each generation imaginatively reproduces its own culture and tradition. See Steven L. Winter, *Contingency and Community in Normative Practice*, 139 U. Pa. L. Rev. 963, 998–1001 (1991) (discussing the concept of *slippage*); Note, *Organic and Mechanical Metaphors in Late Eighteenth Century American Political Thought*, 110 Harv. L. Rev. 1832 (1997) (discussing how organic and mechanical metaphors influenced the thought of the people who designed the American government).

INDEX

GARY MINDA IS a professor of law at Brooklyn Law School where he teaches labor law and jurisprudence. He was educated at Michigan State University and Wayne State University and at Columbia University and Wayne State University Schools of Law. He is the author of *Postmodern Legal Movements: Law and Jurisprudence at Century's End* (1995). He has written extensively in the fields of legal theory, jurisprudence, labor, and antitrust law.